BRITAIN AND THE AMERICAN SOUTH

Britain and the American South

FROM COLONIALISM TO ROCK AND ROLL

Essays by
FRANKLIN T. LAMBERT
HOLLY BREWER
KATHRYN E. HOLLAND BRAUND
S. MAX EDELSON
MARCUS WOOD
R. J. M. BLACKETT
HUGH WILFORD
BRIAN WARD
MICHAEL O'BRIEN

Edited by
JOSEPH P. WARD

UNIVERSITY PRESS OF MISSISSIPPI
Jackson

www.upress.state.ms.us

The University Press of Mississippi is a member of the Association of American University Presses.

Copyright © 2003 by University Press of Mississippi
All rights reserved
Manufactured in the United States of America

Print-on-Demand Edition

Library of Congress Cataloging-in-Publication Data

Porter L. Fortune, Jr. History Symposium (26th : 2001 : University of Mississippi)
  Britain and the American South : from colonialism to rock and roll/essays by Franklin T. Lambert . . . [et al.]; edited by Joseph P. Ward.
  p. cm. — ([Chancellor Porter L. Fortune Symposium in Southern History series])
Includes bibliographical references and index.
  ISBN 1-57806-580-1 (cloth : alk. paper)
  1. Southern States—Relations—Great Britain—Congresses. 2. Great Britain—Relations—Southern States—Congresses. 3. Southern States—Civilization—Congresses. 4. British—Southern States—History—Congresses. 5. Southern States—Foreign public opinion, British—Congresses. 6. Public opinion—Great Britain—History—Congresses. I. Lambert, Franklin T. II. Ward, Joseph P., 1965– III. Title. IV. Series.
  F209.P67 2001
  303.48′275041′09—dc21   2003007161

British Library Cataloging-in-Publication Data available

We are sailing to London. . . . We are a whisper of wind seeking for London, a clean rag from the wash on a straight-up pole, pushing on to London. We are these new people who sail for pleasure. But the wind and the whisper and the rag are part of what I know, and the me in the other we, I am, fears. We are a sailed people. We sailed to America. We taste the path of our abduction in our tears.

. . . I miss the safe inland cities. Nashville, Atlanta. These cities with their front porches on the ocean, Washington, Savannah, Charleston, scare me, like a door left open on a dark night with robbers about.

But I am hungry for the city on the Thames.

—ALICE RANDALL, *The Wind Done Gone*

Contents

Acknowledgments   ix

Foreword: Empire Building and Empire Wrecking   xi
   Joseph P. Ward

Virginia's Religious Revolution: From Established Monopoly to Free Marketplace   3
   Franklin T. Lambert

Power and Authority in the Colonial South: The English Legacy and Its Contradictions   27
   Holly Brewer

"Like a Stone Wall Never to Be Broke": The British-Indian Boundary Line with the Creek Indians, 1763–1773   53
   Kathryn E. Holland Braund

Carolinians Abroad: Cultivating English Identities from the Colonial Lower South   81
   S. Max Edelson

The American South and English Print Satire, 1760–1865   107
   Marcus Wood

British Views of the Confederacy   141
   R. J. M. Blackett

The South and the British Left, 1930–1960   163
   Hugh Wilford

"By Elvis and All the Saints": *Images of the American South in the World of 1950s British Popular Music*   187
  BRIAN WARD

Afterword: On the Irrelevance of Knights   215
  MICHAEL O'BRIEN

Notes   229

Contributors   269

Index   271

Acknowledgments

The Department of History (chaired by Bob Haws) and the Center for the Study of Southern Culture (led by Charles Reagan Wilson) at the University of Mississippi funded the 26th annual Porter L. Fortune, Jr., History Symposium, which was the starting point for this volume. The editor is grateful for their support as well as the help of Betty Harness, Michelle Palmertree, Brian S. Miller, Rusty Cooper, and the staff of the University of Mississippi Libraries. He also wishes to express his appreciation to Nancy Bercaw, J. R. Duke, Charles Eagles, Robbie Ethridge, Sue Grayzel, Winthrop Jordan, Michael Landon, Kevin McCarthy, John Neff, Ted Ownby, Elizabeth Payne, John Shelton Reed, Chuck Ross, Sheila Skemp, Carolyn Ellis Staton, Douglass Sullivan-González, and Elizabeth Young for their assistance with various aspects of this project. At the University Press of Mississippi, Craig Gill has been a great supporter of this book, not the least because he recommended Derik Shelor to be its copy editor. Finally, though chiefly, this book would not have been possible without the energy, ideas, and patience (especially with the editor) of the contributors.

Foreword

Empire Building and Empire Wrecking

JOSEPH P. WARD

"You are very Irish, you know." That pronouncement was made by Captain Rhett Butler to the young widow formerly known as Scarlett O'Hara in the Atlanta of Margaret Mitchell's imagination. The scene was set some time into the Civil War, when most of Mitchell's characters were becoming increasingly aware of the costs of the conflict, but Rhett, as always, had his eyes focused squarely on opportunity. Scarlett and several other ladies were doing their bit for the Confederate cause by selling dances in an effort to raise money for medical supplies. The supplies would be brought from England through the Yankee blockade by that "pirate" Captain Butler. Rhett buys a dance with Scarlett, during which they have a lengthy conversation that concludes with his comment about Scarlett's ancestry mentioned above.

Of course, Scarlett was only half Irish, on her father's side, but Rhett's emphasis on her paternal lineage helps him to argue that Irish planters like the O'Haras and English colonizers like the Butlers had participated in a common project in the American South. During his dance with Scarlett, Rhett tells her:

> *What most people don't seem to realize is that there is just as much money to be made out of the wreckage of a civilization as from the upbuilding of one. . . . Your family and my family and everyone here tonight made their money out of changing a wilderness into a civilization. That's empire building. There's good money in empire building. But, there's more in empire wrecking. . . . This empire we're living in—the South—the Confederacy—the Cotton Kingdom—it's breaking up right under our feet. Only most fools won't see it and take advantage of the situation created by the collapse. I'm making my fortune out of the wreckage.*

At the risk of taking *Gone With the Wind* too seriously (or, some might suggest, taking it not seriously enough), it may be fair to say that *Britain and the American South* traces aspects of the building up and wrecking of the British enterprise in the South. Half of its eight main chapters examine the colonial era, and the other half address the period that followed American independence. The emphasis in the early chapters is on the transplantation of British institutions and customs—the Church of England, the laws of property, ideas of gentility—to the southern colonies and territories in England's (and, subsequently, Britain's) sphere of influence on the North American mainland, and their mutation in their new soil. The later chapters shift their attention to the attitudes of British artists, politicians, intellectuals, and musicians toward the society and culture that their ancestors helped, directly and indirectly, to create in the South. Michael O'Brien's afterword ranges broadly across the entire field of research as well as the arguments presented here and concludes, among other things, "that often Britain and the South have had little to do with one another and, when they have, have usually demonstrated remarkable ignorance and obtuseness about the other."

The relationship between Britain and the American South has hardly gone unnoticed by scholars. Prominent among the many recent studies in this area are James Horn, *Adapting to a New World: English Society in the Seventeenth-Century Chesapeake* (Univ. of North Carolina Press, 1994); Helen Taylor, *Circling Dixie: Contemporary Southern Culture through a Transatlantic Lens* (Rutgers Univ. Press, 2001); Alan Gallay, *The Indian Slave Trade: The Rise of the English Empire in the American South, 1670–1717* (Yale Univ. Press, 2002); and Joseph A. Fry, *Dixie Looks Abroad: The South and U.S. Foreign Relations, 1789–1973* (Louisiana State Univ. Press, 2002). This book contributes to this scholarly discussion by bringing together in one volume a series of microhistories by leading researchers who together can command a range of sources and historiographies across almost the entire chronological span of British interest in the South. Although it cannot claim to touch all aspects of the trans-Atlantic relationship—it is weak, for example, in the area of ties between parts of Britain outside of England with the

South—this book's approach encourages readers to consider the influence of early modern British culture on race relations, religion, and attitudes toward the outside world in the modern South. It seeks not to wreck a field of knowledge but rather to help build it up. Rhett be damned.

Britain and the American South

Virginia's Religious Revolution

From Established Monopoly to Free Marketplace

FRANKLIN T. LAMBERT

In the mid-1700s, the Reverend Patrick Henry faithfully executed his duties as rector of St. Paul's Church in Hanover County, Virginia. As a parish priest, the uncle of his better-known namesake enjoyed all the rights and privileges afforded clergymen under Virginia law: a salary underwritten by the parish levy, prestige ascribed to clergymen of the established Church of England, moral stature as a defender of the "one true faith," and state protection from purveyors of heterodoxy. All of that was placed at risk, however, with the arrival of Samuel Davies, a New Light itinerant preacher from Neshaminy, Pennsylvania, a notorious seedbed of evangelical enthusiasm.[1] Henry's colleagues along the Virginia piedmont joined him in denouncing Davies's violation of their parish boundaries. According to one clergyman, if Davies had come into a country where the Church of England was "in the same state of corruption as the Romish Church was at the time of the Reformation," then the clergy would have supported his missionary activities. But that was not the case. In their estimation, Protestant Christianity was well served by Virginia's parish ministers, and the presence of competing sects could only lead to social strife. The clergymen, therefore, interpreted Davies's presence as that of a proselytizer more interested in winning converts for his Presbyterian sect than in bringing them into the Christian fold. Upon reviewing the case, the Bishop of London agreed, pointing out that the Act of Toleration did not protect an itinerant who traveled "over many Counties to make Converts in a Country ... where till very lately there was not a Dissenter from the Church of England."[2]

Forty years later, Thomas Jefferson noted that a majority of Virginians were Dissenters; unlike the Bishop of London, he applauded their success. By 1776, to Jefferson's delight, Dissenters had created a de facto free marketplace of religion, providing men and women choice among competing sects. In that same year Jefferson proposed legislation that would make religious choice a constitutional right. He opposed Virginia's establishment laws that provided state funds for the Church of England while regulating the activities of Dissenters. He preferred Pennsylvania's more liberal approach, by which religion had "long subsisted without any establishment at all." His opponents contended that, absent state support, religion would languish to the detriment of society. Jefferson replied that that was not the case in Pennsylvania. There, he wrote, "Religion is well supported; of various kinds, indeed, but all good enough; all sufficient to preserve peace and order; or if a sect arises, whose tenets would subvert morals, good sense has fair play, and reasons and laughs it out of doors, without suffering the State to be troubled with it."[3] Jefferson's fight was finally crowned with success in 1785 when the Assembly passed the Virginia Statute for Religious Freedom, which abolished establishment and endorsed free exercise.

Most scholarly attention given to the fight for religious liberty in Virginia has centered on the legislative debates, and in particular the rhetorical battles pitting Jefferson and his chief ally, James Madison, against Patrick Henry. What is often overlooked or given short shrift is the reality underlying the rhetoric, that is, the shift in Virginians' religious choices and allegiances over the previous forty years across Virginia, particularly on the fast-growing frontier. This essay explores that shift within the framework of clashing "religious economies." Among historians, the idea of analyzing religion in economic terms is recent, but its roots are contemporary with the struggle to define the place of religion in revolutionary Virginia.[4] In his *Wealth of Nations*, published in 1776, Adam Smith devoted a section to the state's role in religious instruction. A political economist, Smith explained religious organizations and exchanges in the same terms he used to describe commerce. In his view, established churches operated in a manner similar to that of the great trading monopolies of the day. "The clergy of every established church constitute a great incorporation," he wrote.

Supported by the state and protected from competition, "they can act in concert, and pursue their interest upon one plan and with one spirit, as much as if they were under the direction of one man." He added that "where there is . . . but one sect tolerated in the society," religious teachers give full vent to their "interest and zeal," including the propagation of fear, prejudice, and superstition, and thus can become "dangerous and troublesome."[5] Jefferson's description of religion in early Virginia fit just such a model. The original charter, he pointed out, contained an "express Proviso that their laws 'should not be against the true Christian faith, now professed in the Church of England.'" The laws establishing the Church required all inhabitants to be assessed the parish levy "whether they were or not members of the established church."[6]

Samuel Davies and his Pennsylvania colleagues introduced into Virginia what Smith described as a free marketplace of religion. Extending his advocacy of free trade to the exchange of religious ideas, Smith believed that religion would prosper in a free and open religious market where men and women could choose among contending faiths. In a society without an established religion, there would be "no doubt . . . a great multitude of religious sects." Faced with competition on all sides, "each teacher would no doubt [feel] himself under the necessity of making the utmost exertion and of using every art both to preserve and to increase the number of his disciples." But, just as competition would make religious teachers more industrious, it would also check fanaticism. He argued that religious "zeal must be altogether innocent where the society is divided into two or three hundred, or perhaps into as many thousand small sects, of which no one could be considerable enough to disturb the public tranquility. The teachers of each sect, seeing themselves surrounded on all sides with more adversaries than friends, would be obliged to [exercise] . . . moderation." Finally, a competitive religious market would offer inhabitants choice. "If politics had never called in the aid of religion," Smith reasoned, "it would probably have dealt equally and impartially with all the different sects, and have allowed every man to choose his own priest and his own religion as he thought proper."[7] Smith argued that such a religious market was not some fanciful notion, declaring, "It has been established in Pennsylvania."[8]

A political economy model provides a useful analytical framework for a fresh interpretation of the transformation of religion in Virginia, in particular, and in the southern colonies, in general, during the thirty years before the American Revolution.[9] First, it exposes the fragile nature of the monopoly enjoyed by the Church of England under Virginia's legal establishment. The absence of a resident bishop, the inadequate supply of qualified ministers, and the enormous size of parishes made it impossible to maintain religious uniformity in a dynamic economy that welcomed new residents and workers. Second, it shows, by contrast, how the Pennsylvania model of a free religious market accommodated competition and choice demanded by the fast-growing, heterogeneous, contentious population of the frontier. Moreover, many of the Dissenting immigrants were non-English Britons, especially men and women from Scotland and Ulster whose religious needs could not be satisfied by the Church of England. And, third, the market approach offers a new perspective on the fight for religious freedom in Virginia. As the clash between the two religious economies became politicized, the stakes were no less than the place of religion in Virginia. Would its support and protection emanate from the statehouse, or would it operate among competing voluntary associations of believers? The constitutional answer proved to settle not only the place of religion in Virginia, but, because Virginia's Statute of Religious Liberty became a model for Federalists in 1787, to define church state relations for the new republic.

The Elizabethan Settlement provided the Virginia Company a model for ordering religion in the Chesapeake society. In 1571, Elizabeth I had pushed through Parliament the Act of Uniformity, which called for "one uniform order of common service and prayer, and of the administration of sacraments, rites, and ceremonies in the Church of England."[10] The queen believed that the act did not violate individual freedom of conscience. First, uniformity had to do with public observance of religion, not private beliefs. She was concerned about peace in her realm and believed that religious squabbling between sects could tear apart her kingdom as it had France. Second, the Thirty-Nine Articles prohibited the Church from ordaining "anything contrary to God's word." To Elizabeth, that meant that the public practice of religion would conform to scripture. Surely, she thought, all Protestants could subscribe to common worship based on the Bible. Moreover, individuals, including Puritans, could hold any private belief that did not criticize the Church of England or threaten the peace of the realm. In Elizabeth's judgment, however, Puritans wished to impose their private views on the public practice of religion. Of the Puritans she wrote in 1583: "I see many overbold with God Almighty making too many subtle scannings of His blessed will, as lawyers do with human testaments. The presumption is so great, as I may not suffer it."[11] In other words, she feared that if private judgments are allowed full reign without the cloak of uniformity, the result would be religious and civil anarchy.

Similarly, the first laws enacted in Virginia established the Church of England as the colony's official religion. The law declared "That there be an uniformity in our church as neere as may be to the canon in England; both in substance and circumstance, and that all persons yield readie obedience unto them under paine of censure."[12] The legislature mandated that a church or chapel be erected in every parish "for the Advancement of God's Glory, and the more decent Celebration of his Divine Ordinances." Governance of local parishes was lodged in the hands of a vestry, consisting of "Twelve of the most able Men of each Parish [chosen] by the major Part of the said Parish." Among the vestry's duties was that of "making and apportioning Levies and Assessments for Building and Repairing the Churches and Chapels, Provisions for the Poor, Maintenance of the Minister," and other tasks necessary "for the more orderly managing all Parochial Affairs."[13] With those acts, the Church of England became Virginia's established church, financed by tax funds and protected by the state against all who violated the Act of Uniformity.

The Church had hardly been established before dissenting intruders threatened the colony's religious peace and uniformity. Puritan missionaries arrived in 1642 from Massachusetts for the purpose of preaching the "true" gospel to Virginians. Massachusetts was a Puritan commonwealth where Congregational churches enjoyed a legal establishment similar to that granted to the Church of England in Virginia. Puritans were hostile to the Church of England, believing that it was in need of reform: that its organization and liturgy were still too Catholic and that all teachings and practices not explicitly sanctioned by the Bible must be eliminated. In England, Puritans were persecuted. But in the vast territory of British North America, they could organize their own colony with freedom to follow their consciences. The problem came when they encroached on Virginia's establishment. The missionaries claimed that they came in response to a call from "some godly people in Virginia" who had requested "Ministers of Christ, to be helpful unto them in instructing them in the truth, as it is in Jesus." Accordingly, Reverend Knowls of Watertown and Reverend Tompson of Braintree "preached openly unto the people for some good space in time," and "the harvest they had was plentifull." However, Anglican officials grew alarmed at their success, and in March 1643, the Virginia Assembly passed an act forbidding nonconformists from preaching publicly or privately in Virginia and requiring Governor Sir William Berkeley to expel all nonconformists. To the Puritan historian Edward Johnson, the expulsion was "none other than the thrusting Christ from them."[14] But to Virginian Churchmen, the governor had acted properly. If Dissenters were allowed to challenge the Church, Virginia would be reduced to the same sort of religious contentiousness that had plagued England in the strife-torn decades before the Elizabethan Settlement.

Virginia's leaders in church and state welcomed the restoration of the Stuarts, in particular applauding the new laws that reestablished and strengthened the Church of England. The so-called Clarendon Code severely circumscribed the religious and civil rights of Dissenters, and Virginians were eager to impose similar restrictions in the Chesapeake. Robert Beverley described the process in his eighteenth-century history: "upon the King's Restoration, he sent [Governor] Sir William Berkeley a new Commission" instructing him to regulate religion and trade in strict compliance with English law. Accordingly, the

"Church of England was confirm'd the established Religion." More specifically, "the Parishes were . . . regulated, competent Allowances were made to the Ministers . . . Convenient Churches and Glebes were provided, [and] all necessary Parish-Officers instituted." Further, stricter laws circumscribed the activities of Dissenters. Beverley believed they were too harsh, observing that "anno 1663, divers Sectaries in Religion beginning to spread themselves there; by a mistaken Zeal great Restraints were laid upon them under severe Penalties, to prevent their Encrease." He thought that the measures hurt the economy because they "made many of [the Dissenters] flie to other Colonies, and prevented abundance of others from going over to seat themselves among 'em."[15]

However, political developments in England as well as economic necessities in the Chesapeake soon forced Virginia's leaders to grant a measure of toleration to Dissenters. In 1687, James II issued his "Declaration for Liberty of Conscience and Indulgence in Religious Matters" in an attempt to loosen some of the restrictions that the Clarendon Code imposed upon Catholics and Protestant Dissenters. Virginia Governor Lord Howard of Effingham immediately ordered the proclamation "published in James Citty on Tuesday next, with the beat of Drum, and fireing of the Great Guns, and with all the Joyfullness that this Collony is Capable to Express."[16] Why did Virginians welcome toleration so heartily just a couple decades after they hailed the Restoration policies curbing Dissenters' rights? The answer is found in economic necessity. Virginia's great planters recognized that economic success depended in large part on attracting more settlers and laborers, and that required religious toleration. The hope was to maintain a firm religious establishment while granting enough toleration to support economic development.

Southern Anglicans faced the challenge of maintaining a regulated religious economy without adequate enforcement machinery. Colonial church leaders lacked the fully-developed organizational structure that their counterparts in England enjoyed. No resident bishops supervised the clergy to ensure an adequate supply of well-trained, orthodox parish priests. And, no ecclesiastical courts enforced church discipline.

Instead, powerful laymen, usually the largest planters, held sway, first by enacting legislation in the General Assembly, and second by enforcing local affairs through parish vestries. Vestrymen had no greater responsibility than that of surveying or processioning parish boundaries. Within those lines, the vestry regulated religious affairs to ensure compliance with the establishment laws. Accordingly, on November 19, 1759, the vestry of St. Paul's Church in Hanover County ordered "that the Parish Lines be Procession'd, . . . and the Same be at Large Recorded in the Vestry Book."[17] Just as individual planters wanted to protect their private property lines, the vestrymen wished to ensure the integrity of the parish lines. By the time of the St. Paul survey, however, a new invasion of Dissenters threatened Virginia's regulated religious economy.

Migration from northern colonies fueled the growth of Dissent in Virginia. From Pennsylvania's founding in the late seventeenth century, thousands of European Protestants immigrated, attracted by the promise of fertile land and religious toleration. One newcomer, Gabriel Thomas, explained that the absence of a state-supported church meant that the residents "pay no Tithes, and their Taxes are inconsiderable," adding that "the Place is free for all Persuasions, in a Sober and Civil way; for the Church of England and the Quakers bear equal Share in the Government." Thomas believed that free religion promoted economic prosperity: "there is no Persecution for Religion, nor ever like to be; 'tis this that knocks all Commerce on the Head, together with high Imposts, strict Laws, and cramping Orders."[18]

While religious freedom abounded in Pennsylvania, plentiful arable land did not. Consequently, by the 1740s, thousands of recent immigrants poured through western Pennsylvania and down the Shenandoah Valley into the southern backcountry. South Carolina Anglican itinerant Charles Woodmason described the large-scale migration, noting in particular its Dissenting character. Writing in the 1760s, he informed the Bishop of London that "hordes of dissenters" from Pennsylvania and New England occupied South Carolina's "interior settlements." In an explanation that applied to Virginia as well, Woodmason noted that the Church was weak along the frontier, with few parishes and fewer qualified ministers to counter the popular appeal of itinerant preachers who spread the unorthodox teachings of Dissent. And the varieties of heterodox preachers was dizzying: "Baptists, New Lights, Presbyterians, Independents, and an hundred other Sects—So that one day you might hear this System of Doctrine—the next day another."[19]

To Woodmason, those intruders represented, at best, competition for the established Church and, at worst, chaos. But for the men and women in the backcountry, they represented choice. Like the chapmen, tinkers, and hawkers peddling wares that made the settlers' lives easier or brighter, itinerant preachers brought colorful messages of hope, comfort, and encouragement, and, no doubt to some, provided a moment of diversion. A merchant before he became a minister, Woodmason recognized that on the frontier he was operating in an unregulated religious market, and his success depended on wooing souls for the Church. He knew that his listeners would weigh his claims against those of the many Dissenters they heard and choose to follow the one who most appealed to them.[20] Woodmason saw the competition as formidable and unscrupulous. He reported that the "Synods of Pennsylvania and New England send out a Sett of Rambling fellows yearly," charging that "among this Medley of Religions—True Genuine Christianity is not to be found," claiming instead that the newcomers make "double the Profits I can make." He wrote, "If there is a Shilling to be got by a Wedding or Funeral, these Independent fellows will endeavor to pocket it," adding that "they beat any Medicinal Mountebank." He reported that whenever he gave notice "to be at such a place at such a Time [for preaching services], three or four of these Fellows [New Lights] are constantly at my Heels—They either get there before me, and hold forth—or after I have finish'd, or the next Day, or for days together." And the itinerants had success. Woodmason commented on how rapidly New Light Baptists advanced their cause in the backcountry. Referring to lay men and women in the Carolina interior, he observed that "twelve months past most of these People were very zealous Members of our Church and many of them Communicants." But, he added, the New Lights have had "Success" and have made "rapid Progress."[21] His account also fit the progress of Dissent in Virginia.

While Pennsylvania immigrants played an important role in challenging Virginia's religious economy, it was a group of Virginia laymen who invited the first Dissenting itinerants. To understand what led to that invitation, we return to Reverend Patrick Henry's parish church in Hanover County at mid-century. Primarily of Scottish descent, the dissidents favored sturdier Calvinist fare than they were receiving. One of the Dissenters, Roger Shackleford, said Henry was an "unconverted graceless man" who preached "damnable doctrine."[22] In lieu of worshipping at St. Paul's, the splinter group sought spiritual sustenance through reading works of the great Reformers, such as Calvin and Luther, and sermons of evangelicals, such as George Whitefield, who had more recently led a great revival in Britain and in the northern colonies. Convening in private homes on Sundays, they discovered in the few books they possessed teachings compatible with the religious heritage of their Scottish and Ulster parents and grandparents. With Samuel Morris, a bricklayer, acting as their elder, the Dissenters organized themselves into a lay-led congregation. Morris built a reading-house on his land to provide a place for the group to meet and read from the Bible and other works. In addition to conducting services at that site, Morris became an itinerant reader in Hanover and surrounding counties, establishing several other "reading-rooms" where he proclaimed the necessity of a spiritual new birth.[23]

The Virginia Dissenters desired a minister to lead them in their spiritual growth and spread the gospel to hungry souls in the piedmont. With no suitable evangelical clergymen in Virginia, they petitioned the New Light Presbyteries of New Castle, Pennsylvania, and New Brunswick, New Jersey, to send them a minister "to officiate for some time among them." Although in Hanover for only a week, the New Light preacher, William Robinson, accomplished much. He helped the lay Dissenters put their church "in regular order" according to New Light beliefs. And through his open-air preaching, he attracted people from all over the region to hear his evangelistic message. When Robinson departed, he left "a General Concern about Religion . . . through the neighborhood, and some hundreds . . . were brought anxiously to enquire what shall we do to be saved?"[24] The strong connection between the presbytery at Newcastle and the Virginians persisted, as the New Lights sent John Roan, who was "instrumental in beginning and promoting the religious concern in several places where there was little appearance of it before." Other Mid-Atlantic revivalists followed, including Gilbert and William Tennent, Samuel Blair, and Samuel Davies.[25]

The Anglican establishment could not by number or temperament compete with the zealous itinerants. The Church had too few qualified ministers to fill western parishes, and those that did were unaccustomed to the hard work of seeking converts outside prescribed services. Again, Charles Woodmason's account of South Carolina clergymen helps us understand their Virginia counterparts. Though suspicious of their motives, Woodmason admitted that the Dissenters were an industrious lot, unlike Anglican parish ministers back in the eastern counties. Of the settled ministry, he observed, "none yet among them ever went out of his Parish, nay not even round his Parish to baptize." He said that he had "seen in Charlestown, Children brought to the font to be baptized, and the Minister put them off till another Day, because he was going to Dinner, or Tea, or Company." Woodmason saw a direct link between the clergy's lack of industry and what he observed on the frontier: "I must freely say, that it has been owing to the Inattention and Indolence of the Clergy, that the Sectaries have gain'd so much ground here."[26] He also believed that the vestry-controlled parish system was too rigid to respond to the fluid society along the fast-growing frontier. Within the Anglican polity, "ev'ry Minister has a Particular and distinc[t] Charge. He has a Circle assigned Him, in which He is to move and not stir out of. He cannot leave his Church for one Sunday without leave of the Vestry . . . under Pain of a Fine."[27] By contrast, Dissenting itinerants went wherever they were in demand. Concurring with Woodmason's assessment, Thomas Jefferson noted that the Dissenting teachers' industry in propagating their views contrasted sharply with the established clergy's "inactivity." As a result, "the zeal and industry of sectarian preachers [gave them] an open and undisputed field."[28]

When two Presbyterian itinerants, Samuel Davies and John Todd, invaded his piedmont parish, Reverend James Maury was unprepared to counter the preachers' popular appeal. According to Adam Smith, clergymen like Maury, "despite state support, . . . are ill-equipped to compete with zealous upstart religious groups," because "the arts of popularity, all the arts of gaining proselytes, are constantly on their side." He noted that in late eighteenth-century England, the Methodists with their "very popular preachers" are "much more in vogue" than are the Anglican clergy. The best Maury could do was to warn his colleague whose county was next on the itinerant's well-publicized preaching tour. "It seems not improper to inform You," Maury wrote, "that the revd Davies & Todd have lately been guilty of what I think Intrusions upon me, in having preached each of them a Sermon at a Tavern in my Parish." The unthinkable had happened: competition in the heart of what Maury had considered to be his exclusive jurisdiction. He observed that neither of the itinerants had "obtained any properly authenticated License to exercise their Function," an ecclesiastical regulation that had heretofore protected the clergy's monopoly. Maury closed by reporting that Davies and Todd had promised upon leaving "to range upon our Frontiers," the district where the Church of England's hold was tenuous.[29]

The itinerants' bold advertising flaunted their disregard for Virginia's customary regulated religious market and caused great distress among the settled ministry. Reverend Patrick Henry found the itinerants' advertising particularly disturbing, in large part because it was so effective. In a letter to a fellow clergyman, Henry warned about Davies's advertised plans for June 1747: "Mr. Davies is to preach at Goochland Court-house next Thursday, from whence he is to travel as far as Roanoke, preaching at certain appointed places in his way." Henry based his report on advance publicity he had seen posted about the countryside: "circular Letters and Advertisements are dispersed all over the upper parts of this Colony, that the People may have notice of the times & places of meeting. My informer has one of the circular Letters, and the Advertisement at Goochland Court-house has, I believe, been seen by hundreds."[30] Henry was aware that through advertising, itinerants bypassed parish ministers and invited parishioners to consider an alternative worship experience. He knew that such tactics threatened to forever change the exclusive relationship he had enjoyed with his people. In short, he now faced competition within his own parish.

What Maury and Henry viewed as unwanted competition, other Virginians welcomed as religious choice. Under the Anglican monopoly, men and women were captive to the only religious service available, that of their parish church. However, some lay persons wanted more, believing that worship on Sundays had grown cold and formal and failed to provide the spiritual sustenance to meet their everyday needs. Rather than reading prescribed passages from the *Book of Common Prayer*, evangelical itinerants offered a spontaneous message aimed at their listeners' hearts. Moreover, the sermons conveyed great power to individuals, insisting that God offered his grace directly within the hearts of men and women through a personal conversion experience, not through the doctrines and sacraments presented through church officials. For some Virginians, such a religion was irresistible.

In his chronicle of eighteenth-century Virginia, Baptist minister John Leland discussed religious choice on the frontier. He recorded that "west of the Blue Ridge, a number of Presbyterians emigrated from Pennsylvania, and did not chuse to worship in the Episcopal mode, but set up their own form of worship." Religious choice came at a high cost to the Presbyterians because under Virginia law they still "were obliged to pay to the Episcopal Clergymen, as much as if they had been Episcopalian." Then in the mid-1760s, Baptists began to spread throughout Virginia, in part resulting from the work of ministers from northern states and in part rising from within "the South."[31] Baptists insisted on the right of each person to make his or her religious choices without any state coercion. According to Leland, "every man must give an account of himself to God, and therefore every man ought to be at liberty to serve God in that way that he can best reconcile it to his conscience." A free religious marketplace was the Baptists' ideal. There, "religion is a matter between God and individuals: religious opinions of men not being the objects of civil government, nor any way under its control."[32]

Not every Virginian who heard or read New Light sermons chose to follow the evangelicals; some elected to remain within the Church of England. One couple, Jacob Moon and his wife, were appalled to learn that their friend and Anglican minister Devereux Jarratt had converted to Methodism. They scoffed at his "sudden fondness of 'the new light cant.'" The Moons insisted that "being Church people [Anglicans], . . . they . . . could listen to nothing but what came through that channel." While that statement suggests that the couple blindly followed the Church's dictates, their decision to stay with the Church was more than unquestioning loyalty; it was a considered choice. It was in the Moon's house that Jarratt had found the volume of Whitefield's sermons that so influenced his faith and ministry. Noting the presence of the book in their home, one scholar concluded that "evidently the Moons had explored their religious options and decided to hold fast to their Anglican faith."[33] More important than the different choices that Jarratt and the Moons made is the fact that each considered religious options, and each selected the one that he or she deemed more suitable for him or her.

The presence of a growing number of Dissenters was more than a matter of individual choice; it was also a political problem in a colony where religious uniformity and Anglican establishment had long been keystones of public policy. In 1745, Governor William Gooch convened a grand jury to investigate and bring indictments against the unwanted itinerant preachers complained about by clergymen in western parishes. In explaining his actions, Gooch referred to the recent "Outrage committed against the Purity of the Worship, and the sacred Appointment of Pastors for the Service of the Altar of the Established Church, which some Men, calling themselves Ministers, were justly accused of in my Charge to the Grand Jury." According to the governor, the itinerants had broken two provincial laws. First, their preaching services consisted primarily of passionately delivered extemporaneous sermons instead of the Church of England's published liturgy, thus violating the act of religious uniformity whereby public worship was to conform to the *Book of Common Prayer*. Second, by criticizing Anglican clergymen, the evangelical itinerants had broken the law forbidding public criticism of the clergy. Gooch added that the itinerant preachers propagated "wicked and destructive Doctrine and Practice," a reference no doubt to the evangelicals' insistence that individuals should follow those preachers who declared the necessity of a New Birth, and their accusation that most clergymen did not preach such a message. To the governor, turning religion into a matter of individual choice was tantamount to anarchy. He vowed that this type of Dissent ought to "be Opposed and suppressed, by all that have a serious Concern for Religion, and a just Regard to publick Peace and Order in Church and State."[34]

Governor Gooch made it clear that his opposition to the itinerants did not violate the Act of Toleration. Shortly after he convened the grand jury, he received a letter from the Presbyterian Synod of Philadelphia expressing concern that his opposition included all Dissenters. The Presbyterians explained that the invading itinerants were renegades, "sent out by some, who by Reason of their divisive, censorious and uncharitable Doctrine and Practice, were in May 1741, excluded from our Synod." After forming their "separate Society," the New Light, pro-revival enthusiasts had "industriously sent abroad Persons whom we judge unqualified" to proselytize. Rather than advancing the Kingdom of God, they "divide and trouble the Churches." The petitioners assured Gooch that, unlike the New Lights, ministers sent to Virginia from the Synod of Philadelphia will produce "proper Testimonials" confirming their qualifications and orthodoxy. In his reply, the governor pledged that "your Missionaries, producing proper Testimonials, complying with the Laws, and performing Divine Service in some certain Place appointed for that Purpose, without disturbing the Quiet and Unity of our sacred and civil Establishment, may be sure of . . . Protection."[35] Thus, Gooch granted toleration within a regulated religious economy. Unlicensed, unregulated preaching would not be tolerated. However, legal restraints were insufficient to slow the spreading free market of religion as continued immigration and conversion swelled the number of Dissenters.

Political tension persisted between Dissenters and Churchmen over the de facto free religious market. The former protested tax payments to support the established Church as violating their freedom of conscience. The latter sought to curb Dissenter activity by requiring nonconformist preachers to pledge loyalty to the Crown and Church, refrain from criticizing either, and acquire licenses to signify their compliance. As more Presbyterians entered the colony in the 1750s, Virginians debated the merits of relaxing the establishment laws to encourage continued immigration. In exchanges printed in the *Virginia Gazette* as well as voiced on the floor of the General Assembly, those who thought Dissent desirable squared off against those who feared its spread. Philo Virginia argued that more liberal toleration laws for Dissenters would benefit the colony's economy by attracting thousands of hard-working men and women. He claimed that it was "an intolerable Grievance to pay their Proportion of the County Levy for the Support of the established Clergy; though they should impose upon themselves the additional Expence of affording a tolerable (tho' lesser) Maintenance, by voluntary Subscriptions, to a Minister of their own Denomination." While Virginia's laws "must appear highly reasonable to that Church in whose Favour they are made," Philo pointed out that they were unreasonable to Dissenters contemplating a move to the colony.[36]

In making the case for an "extensive Toleration," Philo invited the assemblymen to observe how Pennsylvania's religious liberty had made that colony the fastest growing in all of British North America. He pointed out that "it is evident in Fact that of all the Plantations in English America, Pennsylvania has flourished most in Trade, and increased in Inhabitants, considering how lately it was settled." Though settled almost a hundred years after Virginia, Pennsylvania was "much better improved, and more closely inhabited." Philadelphia was the largest city of North America, a commercial hub that was indeed "the Mart of Nations." Philo urged the Virginia Assembly to exempt such Protestant Dissenters from paying toward the "Support of the established Church."[37]

While Philo saw economic benefit in a more extensive toleration, Tom Telltruthia envisioned social chaos. Responding to Philo, Tom conceded that all was not right in the established Church; in particular, there was much "useless Lumber among the Clergy." But, he opposed any "Scheme of universal Toleration." He argued that the colony already had one internal "Distemper" in the institution of slavery and reasoned that "if we add that of the Sectaries too, by a universal Toleration, I am afraid it shall bring a greater Load upon our Constitution" than it will be able to bear. In his analysis, both Pennsylvania and Virginia should be content with their present burdens: the former's "Sectaries and divided Interests," the latter's slavery. Tom warned that universal toleration would promote religious competition. Preachers of the Church of England and those of the various Dissenting sects "instead of recommending Virtue and Piety to their Hearers, will get to Daggers drawing among themselves, and mauling one another." Such interfaith rivalry already created a spectacle in Pennsylvania, a "weekly diversion . . . exhibited by the dissenting, and contending Orators." He concluded by expressing his opinion that Virginia needed no more toleration, "that we have not a Bit more of it than is unavoidably pinned down upon us by Act of Parliament, which may happen to be full enough, if not too much."[38]

The writer's suggestion that slavery and free religion were a combustible mixture reflected southerners' worst fear, that of a slave rebellion. Throughout their histories, the slave colonies had placed strict regulations on religious instruction of slaves. Many slaveholders feared that the liberating message of the gospel, if not carefully edited, could give slaves dangerous notions. Some thought that the evangelical revival with its emphasis on individual experience had contributed to the 1741 Negro riots in New York. Even Samuel Davies, who preached the necessity of a spiritual conversion to slaves, expressed alarm that some slaves had placed their own "construction" on his words. To slaveholders interested in absolute control, religious choice among slaves was unthinkable.

Thus, in the 1750s, the Virginia Assembly tabled bills seeking a more liberal toleration. In Thomas Jefferson's view, the colony's leaders "shewed equal intolerance in this country with their Presbyterian brethren, who had emigrated to the northern governments."[39] In other words, both New England Puritans and Virginia Anglicans clung to the principle of religious uniformity for more than a hundred years after their settlement, and each continued to persecute Dissenters. However, when the Virginia Assembly next confronted the question of religious toleration, they did so when perhaps as many as two-thirds of Virginians were Dissenters and the demand for liberty suffused the Revolutionary atmosphere.

Delegates to Virginia's constitutional convention in 1776 renewed the debate over the place of religion in the new state, and they divided according to which religious economy they advocated. Churchmen took the conservative position that only religious regulation could reliably provide the necessary religious instruction for virtuous republicans. Conservatives worried that, if left to a free religious market, religious instruction would be hit or miss, resting on the inclinations and resources of sects more concerned with proclaiming their own theological notions than a common body of beliefs. Dissenters countered that establishments were and had always been engines of persecution, with the state acting as a police force for the favored religion. Further, they argued, a state should have only a negative role where religion is concerned: that of protecting each individual's right of conscience. They believed that one's salvation was an issue between God and the individual, and that the individual must be free to pursue God's grace in his or her own way.

The constitutional battle began with conservatives proposing an Episcopal establishment that granted a liberal toleration to Dissenters. The initiative evoked an immediate and spirited opposition from those who insisted that religious liberty was a natural, divine-given right, not a government prerogative. On November 8, 1776, the clergy of the established Church presented a memorial to the Virginia Assembly calling for a constitutional establishment that would not encroach upon "the religious rights of any sect or denomination of men." They argued that a "religious establishment in a State is conducive to its peace and happiness," and "it, therefore, cannot be improper for the legislative body of a State to consider how such opinions as are most consonant to reason and of the best efficacy in human affairs may be propagated and supported." They added that "the doctrines of

Christianity have a greater tendency to produce virtue amongst men than any human laws or institutions, and that "these can be best taught and preserved in their purity in an established church." Under Virginia's colonial establishment, they maintained, "order and internal tranquility, true piety and virtue have more prevailed than in most other parts of the world." They warned that if the Dissenters succeeded in abolishing establishment, and "all denominations of Christians be placed upon a level," that the resulting competition among sects will produce "much confusion, [and] probably civil commotions will attend the contest."[40]

Dissenters demurred, flooding the Assembly with petitions calling for disestablishment. Presbyterians, Lutherans, and Baptists called for liberty of conscience. In a typical plea, some Prince Edward County Dissenters called Virginia's establishment a "long night of ecclesiastical bondage." They hoped that "all church establishments might be pulled down, and every tax upon conscience and private judgment abolished, and each individual left to rise or sink by his own merit and the general laws of the land." In other words, they called for a secular state where citizens could worship as their consciences directed them without suffering any civil penalty. Such religious freedom, they promised, would make Virginia "an asylum for free inquiry, knowledge, and the virtuous of every denomination."[41]

A petition from the Presbytery of Hanover County called for a complete separation of church and state. First, they argued that America was fighting for freedom and that establishment is antithetical to freedom. "In this enlightened age and in a land where all of every denomination are united in the most strenuous efforts to be free," the petitioners reminded the legislature, "we hope and expect that our representatives will cheerfully concur in removing every species of religious, as well as civil, bondage." Second, they argued that any establishment, including that of the "Christian religion," that is, Christianity itself and not that of a single sect, would amount to surrendering liberty of conscience to the state. They explained, "There is no argument in favor of establishing the Christian religion but what may be pleaded, with equal propriety, for establishing the tenets of Mohammed by those who believe the

Alcoran; or if this be not true, it is at least impossible for the magistrate to adjudge the right of preference among the various sects that profess the Christian faith, without erecting a chair of infallibility, which would lead us back to the Church of Rome."[42] The message was clear: religion is a matter of conscience between God and individuals, and the state should have no role in religious affairs whatsoever.

Faced with petitions both defending and attacking establishment, the Virginia legislature in the fall of 1776 engaged in heated debate. Thomas Jefferson called it "the severest contest in which I have ever been engaged." Leading the proponents of establishment were Edmund Pendleton and Robert Carter Nicholas, "honest men, but zealous churchmen," according to Jefferson. While a majority of Virginians were Dissenters, a majority of the legislators were Churchmen. However, many of them were "reasonable, and liberal men" who tried to safeguard religious liberty within an establishment bill. The bill that passed did in fact make some strides toward religious liberty. Most significantly, it repealed the laws which "rendered criminal the maintenance of any religious opinions (other than those of the Episcopalians)." But it also declared that "religious assemblies ought to be regulated, and that provision ought to be made for continuing the succession of the clergy and superintending their conduct." However, the thorniest problem, that of tax support for religion, remained unresolved and would continue to be debated from 1776 to 1779. The question was "whether a general assessment should not be established by law on every one to the support of the pastor of his choice; or whether all should be left to voluntary contributions."[43]

With the cry for freedom growing louder during the Revolution, the Virginia legislative session of 1779 brought the downfall of establishment in Virginia but failed to enact Thomas Jefferson's bill for religious freedom. In June, Governor-elect Jefferson's bill for complete religious freedom was reported to the House. Again petitions poured into the Assembly supporting and attacking the bill. Some wanted to abolish establishment altogether, including public support of the clergy, while others wished to retain "an establishment . . . under certain regulations" that allowed for considerable freedom. After much debate, the lawmakers ended the establishment to the extent that the "clergy could no longer look for support to taxation." However, they retained possession of their glebes and kept a near-monopoly of marriage fees. As to Jefferson's bill on religious liberty, a majority found it too radical, preferring instead Patrick Henry's "liberal Establishment," which granted toleration to Dissenters.[44]

After the War of Independence, Virginians again took up the issue of the place of religion in the state. As before, Dissenters and Churchmen staked out clear and opposing positions. The former wanted absolute religious freedom—that is, no state support or regulation of religion whatsoever. The latter, reconstituted in 1783 as the Protestant Episcopal Church, advocated a new and more liberal establishment. In late 1784, the legislature debated the "Bill Establishing a Provision for Teachers of Religion," widely known as the "General Assessment Bill." Supporters justified public support of religion by repeating that "the general diffusion of Christian knowledge" was essential for a virtuous republic." They then argued that only the legislature could make "competent provision for learned teachers, who may be thereby enabled to devote their time and attention to the duty of instructing such citizens." They promised that the establishment law would contain the "liberal principle" of toleration "by abolishing all distinctions of pre-eminence among the different societies or communities of Christians."[45]

The issue being debated was not the importance of religion to society. Both sides agreed that religion in general and Protestant Christianity in particular was necessary for a moral citizenry. Further, men on both sides of the debate held strong personal beliefs that they frequently expressed in speech and print. Rather, the question disputed was about the place of religion in society. Henry and his followers thought that religious instruction was too important to leave to the voluntary initiatives of individual sects; therefore, he advocated an establishment with tax-funded ministers. He thought that a liberal toleration would satisfy Dissenters. Leland, Madison, and Jefferson wanted religion to operate with no government interference in a free marketplace of ideas. And they wanted complete religious freedom, not toleration.

Leland explained their position. First, he wrote, "Government has no more to do with the religious opinions of men, than it has with the principles of mathematics." Second, he continued, "Let every man speak freely without fear, maintain the principles that he believes, worship according to his own faith, either one God, three Gods, no God, or twenty Gods." And, third, he concluded, "let government protect him in so doing."[46]

With the passage of the *Virginia Statute of Religious Freedom,* the free marketplace of religious ideas became a constitutional guarantee in Virginia. It also became the model for the new republic. With Jefferson and Madison leading the legislative fight, most historians have credited them with winning the battle for religious freedom. However, they themselves recognized that their success would have been impossible without the thousands of Dissenters who over the previous forty years had poured into the state, many of whom emigrated from Pennsylvania. Jefferson noted that by 1776 a majority of Virginians were Dissenters. Settling primarily along the frontier, where the presence of the established Church was weakest, they had created a de facto free marketplace of religion, providing men and women choice among competing sects. Reflecting on the triumph of religious liberty, Madison explained how the measure passed even though most of the legislators were Episcopalians who favored establishment. "It is well known," he wrote in 1788, "that a religious establishment would have taken place in that State, if the legislative majority had found as they expected, a majority of the people in favor of the measure; and I am persuaded that if a majority of the people were now of one sect, the measure would still take place and on narrower ground than was then proposed."[47]

Critics feared that without an establishment, religion would languish, but Madison predicted otherwise, and he lived long enough to see his prediction validated. In an 1819 letter to his friend, Robert Walsh, Madison observed, "there has been an increase of religious instruction since the Revolution." He noted that while old churches "built under the establishment at the public expense, have in many instances gone to ruin," among the other sects "Meeting Houses have multiplied and continue to multiply." He expressed his opinion that "the number, the industry, and the morality of the priesthood and the devotion of the people have been manifestly increased by the total separation of the Church from the State."[48] In short, religion flourished in the free, competitive market.

For his part, Jefferson lamented the choices Americans made. In the late eighteenth century, he had hoped and even predicted that the next generation would embrace a religion of reason, perhaps Unitarianism. However, he lived to witness a very different outcome: a second great evangelical revival wherein tens of thousands opted for the very kind of religious enthusiasm Jefferson so decried. In the free religious market he had championed, individuals made their own choices.

Power and Authority in the Colonial South

The English Legacy and Its Contradictions

HOLLY BREWER

When historians consider the influence of English ideas about power and authority on colonial America, they have often focused on what colonists referred to at the time of the Revolution as "English liberties," which meant some combination of representation, trial by jury, and freedom of the press, at least for free-born adult men. Of course, the influence of English ideas about authority is a complex question—and many other scholars have addressed the ways that English culture and values influenced the colonies. But to some degree our questions have been ignoring the depth of the changes and struggles that England and Britain burned through during this period. Indeed, any scholar who looks closely at—to take only one example—the role of the jury must admit that it transformed between the mid sixteenth and early nineteenth centuries from a more elite, neighborhood body that was supposed to judge on the character of the accused, to a body that was less elite and supposed to analyze only the evidence presented in the courtroom. Likewise this period was convulsed by sharp confrontations over who could vote (and when and over what) and over freedom of the press.[1] The seventeenth century in England, in particular, was a time of incredible struggle—of two revolutions—fought over principles of power and authority, questions that ranged from high ideology to base laws, with arguments about perpetual status at their center.

Those two revolutions in England profoundly affected the colonies, both practically, by disrupting the political organizations of many colonies, and ideologically, by shaping the debates over laws and principles in the colonies. While the New England colonies, especially during the first revolution, the English Civil War/Interregnum of 1642–1660, felt freer to pursue their own courses, the southern and Carribean colonies most certainly did not: their Royalist Governors and Burgesses were forcibly evicted by Cromwell's troops in 1651–1652. During the Glorious Revolution of 1688–1689, many colonies held mini-revolutions of their own, and the issues of authority underlying it had echoes in debates in the colonies.

I propose to focus on the seventeenth century and the way that these debates influenced the development of the colonies in the colonial South. In particular, I want to trace the opposite side of the "whiggish" history that is normally told, which begins with the founding of the House of Burgesses in Virginia in 1619 and relates the steady growth of freedom and English liberties. Instead, I want to outline the impact of the opposing ideas about authority and power: absolute monarchy, neo-feudalism, and perpetual status. These principles were those supported by the Royalist side during the English Civil War and had some basis in the laws and practice of England. To what extent did southern colonies adopt these precedents and ideology? How receptive were Virginia and Barbados, in particular, to the different sides in the titanic struggles gripping England, particularly the English Civil War? These alternative precedents, which focus on the principle of perpetual status, help to explain both slavery and many other aspects of the legal organization of the southern colonies. Particularly, this study will sketch those elements of English culture and institutions which supported perpetual status, whether in religious and political ideology, land law, or personal law (of which both slavery and monarchy are parts).

These elements interacted with each other: political debates both drew on the law and sought to reshape it. One set of laws (about perpetual land ownership) influenced another (those about personal status). Religion was the arena where much of the debate took place, partly because church and state were one in Tudor and Stuart England: the monarch was the head of the Church. During the seventeenth century, in short, England's struggles over power ranged across religious and political and legal boundaries.

Should authority be based on inherited right or on the consent of the governed? While there were of course legal precedents for both—kings and members of the House of Lords generally inherited their positions, members of the House of Commons were elected (e.g. on the consent of some 5–10 percent of adult males in the population)—what those precedents even meant was sharply disputed. Sir Robert Filmer's Royalist pamphlets of the 1640s, for example, while admitting freely that the House of Commons was elected, argued that its role was only to advise the king, that it was called only at his pleasure, and dissolved at his pleasure as well, and then only infrequently. The king had his authority by divine right (as his father's next heir), and his will was the law of the land.[2] Filmer's principles came from his king, and were preached in pulpits, from sermons to catechisms. Charles I was steeped in his father's ideology of divine and absolute monarchy. James I had laid out the basis of this ideology in his *Trew Law of Free Monarchies* (1598). "The duty and allegiance which the people swears to their prince is not only bound to themselves, but to their . . . lawful heirs and posterity [to] the lineal succession of crowns. No objection may free the people from their oath giving to the King and his succession. As he is their heritable overlord, and so by birth comes to his crown."[3]

The arguments underlying absolute monarchy were largely about perpetual status and the divine basis of birthright. The next king was heir by birthright: he was chosen by God for that status, the same as his father. If primogeniture did not hold, as Thomas Paine so cleverly mocked with statements like "virtue is not hereditary" in 1776, then the very basis of monarchy—hereditary authority—disappeared.[4] Without perpetual status, there is no monarchy.

Perpetual status did not apply simply to the monarchy, however. It applied, potentially, to everyone. Were you born to privileges and/or obligations or were you born with some measure of choice about your fate, whether religious or political? Religion and politics, it must be remembered, were inextricably combined in sixteenth- and seventeenth-century England: the monarch was not only the head of the country; he (or she) was head of the Church. Hierarchies in both ran parallel. Perpetual status was an issue that English lawyers of the sixteenth and seventeenth centuries spent a great deal of time arguing about, whether inside or outside the courts of law.

Perpetual status had many dimensions, but basically the principle was that you were born a subject of a kingdom, or you were born to inherit it. You were born to inherit a freehold or a copyhold or a leasehold, born to inherit a seat in the House of Lords. Just so, you could be born to obligations that fit your status: by the Elizabethan statute of Artificers, you and your children could be forced to labor for someone else if your belongings were not worth a total value of "ten poundes" and you were not heir to someone. Indeed, children from such families could be forced to labor in "apprenticeships" to husbandry (e.g. without pay) if a person who owned at least sixty acres of land needed their help: "That if any person shallbee requyred by any Householder having and using half a ploughelande [about sixty acres] at the least in Tillage, to bee an Apprentice and to serve in Husbandrye or in any other kind of Arte, Mysterye, or Science before expressed, and shall refuse so to doo; that then upon the Complaint of suche Housekeper to one Justice of Peace of the Countye . . . [he] shall have powre and aucthoritee by virtue herof, yf the said person refuse to bee bounde as an Apprentice, to commit him unto Warde [prison], *there to remayne untill he be contented and will bee bounden to serve as an Apprentise* should serve. . . ." The statute of Artificers built upon elements of feudalism, such as they had existed, by which the children of villeins had their parents' status.[5]

Likewise, you were born a subject of both church and state. You were born a member of the Anglican Church (it was assumed) and were supposed to be baptized within three weeks of your birth, which reaffirmed that membership. If not, your parents could be prosecuted. You were born owing allegiance to the king—and to all magistrates and lesser officials justly put in authority over you, as literally millions of catechisms, published across the land, emphasized. "What dost thou learn from these commandments? . . . My duty [is] . . . to honour and obey the kyng and his ministers. To submit myself to all my governours, teachers, spiritual pastors and maisters. To ordre myselfe lowly and reverently to all my betters."[6] The mainstream catechism, in short, inculcated principles of perpetual status: you were born a subject, with obligations, just as the king was born your overlord.

The political support of birthright and birth status influenced religious positions and vice versa: the religious debate over birthright connected ideologically to other questions of birth status; just so were people born subjects or born slaves. As Stephen Marshall expressed it so beautifully in 1644, while arguing for the Anglican position that children are born members of the same church as their parents, with consonant privileges and obligations: birthright is everything. "As it is in other kingdomes, corporations and families; the children of all subjects born in a kingdom, are born that prince's subjects; where the father is a free-man, the childe is not born a slave: where any are bought to be servants, their children born in their master's house are born his servants. Thus it is by the Lawes of almost all nations, and thus hath the lord Ordained it shall be in his kingdome [i.e., in the church]." For Marshall as for the Church of England, a child inherits the status of the parent as a Church member just as a child inherits the status of the father as a subject, free-man, slave, or servant. Marshall pointedly did not distinguish himself from the "Orthodox Church [the Anglican]": his point was to argue for infant baptism as a possibility (except for "Indians" and "Turks,") although he did focus on the easiest case, the children of professed believers.[7]

Perpetual status was also enshrined in land ownership, by means of the legal institutions of primogeniture and entail (which also governed the transmission of titles). The statute "De Donis Conditionalibus" (1285) that formed the core of "feudalism" in England (such as it existed) dictated that the natural way for land to descend after a person's death was according to the rules of primogeniture. (In England this meant all land would go to the eldest son, or if no son, to the daughters). Those who owned land could not freely designate the person who would next inherit it. After some reforms (especially a law of 1540 passed under Henry VIII, and also Henry VIII's liquidation of the monasteries) it became easier for testators to choose who would inherit their land, but only for a while. Due to that thirteenth-century statute, "De Donis" land once again began falling into a kind of locked inheritance, despite Henry VIII's reforms. If a testator once designated that the land should descend via primogeniture, it was supposed to do so "for ever." This permanent inheritance by primogeniture was called an entail.

Entails in their ideal form were impossible to break. The land could not be sold or mortgaged. It could be leased only under certain conditions. In practice, English lawyers developed some strategies for breaking entails (fines and common recoveries), so that the land could be sold to pay off a debt, for example. But even these were difficult to invoke. Several of Jane Austen's novels, for example, revolve around entails—which the families are unable to break, and lead to the women, in particular, being put in difficult positions. In *Pride and Prejudice,* Mr. Bennet had inherited his estate in a male tail (a type of entail that barred females from inheriting). The rules required that the consent of the "next heir" be gained before such an entail could be broken; in order to revoke an entail, the person who was supposed to inherit thus had to agree that he would not receive the land. The problem is obvious: The distant cousin who was to inherit, Mr. Collins, would never have agreed to breaking the entail; he was not even asked.[8]

Likewise, lesser forms of land ownership could be hereditary. A person could lease a farm for "three lives," meaning his own life and that of his next two heirs by primogeniture—although these usually also specified a maximum of twenty-one years. Copyholds—the remnants of feudalism—also descended by primogeniture.

These three interrelated types of perpetual status—political and religious and economic identity—were key parts of the laws of England in the late sixteenth and early seventeenth centuries and were approved of by many, particularly those in authority. This was the way the world should be.

They were not, however, completely traditional. Indeed, the first "historians" to discover and define medieval feudalism were doing so in the context of the ideological debates over perpetual status in the early seventeenth century. In defining medieval feudalism, they were searching for legal precedents and principles to justify their ideals of absolutism. They were trying to create a model of a past that should influence the present. Others, by labeling "feudalism" as a product of the Norman conquest, sought to idealize different precedents and ideals, in pre-Norman, Anglo-Saxon laws and norms.

This historical debate over feudalism had wide political impact and implications. More than a century later, for example, Thomas Jefferson would glorify Anglo-Saxon freedoms and repudiate Norman feudalism.[9] Feudalism in seventeenth-century England, then, was hardly dead. Pure feudalism, with its double-sided obligations and services and oaths of loyalty, undoubtedly was, if it had ever existed.[10] But important elements of what these seventeenth-century historians labeled feudalism were embedded in the law and, in the context of these debates, were being idealized and glorified. These included the entails, discussed above, and some types of personal status (e.g. the statute of Artificers drew on principles related to villenage).

Elements of feudalism and hereditary status also included the layers of land ownership. Often king, lord, and commoner all had some claim, layered claims, if you will, to the same piece of land. The king gave the land to his "tenant in knight service"—a lord—and in exchange the lord owed some obligations (and the land still really belonged to the king and could revert to him). The tenant in knight service in turn leased the land under, for example, a copyhold, to the commoner. And that copyhold could itself contain certain rights, including access to common land. These claims were often hereditary.

Indeed, the enclosure movement in England between the sixteenth and the early nineteenth centuries, which historians have usually seen as capitalist, was in other ways neo-feudalistic, albeit invoked to limit the traditional rights of the poorer and middling sort. By enclosing common lands and using them for their own purposes (and preventing common people from growing crops or grazing cattle or sheep on them) the lords increased their own hereditary authority. While this did lead to a concentration of capital, it also grew out of a glorification of, if you will, absolute lordship. Even the terms under which the new enclosures were created invoked older feudal norms: they wanted to make it seem as if these reforms had some basis. Modifications of the term villein, for example, were used to describe those who would be tenants in new cottages built to replace the old.

These legal norms about feudalism and perpetual status were fiercely debated and even fought over in the English Civil War and the Glorious Revolution. The debates and wars made the connections between laws and systems of power explicit; they illuminated the connections between monarchy, aristocracy, and inherited status generally.

The key group to lead the opposition to inherited status, whose effort to limit the authority of Charles I led first to civil war and finally to beheading him, were those we now call Puritans or, after the Civil War, Dissenters (meaning they "dissented" from the Church of England and refused to worship there). Many Puritans (not all) moved from arguments about consent to church membership to arguments about consent to government. John Milton, for example, wrote political pamphlets in the 1640s that celebrated the legitimacy and rightful authority of the commons—true government should be based on the consent of the governed. Whether one looks at the Putney debates (wherein Cromwell's soldiers debated the legitimate boundaries of consent) or the laws passed by the House of Commons, which required oaths of allegiance from all men—consent of some kind, as opposed to hereditary obligation, was clearly critical to those who fought with Cromwell on the side of Parliament. As Colonel Rainsborough stated during the Putney debates of 1647: "every man that is to live under a government ought first by his own consent to put himself under that government." Indeed, the question of consent was arguably the most important issue during the trial of Charles I.[11]

The religious argument—that they were born to be members of the Church, just as they were subjects of the kingdom—honed their objections to their political status. Indeed, one of the critical questions of the seventeenth century was "infant baptism," about which literally hundreds if not thousands of tracts were written. John Tombe, a self-described "antipaedobaptist," took the lead in arguing against the Anglican position about Church membership. "Christianity is no mans birth right" but comes only by "free election of grace, and according to Gods appointment." Baptism should be a matter of election and choice, not inheritance: "In the confession of baptism, every ones free choice is shewed. . . . None were to be baptized, but such as shewed their own free choice by confession."[12]

Under Cromwell (a Puritan) they not only executed King Charles I in 1649, ending his lineage and kingship itself, but also abolished the House of Lords. They thus destroyed the twin bastions of hereditary authority in the English system. While Cromwell anointed himself Lord Protector and did not hold viable elections for Parliament (partly because of a fear that those elected might literally condemn those who had participated in the execution of the king), the Interregnum rump parliamentary sessions are marked by constant discussion on the topic of consent and new elections.

At the restoration of Charles II in 1660, not only the king was restored (and his progeny by primogeniture) but also the hereditary House of Lords. At the same time, one of the critical questions asked of ministers (many of whom had received their positions during the almost twenty years of Puritan control) was whether they held to the Anglican position on hereditary Church membership. If they did not, they would be dismissed. More than two thousand were thus removed by 1662.

Literally all of the authors writing in seventeenth-century England whom the American Revolutionaries cited and quoted as the basis for their Republican ideology were Dissenters. Whether writing in the context of the English Civil War, or of the Glorious Revolution in 1688–1689 and the decade of crisis that preceded it, they extended the religious arguments against inherited status and for consent to political theories. While John Locke developed these most clearly (and was undoubtedly the most influential), others, from James Harrington to Algernon Sidney, were inspired by the religious controversies to shape new theories of government based on the consent of the governed.[13]

The Glorious Revolution was undoubtedly only a partial revolution, in that it did not fully adopt the new theories. Parliament got rid of one king but chose other monarchs (a queen and her husband). They exerted some control over the dominance of inherited right and limited the absolute power of kings, but did not dispense with the principles. Still, many of the books written during the decades before and after had more radical positions about inherited right. Indeed the clear implication of popular books such as Gordon and Trenchard's *Cato's Letters* (published first in serial form in the 1720s and reprinted four times in the colonies) was that inheritance was the worst way to choose a king. A prince always grows up spoiled and without self restraint, by definition.[14] While they did not propose doing away with the position of monarch altogether (and indeed, one could not do so openly without threat of prosecution for treason, and had to fight to evade the official censors), their implication was that rulers should be chosen.

John Locke, who came from a Dissenting background (his father fought with Cromwell), was one among many obsessed with questions of hereditary status, although he argued more strongly against some aspects of it than others. His *Essay on Toleration,* for example, contends that "nobody is born a member of any church; otherwise the religion of parents would descend unto children, by the same right of inheritance as their temporal estates, and every one would hold his faith by the same tenure as he does his lands, than which nothing can be imagined more absurd."[15] Whereas Locke expressed some tolerance for hereditary lands, he did try to modify it by critiquing primogeniture: The first treatise of his *Two Treatises of Government* is an argument against inherited power and inherited status generally. Indeed, Puritans—including John Winthrop, who was a member of Parliament in the 1620s, tried to modify the rules about inheritance of land via primogeniture: they argued that all of a father's children deserved some share. Granted, this was not as radical a position as might be taken (they were not arguing that all children in the kingdom deserved a share of land), but it was still a significant amendment to hereditary norms, in that such a policy would gradually break up estates.

Republican/democratic ideology challenged that older system of status. Should the child have the status of the father—or the mother? Can the status or the actions of the father or the mother bind the child permanently, and all their posterity? The answer for the democratic/republican political theorists of the seventeenth century was a resounding no. They gave a very different answer than the Royalists had given.

On the question of hereditary slavery, Locke, for example, was unequivocal. Even in the case where a father has made war in an unjust manner, and agrees to serve another in exchange for his life (the only case where Locke allowed any semblance of slavery), the father can never bind the child. "I say this concerns not their children who are in their minority; for since a father hath not, in himself, a power over the life or liberty of his child, no act of his can possibly forfeit it. So that the children . . . are freemen." He continued in the same vein at length.[16]

Locke's *Two Treatises of Government* offers a resounding critique of slavery on the grounds that slavery cannot be inherited:

> *The absolute power of the conqueror reaches no farther than the persons of the men that were subdued by him, and dies with them; and should he govern them as slaves, subjected to his absolute arbitrary power, he has no such right or dominion over their children. He can have no power over them but by their own consent, whatever he may drive them to say or do; and he has no lawful authority whilst force, and not choice, compels them to submission.*[17]

"He can have no power over them but by their own consent" gets at the heart of the political system that Locke was constructing. One is not born to a status. One can choose one's status, and that choosing must not be forced. This ringing indictment of slavery as it was then developing in England's empire is unequivocal. The only bound labor that Locke condones is in fact a kind of contract-bound indentured servitude, within which the servant has significant rights. Throughout his treatise, he develops ideas about what free choice means: in the case of labor contracts, as others, valid consent should be free from influence and force. The person agreeing to labor had certain rights which he cannot grant to another, which he cannot alien, including the responsibility of providing first for himself and his family. And the implication of Locke's extended meditation on political contracts is that unjust contracts, whether political contracts or for one's labor, can be broken (are voidable).[18]

Although Dissenters tended to cluster on one side of these arguments (to support consent) and Royalists and many mainstream Anglicans on the other (to support hereditary authority), one should not be too simplistic about these categories. While religious arguments were affecting and shaping the political, the arguments were far from simple. The Reformation bore within it divergent claims for the basis of authority, whether in birth or consent. Ironically, both the absolutist arguments about monarchy and the most radical ideas about consent and equality were strengthened by the Reformation. The divine authority of kings and their role as "fathers" of their country—and even the emphasis on the fifth commandment—were profoundly strengthened by arguments coming out of the Reformation. On the other hand, Luther's priesthood of all believers, who could interpret the Bible for themselves, had radical egalitarian implications. Thus in some sense both sides in the English Civil War were making arguments that were partly shaped by the legacy of the Reformation.

These English controversies helped to shape the institutional structure, legal norms, and culture in the colonies. Since the focus of this essay is on the colonial South, I can only say a few words here about the "Puritan" colonies. Suffice it to say that in reading the laws of Massachusetts side by side with those of England and Virginia, it is clear that Massachusetts was anything but traditional. The Puritan colonists fashioned a new set of inheritance laws that favored partible inheritance and they refused to enforce entail. They wrote a new set of laws and reconsidered nearly every English norm, from criminal to civil laws. Who should vote? They connected it to church membership, age, gender, and property ownership. Neither of the first two applied in England, and New England Puritans set property qualifications lower. They elected all levels of their political and religious authorities. This is not to argue that the Puritans who settled in New England were as radical as Protestants potentially could be—they were not. On questions from elections to banishments from church membership (which by the 1640s they had agreed could be quasi-hereditary), they compromised. Most were not "levellers."

Still, in 1641, Massachusetts took a very similar position on slavery to that which would be taken by Locke forty years later. In a law entitled

"Bond-Slavery" they wrote: "There shall never be any bond-slavery, villenage or captivitie amongst us; unlesse it be lawfull captives taken in just warrs, and such strangers as willingly sell themselves." While they did capture and sell prisoners from their Indian wars, and did eventually allow some slavery, they never developed the complex of laws that many other colonies did.[19] The nature of their exception is very important to understanding the debates over slavery and bond labor in the seventeenth century: they allowed it only, essentially, as punishment for what they regarded a crime (as punishment for starting, they argued, an unjust war), and/or on the basis of direct consent (so it was neither forced nor hereditary).

While historians have often seen Puritans as traditional—pointing to the ways, for example, that New England towns modeled themselves after small towns in southern England—their stands on the question of hereditary status were anything but. With respect to those towns, for example, they made one especially critical institutional difference—there was no lord who owned the town and from whom the townsfolk leased their land. Instead, each settler family was given roughly equal portions of land, which they owned free and clear. There were of course some freeholds in England in the seventeenth century, but they were the exception, not the rule.

In short, New England was not traditional—but in many ways the southern colonies were. With the exception of the slave code, Virginians made virtually no criminal laws, for example, and simply followed British ones. Indeed, it is striking the degree to which Virginia seemed to follow English laws (and not create their own). Even when one focuses on the slave code, it becomes clear that they were basing it on English norms as imprinted in their law books. Winthrop Jordan's *White over Black* suggested some years ago that there might be a link between the "feudal laws" on the law books of England and the origins of slavery, although he was quick to point out this was only a mild influence. I see a much stronger connection. While medieval feudalism, such as it existed, was dying out in England, it was being given a new lease—and a new form in the colonies—by the ideologies underlying absolute monarchy and perpetual status.

Much of the basic structure of colonial Virginia laws favored the development of an aristocracy via laws that encouraged perpetual status. Whether one examines issues of land distribution, laws of status and inheritance, or the structure of government itself, all favored the development of a society modeled after England and (after Virginia was taken over as a Royal Colony in 1624) ideally the creation of a society that was shaped by the king. Unlike Maryland, Virginia headright policy, for example, sharply favored the master. During the 1610s, most servants who went to Virginia were promised the right to fifty acres of land as well as other freedom dues after they completed their term of service. But after about 1620 the right to patent fifty acres of land went not to the imported servant, but to the person who imported that servant (or later slave). Indeed, at certain points, the importers of multiple servants/slaves were actually given what can only be described as bulk bonuses. In the law of 1705, for example, the owner of five slaves was allowed to patent five hundred acres of land (or one hundred acres per slave). For each additional slave he owned, he could claim two hundred more acres, up to a total of four thousand.[20]

Even if one had a headright claim (which could be bought by a freed servant), in order to translate that into actual land one needed to have land properly surveyed and approved by the secretary of the colony (a position appointed by the governor). Depending upon the secretary, this could involve substantial difficulties, unless one were a friend (or made oneself into a friend). The ability to gain new land also depended upon its availability (it also had to be obtained from the Indians first). Tensions over these questions came to the surface during Bacon's Rebellion, but they never rested long underneath. Freed servants could become squatters, of course, but they had no legal title to the land they occupied—nor to any improvements they had made upon it.

One other important way that land distribution policy favored the formation of an aristocracy—and in some ways an explicitly feudal one—was a policy set in England by the Stuart kings: the great proprietorships. Various kings—especially Charles I and Charles II—regarded the empire on the other side of the Atlantic as so many potential gifts at their disposal. Granted (indeed, sometimes doubly granted in competing claims) by these kings as favors and rewards (or in exchange for large sums), much of the land (sometimes including the ability to choose political authority, as well) went to great proprietors. Barbados, Bermuda, Maryland, the Northern Neck of Virginia, the Carolinas, Maine, Pennsylvania—all were granted to great proprietors. These proprietors, in turn, rarely sold the property in their colonies free and clear. They retained ownership and distributed land with attached quit-rents. The layers of ownership are part of what was then called feudalism. To give only one example of what this meant: to get rid of the Penns' claim to Pennsylvania, the revolutionaries there confiscated all of the 21 million acres.[21] The proprietary right descended by the rules of primogeniture, and often included official titles for the proprietors. The fact that these lands were given away on these terms by Charles I in the 1630s and Charles II immediately in the wake of his restoration, particularly to those who helped place him on the throne, should tell us something about the connections of these rights to monarchical structures and hereditary ideology.

The connections between hereditary slavery and the Restoration are even stronger, in both time and ideology. Hereditary slavery, where the child inherits the status of the mother, became the law of Virginia in 1662, in the wake of the Restoration. The laws welcoming Charles II and his lineage back to the throne were passed in close conjunction with that justifying hereditary slavery. Before 1662, those forcibly imported from Africa were treated similarly to the whites who came as servants in that they were both freed after some years. Likewise, the first laws in Barbados creating a slave code date to 1661. While keeping people of African descent as "perpetual" servants, and making their descendants into servants or slaves as well might have antedated the laws in practice (more clearly in Barbados than in Virginia), formalizing these practices and giving them a structure of enforcement was critical to creating these societies.[22]

Colonial historians like to imagine that the politics of the colonies and those of the mother country are somehow separate. Yet they were anything but. William Berkeley, first appointed governor of Virginia by Charles I in 1642, was a devout supporter of the monarchy for the next thirty-five years, so much so that Charles II rewarded him in 1663 with an hereditary proprietorship of Carolina for his help in "restoring" him to his throne. Berkeley's Royalist pedigree was well formed and consistent; his ideological awareness acute. When he heard that members of Parliament had tried and beheaded Charles I, Berkeley called together the Assembly and Council of Virginia, which passed a law under his direction that made it high treason (punishable by hanging, drawing and quartering) to even speak about the trial or beheading of the king (or the legitimacy of Parliament's actions) with any favor.

Anyone who questioned the legitimacy of Charles II, or the authority of Berkeley himself as governor, was likewise to be punished. "Whereas divers [people] out of ignorance, others out of malice, schisme and faction . . . asserting the cleerness and legality of the said unparalleled treasons, perpetrated on the said King, doe build hopes and inferrences to the high dishonour of the regall estate and in truth to the utter disinherison of his sacred Majesty that now is [Charles II], and the devesting him of those rights, which the law of nature and nations and the known lawes of the kingdom of England have adjudged inherent to his royal line, and the law of God himselfe . . . hath consecrated unto him."[23] The text of the law makes clear the legitimacy of monarchy, and of Charles II. The right to be king is "inherent to his royall line" as "consecrated" by God himself. The word "disinherison" is important: it refers explicitly to the legal manner in which Charles II became king (by inheritance by primogeniture) with the death of Charles I. This was a law that honored perpetual status: the "law of nature and nations" as well as those of England had lodged the right to be king "to his royall line."

In a larger ideological sense, Berkeley opposed all of those institutions which might encourage anyone to think differently about monarchy. In 1671 he wrote in a letter to the Lords of Trade and Plantations, "I thank God there is no free schools nor printing [in Virginia] and I hope wee shall not have these hundred years, for learning has brought disobediences and heresy and sects into the world and printing had divulged them, and libels against the best government. God keep us from both." Under his rule, the nascent college established in Virginia in the 1630s had dissolved by the 1640s.[24]

Virginians of all sorts, in other words, richer and poorer, could hardly have been unaware of the political disputes in England. The story of the public trial and beheading of Charles I, in particular, was one that traveled far and fast. When the British fleet actually sailed up the James in 1651, however, it was clear that the Royalist Virginians had no real defense. Commissioners sent by Parliament negotiated a new government with the House of Burgesses, which led to a more powerful House of Burgesses, with a governor elected by themselves (rather like a prime minister) and Puritans in some prominent positions. Only those who swore an oath of allegiance to the new ascendancy of Parliament were permitted to vote, and the commissioners supervised the election of the new House of Burgesses. Upon rumors of a possible restoration of Charles II to the throne in 1660, however, Virginians—with Berkeley newly restored as their proper head—were among the first to offer their support. Royalist supporters of Charles I fled to Virginia in the 1650s and continued to be welcomed there in the 1660s.

If one sees the English Civil War as a struggle between authority based on hereditary right versus one based on consent, then restoring the king and his lineage to the throne was parallel to making slavery hereditary. One was born to a status. That was the ideology that had just been restored to the throne of England.[25]

Virginia laws after 1661 drew deeply on the precedents set in Barbados. Even before Barbados set a slave code in 1661, one observer, Richard Ligon, claimed that sharp differences already demarcated the treatment of "servants" from "slaves" by 1650, in that slaves were held perpetually and their status descended to their children. At least one Barbadian planter thought he was following the "laws of England" in his treatment of servants and slaves and the distinctions between them: "by those Lawes, we could not make a Christian a slave" yet it was fine to make a heathen one. (Ligon had asked him to let one of his slaves be baptized, to which the planter replied no, because then he would have to free him, and it would set a bad precedent for other slaves.) Another visitor, Charles de Rochefort, tried to offer a justification for slavery. He maintained that the "slaves, and such as are to be perpetual servants, and are commonly employ'd in these islands, they are originally Africans." He claimed that some entered slavery voluntarily, both for themselves and their children: "some are reduc'd to a necessity of selling themselves, and entering into a perpetual slavery, they and their children, to avoid starving." Others, he claimed, "are sold after they have been taken Prisoners in war by some petty neighbouring Prince." While Rochefort's comments were superficially similar to Locke's justification (which drew, by the way, on Hugo Grotius), they were different in several critical respects: fathers also sell their children, it is perpetual (not temporary), and de Rochefort did not care whether it was a just war or not. The latter arguments, of course, could apply to anyone, whether English and Christian or not.[26]

It is critical to note that Barbados was almost completely controlled, even more than Virginia, by Royalists. There, the Commonwealth takeover was brief. Barbadian politics were complicated, partly because of overlapping and disputed grants of the island by King Charles I (so that at least two different men had claims to be Lord Proprietor, with the right to choose a system of government). Royalists set the earlier policy of perpetual enslavement, even if not yet legally enshrined.[27]

While hereditary and perpetual slavery was different from what then existed in England, it is not as different as we would like to believe, as the practice of kidnaping makes clear. Many English subjects were forced into servitude in the New World, just as Africans were, neither signing contracts nor consenting in other ways to their transport or labor. Both English and Virginian authorities essentially agreed to allow, if not encourage, kidnaping during most of the seventeenth century, as both laws and practice reveal. Historians have long acknowledged the many court records from seventeenth-century Virginia that adjudge the age of imported servants. Servants who arrived without contracts served a length of time that was determined by their age. If imported at age eleven in the 1680s, for example, as some were, one would have to serve thirteen years (until age twenty-four). If imported at fifteen, then nine years. If imported at twenty-one (or any age above nineteen) then five years.

But why were these servants arriving without contracts? To fully answer that, one must turn to the English courts and to broadsides and legal debates, debates which finally culminated in kidnaping laws with teeth, but only by the early eighteenth century. Basically, the answer is that as long as the persons taken were poor, and especially if they were poor children (and not heirs), the English authorities—and the English laws—did not much care whether they consented to go. After 1682 (strengthened in 1717), those who left were supposed to consent in front of a magistrate and "searchers" were sent onto ships to ascertain this, and lists were supposed to be kept of those departing. Even these rules were not always enforced, however, and some of the eighteenth-century narratives of former indentured servants relate being kidnaped. That it still went on is supported by English broadsides reporting "Grand Kidnapper at last Taken" and by the continuing Virginia records of age being adjudged for those who arrived without contracts (at least through the mid-eighteenth century).[28]

What does the kidnaping mean? Quite simply, especially when put together with the English poor laws, it means that to a certain degree English society assumed that you were born to a particular status and that the poor would have to work—and did not mind their being forced to work. If an elite person were kidnaped, however, like a four-year-old heir, the authorities rigorously traced the child.[29] Once such kidnaped poor children arrived, they faced a life of similar status, if not worse, than the one they had left. While some mobility was possible for those who came as indentured servants, particularly if they arrived during the first half of the seventeenth century (and survived), the structure of that society made it difficult.[30]

The connections between kidnaping and slavery were clear to the Burgesses as well. The law that made slavery hereditary for the children of an enslaved "negro woman" was passed directly after one of the laws about "servants" who arrived without contracts, requiring that their ages be adjudged, if under sixteen.[31] The Burgesses' minds were clearly on the subject of the status of laboring children and how long they should serve. Still, while admitting that both slavery and kidnaping grew out of norms that accepted hereditary status, freedom at age twenty-four was better than never, even if one did not live for very long afterward, or begin freedom with many resources. The Burgesses were also forming distinctions between "Christians" and heathens, between "Englishmen" and "Negroes." Instead of seeing forced, hereditary slavery as from the beginning associated with blackness (and climatic necessity), we should see it as part of English norms about status. As the treatment of whites and blacks began to be differentiated, religion played more of a role than race.

After 1705, in reforms that began in the late seventeenth century, the Virginia laws about slavery became ever more connected to a larger complex of laws about perpetual status. Virginia laws allowed people who were enslaved and their progeny "for ever" to be entailed (so that they could not easily be sold away), with both slaves and land belonging to the "head" of a family lineage "for ever," such that ownership descended by primogeniture. Both entail and slavery enshrined perpetual status. While entails were honored from the very beginning of the seventeenth century in Virginia, after the 1705 legal revision entails became much more difficult to break than they had been in England. To break an entail after 1705 required a specific act of the legislature. A revision of 1727 allowed masters to attach slaves to a parcel of entailed land (perpetually) rather than directly to a personal lineage. In principle, this meant that slaves could not be sold. However the way the law was written did allow entailed slaves (unlike entailed land) to be attached for debt, so if the owner was willing to do a legal run-around, it was possible to sell an entailed slave.[32]

These laws (which books like Morris's *Southern Slavery and the Law*, which focuses on the nineteenth century, do not mention) were very different from those of the nineteenth century. Slaves, while designated "real property" under these laws, were also very much people. Indeed, the comparison to medieval villenage is more than an imaginary one. Virginia legal authorities saw the similarity as explicit. St. George Tucker's edition of *Blackstone's Commentaries . . . [for] Virginia*, probably the most important single legal text published in Virginia in the early nineteenth century, claimed that before the Revolution in Virginia all slaves had the status of villeins. As late as 1848, Henry Augustine Washington blamed entail, which he saw as feudal land law, for slavery (which he saw as feudal personal law). Despite the

Revolutionary dispersing of entailed estates, slavery was left, "a fragment of the feudal system floating about here on the bosom of the nineteenth century."[33]

For the 1705 revisions, in particular, we have some information about who wrote them and supported them, unlike for earlier Virginia slave laws. William Fitzhugh seems to have been the primary author of the 1705 reforms—even though he died in 1701. He had been working on revisions for some time, and seemed to have based his legal knowledge on an extensive reading of the various volumes of Sir Edward Coke's *Institutes of the Laws of England* and the *Statutes of the Realm* of England, for it was these he cited most frequently in his legal notations. He also carefully collected all previous Virginia laws. The most important of the *Institutes* was Coke's volume one, which was often called by contemporaries *Coke upon Littleton*. Realizing this is critical, because Littleton, on whose treatise Coke commented in this volume, is the classic feudal treatise on land and personal status (but especially the former), written in the late fifteenth century. One does not necessarily have to embrace feudalism after reading *Coke upon Littleton* (indeed, Coke offered subtle critiques), but Fitzhugh was certainly well familiar with this part of English legal tradition. If he wanted to provide "precedents" for Virginia slave law, he had them laid out before him. Fitzhugh entailed the whole of his estate (some fifty-one thousand acres) on his five sons. Fitzhugh left few overt statements of his political opinions, but the few clues indicate he was high Tory. Indeed, he was prosecuted in 1693 for asserting that James II's son was a rightful heir to the throne and criticizing those who questioned the legitimacy of James II's lineage: "[Fitzhugh] wondered what they would have to say now about the legitimacy of that prince."[34]

Robert "King" Carter, who pushed through the later revisions, was also well-versed in English feudal law. Although he claimed to be "no Tory" (the term was tainted after 1715 and the accession of the house of Hanover, during which "Tory" Royalists tried to restore the line of James II to the throne), he clearly supported hereditary and proprietary interests (he was agent for the proprietor of the Northern Neck, during which he acquired much of his fortune). He owned more slaves and land than any other Virginian at his death in 1733, and left all—slaves and land—in perpetual entail, with the slaves and their progeny attached to the land.[35]

Entail became a powerful institution in colonial Virginia, one that probably controlled three-fourths of the land in Tidewater Virginia by the time of the Revolution. Thomas Jefferson, who led the struggle to get rid of it in 1776, claimed that its was the most important single thing he did in implementing Republican ideology and "striking at the root of landed aristocracy."[36]

Many other key institutional elements of English origin helped to create a society that encouraged hereditary status. Government was based only partly on the consent of the governed. Although there were no hereditary titles in the colonies (aside from the Great Proprietors), in most colonies many officials, from governor to council to judges and other officials, were appointed either directly by the king or indirectly via the governor. The Anglican Church was the established church in Virginia, as well as much of the rest of the South. It exerted a powerful influence in Virginia, especially. Its catechisms and set sermons (prepared in England and performed in a rote-response manner) often encouraged obedience to authority and the divine right of the king and his lineage to rule.

The sermons of Richard Allestree (one of Charles II's favorite ministers), which went through dozens of editions in the late seventeenth and early eighteenth centuries (including one in Virginia in 1748), embody both of these traits. He encouraged passive obedience to all superiors. He said nothing about consenting to that authority: God places you in a condition to which you must accustom yourself. Allestree was very popular in Virginia, and was in almost every gentleman's library in the early eighteenth century. An almost direct echo of Allestree was published in Maryland in 1750, but it was adapted especially for slaves. It instructed slaves that obeying their master was equivalent to obeying God. They were told to obey their master even if they believed he was ordering them to do something evil, on the grounds that only God (not they) could judge him. This sermon thus explicitly enshrouded a master in the king's divine robes.[37]

The continuing articulation of slaves as "property" after the American Revolution was part of a neo-feudal ideology where property and status were, ideally, fixed by lineage and within which people—villeins, tenants, servants—were also property. But it was also different: in some ways, after the Revolution, those enslaved became, legally, less people, and more property, in a shift of the balance. It did so because the Revolutionary ideology explicitly rejected these norms that honored hereditary status.

In short, I am seeking to raise a significant challenge to traditional interpretations of the origins of slavery in the southern colonies based simply on arguments about climate and the ability to grow staple crops. Instead, I question how and why land and status became distributed and inherited as they were, how the laws shaped these patterns of distribution and inheritance, and why these laws were passed. Only then can we return to how patterns of distribution and inheritance shaped the desire to produce intensively for markets, the question on which most historians have focused. Ideology needs to be woven back into a much more prominent position. It is only by understanding the law of perpetuities and the pattern of the implementation of those laws that we can unravel the powerful role of ideology. Exploring how these laws were implemented and what patterns were followed can give critical insight into the way that ideology shapes laws and how those laws can in turn set patterns of development within the British Empire as a whole.[38]

The ideas about perpetuity, although restored in 1660 with Charles II, were not new. As the evidence from Marshall in 1644 suggests, there were deep strands in English thought and practice which emphasized birth status, whether in terms of subjects, church members, servants, or slaves. In adopting this strand in their colonies in the seventeenth century, Virginia (and Barbados, and later South Carolina and other colonies) were not creating something altogether new. They were modifying an older set of ideas to a new situation.

By emphasizing the ways they incorporated birth status, I do not mean to suggest that they repudiated the opposing strand of English liberties. They did not. Especially during the eighteenth century, that strand grew in strength in Virginia, with the establishment of a printing press, a college, and the growth in power of the House of Burgesses by the mid-eighteenth century. With the Revolution, they repudiated inherited right in many ways—abolishing entail, creating an elected governor and senate, etc. Yet slavery remained.

For Americans today, perpetual status is a very difficult issue to get our minds around. Even for Britons today, it is difficult, but they understand it, because their newspapers still debate it. (Witness the recent loss of power among hereditary peers in the House of Lords. The newspapers in England in 1998 and 1999 repeated many of the ideological debates of the American Revolution over hereditary right. During the summer of 2001, the Scottish parliament was debating abolishing the remaining feudal rights of lords (which give them immense power over leaseholds) because some of those have recently been invoked, and too harshly. Only about two hundred people own most of the land in Scotland, and the rest live on long-term leaseholds. The recently deceased Duke of Sutherland owned about 1 million acres in England and Scotland, virtually all of it entailed. The Duke of Westminster owns a large part of London (two-thirds by some estimates), and most of the houses for sale in London are available only as long-term leases (not freeholds) as a result of an entail broken only in this century (because of inheritance taxes, the family sought to skip a generation).

Fully understanding these ideas about hereditary right and obligation will take more work. They were, for example, not only English. Spanish colonization enshrined many of these ideas before the English did, and provided a model for them. Its encomienda system was a variant of entail, and they also practiced, earlier, hereditary and perpetual slavery. While the Spanish colonial model clearly influenced the English in practice, it may also have done so in principle. Yet they might also have common roots in European feudalism, such as it existed and was expanded into empire.

Two sets of conflicting ideas about power and authority were pouring out of England in the seventeenth century, one of which emphasized the consent-based authority of an elected legislature, and one of which emphasized hereditary authority and obligation. The latter was, in many ways, the more traditional, and deeply embedded in law and practice. Until we acknowledge both we will not understand colonial British society, particularly in the South. Arguably, we would still have slavery today without the ideological shift that emerged in religious debates over consent and status, and took fuller form during the American Revolution.

"Like a Stone Wall Never to Be Broke"

The British-Indian Boundary Line with the Creek Indians, 1763–1773

KATHRYN E. HOLLAND BRAUND

The late Professor J. Brian Harley, one of the outstanding figures in the history of cartography, wrote that "European maps . . . can be viewed as statements of territorial appropriation, cultural reproduction, or as devices by which a Native American presence could be silenced." He noted that "lines of demarcation drawn on the maps became symbols as well as records of the division of the [land] . . . into . . . spheres of influence." "In America," he concluded, "cartography is part of the process by which territory becomes."[1] Harley's statements would seem to be true in regard to the American southeast, where in the years preceding the American Revolution the exploration and survey of Indian territory and the establishment of negotiated and marked boundary lines dividing Indian and British lands became a visible symbol of the transfer of dominion over the land from native peoples to the British colonies. Yet Harley's observation is neither complete nor completely accurate. For European maps and supporting documentary evidence also reveal the Native American presence and provide information on tribal composition, governance, and concepts of land tenure. Moreover, boundary lines—whether notched on trees or drawn on maps—do not always mark a division but sometimes a point of juncture.

Between 1763 and 1773, Creeks and Anglo-Americans came together for six major conferences to discuss the matters that bound them together and to establish boundaries to divide them.[2] The boundaries ultimately negotiated were meant to be, at least from the Creek point of view, permanent.[3] Emisteseguo of the Little Tallassee was only one of many headmen who declared "that when the Boundary was settled he hoped the Transaction of that Day would not be confined to the Knowledge of the present Generation but would be remembered by the Posterity of both white and red People, and he hopes that the Trees marked on that line will stand as a great Stone Wall to mark the Partition between them."[4]

This then is the heart of the matter: lines dividing and defining empires and paths linking friends in trade and peace. What is interesting—what is important—is not merely the process, but the polities involved, particularly the Creek confederation of towns. This essay will focus on how the Creek political structure operated, what value the Creeks placed on their land, and how they developed a coherent policy that reflected their views as they faced escalating demands for their territory by their trade partners.

Creek political and social structure was built around the concept of *italwa*, the Muskogean word for the town, which denotes not only the physical elements of a town, but its people and their ceremonial and civic responsibilities in maintaining the community.[5] The sixty-odd towns of the Creek confederacy were actually arranged into two geopolitical divisions, which the British called Upper and Lower Creeks. These divisions were dominated by Muskogean tribes, although non-Muskogean towns were important components of the confederacy. The Upper and Lower towns, or nations as they are sometimes called, recognized themselves to be "one People."[6] Matters of importance, particularly in regard to territorial sovereignty and foreign relations, were dealt with by groups of headmen meeting in regional meetings.[7] And though they sought the advice and support of their opposite division and were often unified in their sentiments and actions, the Upper and Lower Creeks conducted foreign policy independently.[8]

The Lower Creek towns, dominated by Muskogean Coweta and Cussita, were primarily situated on the Chattahoochee River and claimed territory that extended to the Atlantic coast, southward into the Florida peninsula, and northeast to a Savannah River border with the Cherokee Indians. The Upper Creek towns were arrayed along the Tallapoosa and Coosa Rivers and claimed lands southward to the

Gulf Coast, westward to the Tombigbee River, and north to the Tennessee River. The majority of the Upper towns were actually Tallapoosa and Abeika (or Coosa) Indians, both Muskogean peoples whose towns dominated Upper Creek negotiations with the British. The Alabama, whose towns were located at the junction of the Coosa and Tallapoosa Rivers, were ethnically distinct from the Muskogean Tallapoosa and Abeika but were an important component of the Upper Creek coalition.[9]

Among the Creeks, all land was held in common.[10] Emisteseguo of the Little Tallassee, in articulating Creek notions of ownership, told the British in 1771 that "every child in it [the Creek nation] has an equal property in the land with the first warrior."[11] William Bartram, who visited both Upper and Lower Creek towns and wrote extensively about them, reported that "the soil, with all its appurtenances ... is equally the right and property of every individual inhabitant." Bartram noted that even though Creek territory was "divided by lines & boundaries amongst the different Tribes ... every individual citizen of the Confederacy have the same equal right to hunt and range where he pleases, in the forests and unoccupied lands, and to range stocks of cattle, horses, &ca."[12]

Though individuals were what the British would have deemed tenants in common and enjoyed the right of usufruct, they did not possess the right to alienate tribal property. Town councils held sovereign authority over the land, including the right to determine its use and to transfer ownership. But town councils sought to achieve widespread agreement and support for their actions before ceding land. As Emisteseguo of Little Tallassee noted, "making any alteration in the boundary without the consent of the whole will be improper."[13]

The town's public square, like other public structures, was erected and maintained by the joint effort of the male citizens of the town. A sacred fire, enclosed by four cabins, sat in the center of this symbolic and consecrated square that dominated the town proper and served as the location for government and served as the heart of Creek ceremonial life.[14] The town center and the residential areas of the Creek towns were surrounded by large communal corn fields. These fields were the most

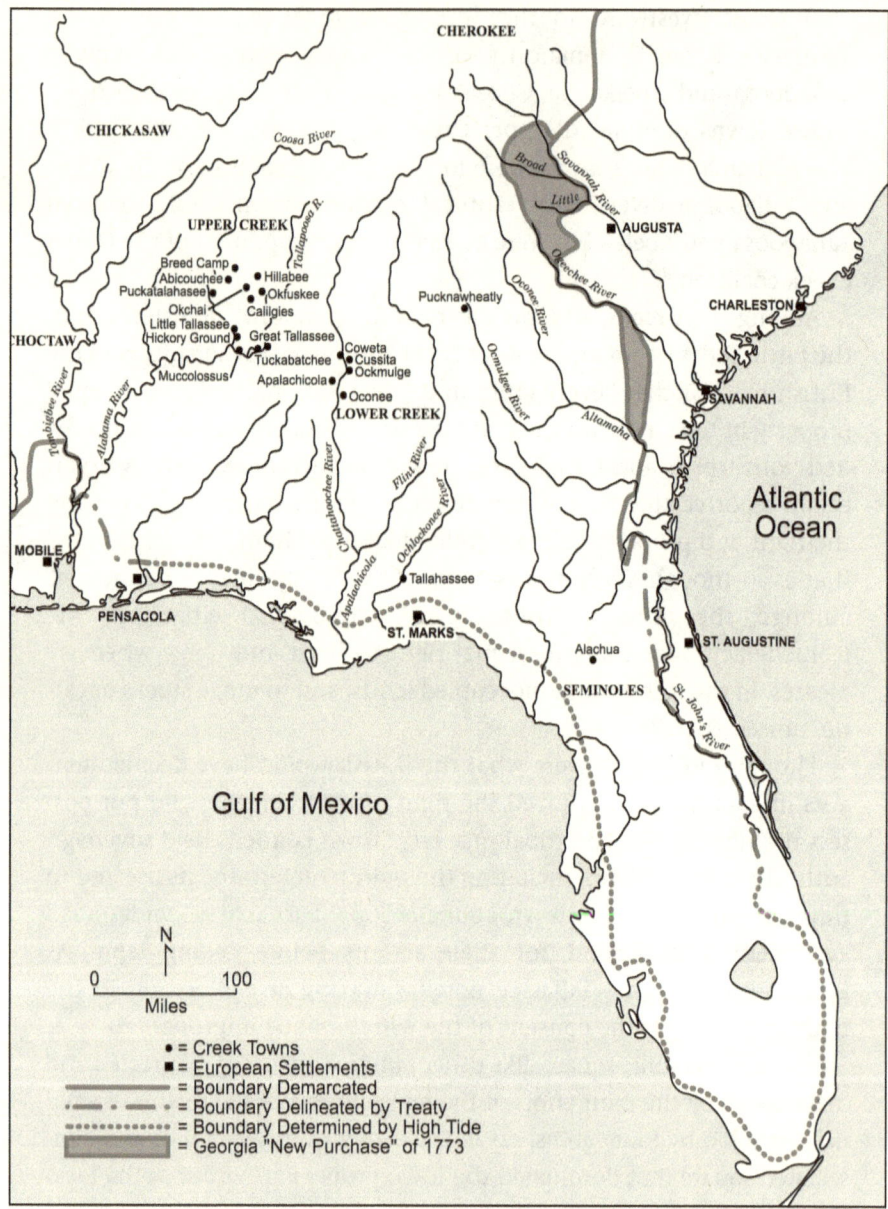

Fig. 1. The Creek Towns and their Boundaries, c. 1773. Boundary based on the work of Louis De Vorsey, Jr. Map drawn by Sarah Mattics, Center for Archeological Studies, University of South Alabama.

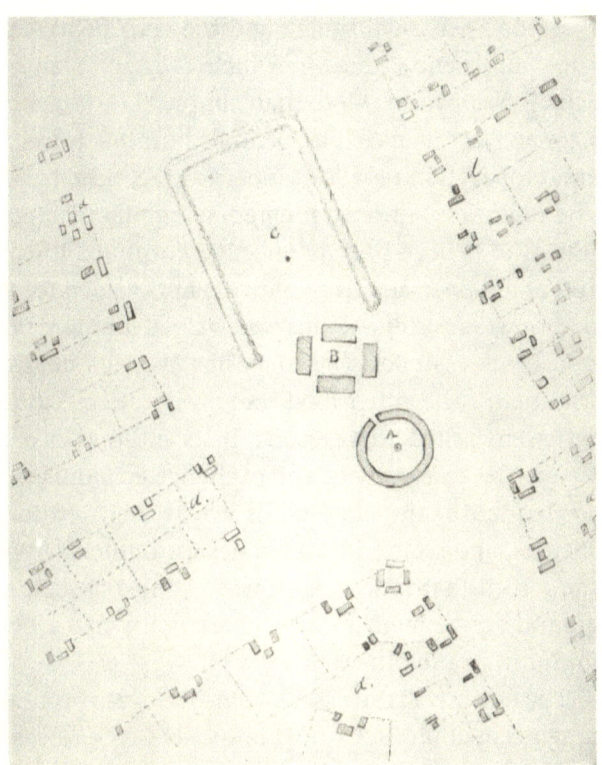

Fig. 2. William Bartram's "A Plan of the Muscogulge or Upper Creek Town," showing the public square (B), as well as the winter council house (A), chunky field (C), and residential compounds. Tracing made by Edwin H. Davis. Courtesy of National Anthropological Archives, Smithsonian Institution.

visible and easily identifiable example of a town's sovereign rights in regard to land.[15] Every Creek town had long-established claims to river bottomland, and town leaders routinely allotted and subdivided the town's agricultural lands among matrilineages, according to need and family size.[16] William Bartram called the large fields the "town plantation" and noted that family (clan) allotments were "divided or bounded by a strip of grass ground, poles set up, or any other natural or artificial boundary,—thus the whole plantation is a collection of lots joining each other, comprised in one inclosure, or general boundary."[17] The harvest was the property of the matrilineages that worked the plot, but each matrilineage also contributed a portion of the harvest to the public granary, controlled by the town headman, who dispensed the food as necessary for public occasions, for travelers, or for those in need.[18]

Beyond the town square and the corn fields, Creek towns claimed large subsistence zones in which they maintained an active, if not actual, occupation. More than simple "hunting grounds," these lands were actively managed by periodic burning as well as selective culling and propagation of wild plants to attract deer, bear, and other game—essentially a well-honed program of habitat maintenance. There is also reason to believe that by selective burning and culling, they assisted and maintained stands of native plants valued for food and medicinal purposes. Subsistence lands were valued for more than simply hunting: cane breaks, salt licks, clay deposits, fisheries, nut tree stands, bee trees, wild herbs, and other food resources scattered throughout their territory were visited on a seasonal basis and provided an important boost to the Creek subsistence and exchange economies. In addition, Creeks created and maintained paths across their territory, erected hunting shelters, and established granaries for hunters.[19] While it is clear from the record that individual towns claimed specific regions as hunting grounds, any member of the Creek polity had a right to use the lands for hunting and other purposes.[20]

The extensive land claims of the Creek towns resulted not only from long occupation, but from conquest. Creek towns and their warriors had been especially active during the wars of the eighteenth century. Like their British trade partners, they too had been engaged in territorial expansion. In the early part of the eighteenth century, Upper Creek warriors had clashed with Gulf Coast tribes as well as the Choctaw and their allies for territory along the Tombigbee River. Lower Creeks headed northeast, taking from the Cherokee hunting lands along the Savannah River in a series of wars.[21] But these conquests were not nearly so spectacular as that of Florida, and by 1763 the Creek towns claimed the entire Florida peninsula. The British acknowledged that claim, noting repeatedly in public documents the cooperative efforts waged by the Creeks with colonists from South Carolina and Georgia against the Spanish missions and St. Augustine. The Creeks continued long after the Georgians gave up.[22] By the time the Spanish withdrew from Florida following their defeat in the Seven Years' War, the Creeks had already established new settlements as far south as modern Tampa

Bay, erected hunting camps deep in the Everglades, and in north peninsular Florida had taken over a string of abandoned missions and plantations stretching from the old fields of Apalachee (now still known by its Creek name Tallahassee) to the Alachua savanna. These Creek colonies had already acquired a new designation in the Creek geopolitical panoply as "Seminoles," derived from the term the Spanish applied to them, "cimarrons," which translates roughly into "wild people."[23]

In addition to the conquered, many refugees and remnant tribes joined the Creek confederacy of towns. The leading Creek towns claimed as their prerogative the right to allocate tribal land for these refugee groups. As far as the historic record can reveal, the process involved a request by leaders of the refugee group before a town council, who then set aside land for the new town. Among the more notable refugees who joined the confederacy in the eighteenth century were bands of Shawnee, Chickasaw, and Natchez, all of whom built towns among the Upper Creeks. Yuchi Indians established a town on the Chattahoochee River, near Cussita. Amalgamation as part of the Creek body politic meant that a displaced or remnant group might conduct their internal town affairs as they saw fit, but they agreed to Creek jurisdiction in external matters. Moreover, the appropriate Creek division thereby acquired the right to lands claimed, abandoned, or formerly conquered by the new member. This meant little for the landless Shawnee, but in the case of other tribal groups, including assimilated Apalachee and Yamasee, Creek councils extended their sovereignty by devolving land claims. Although Creeks did not incorporate Natchez lands as part of their confederacy, they did claim the right to hunt on the land once inhabited by the Natchez and other assimilated groups.[24]

Following the establishment of the British colony of South Carolina, the Creek towns had established a trading alliance with their new neighbors that had occasionally teetered but never fallen since the first caravan of Carolina traders had entered Coweta in 1685. British land claims did not conflict with those of the Creeks until the establishment of Georgia. The Creeks gave the Georgians land upon which to "sit," in much the same way town councils welcomed others who came from afar. That grant, made in 1735 with General James Oglethorpe, confined the colony to a tidewater boundary. Even this was less generous than one might imagine, as this land had been the property of extirpated coastal tribes largely destroyed by disease. The Creek world view expanded to include both the "fires" of Charleston and Savannah, and the trade in deerskins for manufactured goods enriched both sides, although nefarious trade practices and boundary violations caused resentment and occasional breaches of the Anglo-Creek peace. As a result, the French acquired a toehold among the Alabamas, at the junction of the Tallapoosa and Coosa Rivers, just upriver from their colony at Mobile.

By the terms of the Peace of Paris, which ended the Seven Years' War, France and Spain agreed to abandon their colonies east of the Mississippi River, thereby extending British dominion to the Mississippi. Most of the territory so cavalierly traded by the great powers of Europe did not belong to them. Rather, most of it was claimed by numerous Indian nations, and uneasiness among tribal peoples was widespread, for many looked upon the withdrawal of the French and Spanish with foreboding and feared the unchecked power of the British empire. Creeks at once protested the right of European powers to transfer Creek lands without their consent. Creeks were equally concerned by the expansion of Georgia, which had outgrown its narrow tidewater boundary of 1735 and was rapidly becoming a populous and powerful nuisance, as settlers with slaves and cattle spilled into Creek hunting territory.

At war's end, Governor James Wright reported to London that it was "impossible for affairs to be more Critical" with his Creek Indian neighbors.[25] The Creeks were particularly concerned over boundary violations by "Virginians," as the Creek derisively dubbed the illegal settlers on the upper reaches of the Savannah River.[26] And as news of the Paris agreement spread, so did wild rumors that Great Britain intended to land troops at newly ceded Pensacola and Mobile, and march against the Creek towns to "punish them for their past Misbehaviour and make them tame."[27]

Leading Creek men convened town meetings to discuss the new world order and to prepare "talks" to their allies, expressing their concerns.[28] Their communications to Governor Wright, the most accessible British official, revealed not only a desire for peaceful coexistence and trade, but a steely determination to defend their territorial integrity. The Mortar of Okchai, a noted Upper Creek chief with pro-French proclivities, expressed Creek surprise that the French and Spanish could "give away Land that does not belong to them" in the Floridas and along the Gulf Coast. The Creeks maintained that the land had merely been "lent" to the French and Spanish. The Mortar's words, translated and relayed by an interpreter, were blunt: "it makes their Hearts cross to see their Lands taken without their Liberty. That he knows white People's Physic is strong for War, and he thinks their Head Warriors have strong Physic likewise— ... he thinks the White People intend to stop all their Breaths by their settling all round them."[29]

In his talk, the Handsome Fellow of Okfuskee pointed to encroachment along the border with Georgia and urged Governor Wright to remove "all these stragling People" settled illegally on Creek hunting lands.[30] The Lower Creek towns sent their own complaints to Georgia, repeating Upper Creek grievances about illegal settlements and providing details on unauthorized trading posts. They also complained that the free-range livestock of white squatters strayed onto Creek hunting grounds. The speaker who delivered the talk from the Lower towns was direct as well, relating that he had been sent to Georgia to determine whether the rumors of the British takeover of the Floridas were true and "whether it was to be Peace or War between the white People and the Creeks."[31]

The Creeks, ostensibly allies of the Georgians, realized their talks were stern and unseemly by the usual standards of friendship that governed Creek diplomacy. The Mortar, in evocative prose undiminished by clumsy translation, explained that their talks were sharp because they concerned the thing that was most important to them—their land. And the Mortar's words left no doubt as to the spiritual as well as economic significance of the Creek domain: "when the King sees this Talk he may think we are cross and love our Lands a great deal, and so we do, the Wood is our Fire, and the Grass is our Bed, and our Physic when we are sick."[32]

Even as the talks went to Georgia, Upper Creek warriors scouted the Gulf Coast, waiting to greet the British and present them tokens of friendship.[33] The wary British officers who landed at Pensacola, Mobile, St. Augustine, and Fort St. Marks were alarmed to find the Indians "numerous and near." In addition to attempting to satisfy the scores of watchful Creek warriors of their peaceful intent, the British commanders promptly noted the weakness of the fortifications they had inherited, and reported home that the Creeks had virtually kept the French and Spanish confined behind them. All concerned recognized that the unexplored Florida peninsula was virtually a Creek hunting preserve.[34]

As Union Jacks were raised along their periphery, Creek councils cogently surmised their situation, "look to the rising of the sun, to its setting, to the right hand, and to the left hand, and on all sides . . . we are surrounded with English."[35] But the converse was also true and the British found themselves confined to narrow coastal garrisons, pressed on all sides by Indians who not only had legitimate claims to the land, but were ready, if necessary, to defend their claims. Creek warriors had the potential to spoil any hope of peaceful development and prosperity in the Floridas. Clearly, British administrators realized the need to honor the sentiments of the Indians in regard to their lands.

With the Proclamation of October 7, 1763, the British government did just that. In addition to officially establishing the colonies of East and West Florida, the decree prohibited surveys and the issuance of land grants beyond the Appalachian divide or on "any lands whatever" that had not been ceded to the Crown or legally purchased from Indians. Citing the action as "just and reasonable, and essential to our interest and the security of our colonies," the proclamation further prohibited individual purchases of land directly from the Indians, reserving that right to crown officials. Moreover, the proclamation ordered any who had "either wilfully or inadvertently" settled on unceded land to immediately remove themselves.[36] The ban on land purchase and settlement "for the present" seemed a logical way to avoid conflicts with the numerous Indian tribes whose lands were the primary subject of the proclamation. More to the point, the attendant military expense that any such border conflicts would generate were clearly unacceptable. In fact, preliminary instructions from London had reached Wright by mid-1763, and in his answer to the Creek talks, he apprised them of Britain's determination to respect their land.[37]

Implied by the proclamation's ban on survey, purchase, and settlement of "unceded" land "reserved" for the Indians was the notion that a mutually agreed upon and clearly marked boundary should be established to clearly delineate British land from that of the Indian nations. The Indian boundary line, as it came to be known, was, as Professor Louis De Vorsey Jr. aptly observed, "a geographic and conceptual force along the frontier zone of the Southeast. . . . the principal point of focus for Anglo-Indian relations throughout the pre-revolutionary period in the Southeast."[38]

The driving force behind the issuance of the proclamation was the desire for peace, the fervent desire of imperial policy makers to avoid Indian wars. This desire to check settlement and divide potentially hostile colonists and Indians had a number of flaws, the most notable of which was the absolute need—at least from the perspective of the colonists—for more land. If imperial policy clashed with the needs and desires of colonists, it was not necessarily different from the goals of Creek headmen, who repeatedly articulated two aims: maintaining peace with the British colonies in order to continue the deerskin trade, upon which they were economically dependent, and securing their borders and protecting hunting grounds from encroachment.[39]

To realize their goal of achieving both peace and a mutually agreeable boundary, Creeks and Britons came together for three postwar congresses, each devoted to adjusting matters relating to land and to peaceful coexistence in each of the three British colonies now contiguous to the Creek domain. The first, the Congress of Augusta, Georgia (November 1763) was a general congress and had been planned prior to the issuance of the Proclamation of 1763. In addition to the Creeks, representatives from the Cherokee, Chickasaw, Choctaw, and Catawba tribes also attended. West Florida-Creek affairs were discussed at Pensacola, West Florida, in May 1765. East Florida-Creek negotiations were conducted in November 1765 at Fort Picolata. Each of the congresses resulted in cessions of land from the Creeks to the British and, taken together, established a continuous—and often contentious—boundary that ran from the Savannah River to the Alabama-Mobile River watershed. The congresses are noteworthy not only for the boundary agreements that resulted, but for what the negotiations reveal about the Creeks.

Creek opposition to the transfer of French and Spanish lands faded as British troops actually took possession of their new holdings and reassured the Indians that they did not intend a war of conquest. Instead, in their speeches and talks, British diplomats stressed the benefits their presence in the Floridas would bring, the most important of which was trade. West Florida's governor, George Johnstone, wasted no time in telling the Creeks that the British needed land for their very subsistence: land on which to settle and raise crops to support a colony that would sustain trade with the Indians. British diplomats also minimized the amount of land they sought and pointed out the value of mutually defined and marked boundaries. As Johnstone told the Creeks at Pensacola, "we are far from asking any large Tract of Country; what we wish most is to avoid Disputing; to fix a certain limit rather than Large Possessions."[40] It was a triumph of realpolitik, since, short of all out war, the only solution was accommodation. Thus, the British were allowed to peacefully occupy coastal towns and forts, including Pensacola, Mobile, St. Marks, and St. Augustine, but the Creeks were adamant that interior posts, such as Fort Toulouse, would revert to Creek ownership. Likewise, virtually all the interior Spanish mission sites, most long abandoned, were deemed Creek property.[41] John Stuart, who served as the British Superintendent of Indian Affairs for the Southern District, stressed that "fixing and clearly ascertaining a Boundary Line" between Creek and British lands was an essential step toward harmonious relations.[42]

That essential step was taken by a coterie of leading men who represented the Upper and Lower Creek towns. Boundary negotiations with the British throughout the period highlighted Creek devotion to the principle that their lands were held in trust by their towns for the benefit of all their people, reserving to regional councils of headmen the right of alienation of land tenure. This was accomplished by achieving widespread consensus among individual town councils, who then delegated the authority to leading chiefs—representatives from the leading towns of the each Creek division.[43] In his opening speech before the assembled dignitaries at Augusta, Captain Allick made it clear that he spoke for both Upper and Lower Creeks, noting, "It is not his own speech but of the whole nation put into his mouth by them," and promising that those headmen not in attendance "have sent word they will abide by the Proceedings of those Present."[44] On the one occasion when a Creek leader tended an offer of land to a subordinate commander at Pensacola without the consent of the other towns, the cession was quickly disavowed by both the British and the Creeks.[45]

The boundary negotiations with the British colonies clearly revealed the divisional nature of the Creek polity, and the fact that it was left to each division to decide the fate of lands under its jurisdiction. This distinction was most notable at Augusta, where Upper and Lower Creek delegates differed on the matter of the land cession to Georgia. The leading man from Lower Creek Cussita reminded the Upper Creek representatives that he was "their elder brother," thereby invoking Lower Creek pre-eminence in the relative pecking order of Creek towns.[46] More importantly, the Lower Creeks asserted that the hunting grounds they proposed to cede were those of the Lower towns "to which you [Upper Creeks] never had any Claim."[47] The Upper Creek delegation acquiesced to Lower Creek preeminence in the matter. They would later recall that at the congress "the lower Creeks would not let us speak a Word."[48]

In West Florida, the Upper towns claimed the exclusive right of alienation for land from the Chattahoochee drainage to the Mobile watershed, which the Lower Creek representatives acknowledged.[49] In East Florida, Lower Creeks from established Creek "mother" towns located on the Chattahoochee River, considerably distant from East Florida, claimed the right to alienate land in the Florida peninsula. The two most populous East Florida Creek settlements, the Apalachee Old Field (Tallahassee) and Latchawie (Latchoway), later called Cuscowilla, were also represented at the congress, but their leaders were not allowed the honor nor responsibility of speaking publicly, and events would seem to indicate they had little input in the decisions made by the Lower Creek delegation.[50] Superintendent Stuart also met with five minor Lower Creek villages from near the junction of the Chattahoochee and Flint Rivers between his meetings in Pensacola and Picolata. Discussion there was limited to lands around the isolated fort at St. Marks, where the Spanish had established a port in what was once Apalachee territory. The Creeks had helped destroy the Apalachee at the beginning of the eighteenth century and were now engaged in town building on Apalachee Old Fields.[51] When Stuart arrived, Lower Creek chiefs reiterated that the land had only been "lent" to the Spanish, but declared that their British "brothers" could assume the grant made to the Spanish.[52] The congress is of particular interest in that it reveals the Chattahoochee-Flint River drainage as the extent of Lower Creek land claims, with the non-Muskogean towns on the lower part of the Chattahoochee speaking for the territory there. Whether they did so with or without the blessing of Cussita and Coweta remains unclear. In either case, they agreed to what Lower Creek delegates had previously stipulated in Augusta.[53] Following negotiations and treaty signings, the regional divisions, when necessary, called general meetings of town leadership to explain and "ratify" the proceedings. For example, the Upper Creek delegates called a general meeting of Upper Creek towns following the 1763 conference at Augusta and later sent word to Superintendent of Indian Affairs John Stuart that they had formally agreed to support the treaty.[54]

For their part, the British had no choice but to recognize the traditional town leaders of the Creek polity and work through them in order to ensure acceptance of boundaries and other treaty agreements by the entire tribe. After 1763, the British government sought, through the distribution of special medals and titles, to recognize and support cooperative allies.[55] The medal chiefs, as they came to be known, received considerable personal property in the form of clothing, presents for their wives, guns, saddles, and other special gifts. Among the Creeks, the British prudently appointed representatives from all tribal entities, and even sought out malcontents, like the Mortar of the Okchai and Tupulga of Conchatys, previously supporters of the French. Though flattered by the attention, most of the Creek medal chiefs proved to be independent-minded spokesmen rather than pawns.[56] Moreover, as death claimed some of the chiefs, Creeks nominated their replacements. Granted, the British looked to their firmest friends for these nominations, but it is clear that the Creeks had a voice in the award of British titles. Medal chiefs were always chosen from among the most prominent leaders and spokesmen for Creek councils in line with traditional notions of power and authority, and only secondarily were they recognized and rewarded by the British as those with whom business could be done. In 1768, the Second Man of the Little Tallassee, after delivering talks from Emisteseguo and Otis Mico (the Mortar), who were great medal chiefs, felt compelled to state his credentials. In addition to the small medal he held from the British, he informed the assembly at the Congress of Augusta in 1768, "I am also a great beloved man, and a ruler amongst my people, what I say deserve credit."[57] Medal chiefs, both at meetings with the British and in talks dispatched via interpreters, were always careful to note that their words were not their own, but the views of their councils. The Creeks, ever mindful of the need for consensus, repeatedly reminded the British that they should heed only the talks and speeches from regional town councils and ignore the talks of individuals who were not authorized to speak for the entire nation.

Less appreciated but of equal importance is the fact that the Creeks likewise laid honors—and concomitant responsibilities—on British colonial governors and military officers, enjoining these newly appointed Creek *micos* to look out for Creek interests. When thus adopted, the new "brothers" and "fathers" were duly instructed as to their responsibilities. In 1771, the Creek delegation made the governor of West Florida the Apalachicola Mico. It was "the highest title we can confer," they told him, since the Apalachicola were deemed to be "the original proprietors" of the land. The Creeks suggested to the new *mico* that it was his responsibility to protect Creek land for his "children" rather than attempt to gain control of it for white settlers.[58] By establishing fictive kin relationships with the British, the Creeks essentially fixed them in the Creek world order, extending to them recognition as people with rights and responsibilities. This fictive extension of Creek social and political order reached to the very pinnacle of the British empire, for King George III was designated as a headman of the Tyger clan.[59]

The awarding of medals to carefully selected leading men was an attempt by the British to establish order among the "many united Republics." Both Johnstone and Stuart recognized the "Competition for Power" in Indian government, but mistakenly viewed it merely as the clashing ambitions of leading men, whom they sought out and hoped to manipulate by "particular Attention and management." Indian diplomacy was, as the British diplomats observed, "not cheap."[60] Nor was it simple, for authority among the Creeks was more complex than individual egos and revolved instead around the ancient relationship of the regional town divisions and internal political divisions and clan networks. The British, far from achieving subtle and suave "management" of authority, merely recognized the influence already established by the Creek towns themselves.

At the three transition congresses, the transfer of land from Creek towns to British colonies was far more than the wholesale appropriation of native land by stronger parties. Rather, the Creek people negotiated with certain goals in mind and they expected value, both tangible and intangible, in return for their land. Creeks assigned the highest value to the land upon which their interior towns were located. They also placed enormous value on their hinterland, which was valued for hunting and other resources. Often overlooked is the fact that much of the land on the Creek periphery was conquered and acquired territory. Conquest of certain peoples and their territory had brought prestige, wealth, and power to the Creeks, and by the end of the eighteenth century that territory also proved a useful commodity. In exchange for their land, Creek headmen sought trade concessions such as more favorable exchange rates and outright "presents" of trade goods—cloth, weaponry, and rum worth thousands of pounds sterling. In 1763, land served as payment for atrocities, providing a relatively painless way to escape the unpleasant and often impossible task of executing fellow Creeks for deaths of British subjects. At the end of the period under discussion, land would become payment for trade debts to British subjects—a dangerous and precedent-setting event.

From the beginning of the Anglo-Creek alliance, the gift of land was a mark of friendship and an expression of generosity, a trait highly valued in Creek culture. Creeks, when awarding their acres to British diplomats in both the Floridas and in Georgia, frequently noted that their land would yield food crops for British settlers, timber for houses and ships, and provide a place for trade depots. In return, the Creeks expected reciprocal generosity in the form of a steady and fair trade to their towns. In a real sense, Creek grants were genuine expressions of concern that a valued ally's needs be met. At the same time, these needs weighed heavily on Creek sensibilities.

In most cases, the Creeks found myriad reasons to make land grants to the British colonies. At Augusta in 1763, Georgians lobbied for a land cession, most likely devised the extent of the grant, and made a general pardon for Creeks who had assisted the French in the war or previously killed British subjects, contingent upon Creek approval of the grant. Those in need of pardon included highly placed Upper Creeks. The grant consisted primarily of the finger of land lying between the Savannah and Ogeechee Rivers as far north as the Little River, and moved the tidewater boundary between the St. Marys and Altamaha Rivers slightly westward. The land grant encompassed all existing Georgia settlements made in violation of the 1735 treaty.[61] The cession ended contention about these settlements and offered the prospect of a boundary that would be understood and honored by both sides.[62] In addition, Superintendent Stuart distributed considerable "presents" to the delegates for distribution to their towns and made promises to better regulate the deerskin trade.[63] Even those reluctant to part with the property could see the many benefits of accommodation, but it seems clear that it was "due regard to the Great King's pardon" which won Creek acceptance of the proposed cession. In speeches to the Upper Creeks, the Lower Creeks were clear: "We hope your future Behavior will be such as may not lay us under the Necessity of giving away more Land to attone for your Crimes."[64]

At Pensacola, British diplomats attempted to shame the Creeks by pointing out that the Choctaw had been more generous at an earlier congress with West Florida than the Creeks seemed willing to be at their congress. The chiding led Creek delegates to make a larger grant than they had intended—but less than West Florida wanted.[65] Of even greater importance in winning agreement for a cession was the public assurances from Superintendent John Stuart of better trade regulations and a reduction of trade prices, long a prime cause of the Abeika Creeks. Stuart proved worthy of Creek trust, and by 1767 he had managed to convince traders to agree to regulations and to roll back prices.[66] The cession was actually meager, consisting of a narrow ribbon of land that extended some fifteen miles inland and curled around the seacoast from Pensacola to Mobile Bay, terminating at the rich soils of the Alabama River. The British, much to their dismay, remained confined to the sandy coastal soil.[67] The territory above the new boundary, regarded by the Creeks as some of their best hunting lands, was also some of the most desirable agricultural lands in the region. And the Creeks would not part with that, regardless of appeals to their generosity.[68]

At Picolata, it was not until Superintendent John Stuart and Governor James Grant questioned Creek generosity and threatened to withhold substantial reciprocal "presents" that the negotiators agreed to what East Florida wanted. Lower Creeks then parted with a strip of land that reached roughly twenty-five miles inland and stretched several hundred miles along the peninsula, from the St. Marys River to the lower reaches of the St. Johns River, before retreating again to a tidewater limit all the way around the Florida peninsula to West Florida. The new boundary left the vast interior expanse, including the best agricultural land in Florida, to the Creeks. Promises were made regarding placing adequate numbers of traders in Creek towns and more favorable exchange rates, which were eventually kept, if only briefly. Moreover, the Creeks retained the right to visit and hunt on the ceded lands. Most importantly, the Florida boundary, like that in Georgia and West Florida, was believed to be permanent.[69]

Creek headmen only grudgingly parted with their territory, and at both Augusta and Pensacola they made it clear that the British would have to prove themselves worthy of further consideration before additional land would be given, devising, in effect, a probationary period. When Upper Creek headmen ratified the Augusta cession at a general meeting of towns in April 1764, they indicated they would know that the British were trustworthy if they kept promises not to encroach across the boundary for four years.[70] At Pensacola, the Creeks promised the British that they would make further concessions "after they knew the English better, that if, after having passed some years with them, they found them good, they would cede as much land as they might need."[71]

As a result of the three congresses between 1763 and 1765, the British and Creeks recognized the legal right of the other to specific land, established detailed boundaries, and maintained the peace, ensuring trade and a continuation of the Anglo-Creek alliance that had been the source of prosperity for both. The Creek headmen quickly concluded that the treaty process had been worth it, and earlier references to future cessions were forgotten as the Creek people came to embrace the concept of a fixed, immutable boundary. When the Creeks returned to Augusta in 1768 to reaffirm the boundaries agreed at the various congresses, Tallachea summed up his people's view of their newly negotiated border. It would be, he noted with satisfaction, "as a strong stone wall that will last to the latest ages."[72] The assertion is extraordinary, and reveals a maturing conception of statehood and territorial integrity among the loosely organized Creek towns. The boundary itself—as well as the Creek political process that achieved widespread consensus and effectively created a Creek territorial entity—was a stellar achievement.

While the Creeks believed the boundary was now "fixed," British governors, military leaders, and the superintendent of Indian Affairs were not satisfied. At the same time they pushed the Creeks to adequately mark the newly agreed upon boundary line, they sought ways to enlarge their holdings, including bribing the Indians sent to mark the line. They also called for new congresses to renegotiate the boundary.

West Floridians were particularly restive, having realized that Creek obduracy in regard to the boundary line had left them with "barren sand" and little more.[73] By the late 1760s, the push was on for a larger cession. Three issues were particularly troublesome. The first involved the land around Mobile and along the Mobile and Tensaw Rivers. This was land once claimed by extirpated tribes who had been allies of the French, notably the Mobilian, Taensa, Tomé, Towasa, and Naniaba around the Mobile Bay.[74] The most important area was the land of the Naniaba Indians, located at the forks of the Tombigbee and Alabama Rivers. There, numerous streams and rivers effectively created a rich, alluvial "island," coveted by both West Florida planters and Indians. The Naniaba, along with the Tomé, were caught up in the rivalry between the Creek and Choctaw confederacies, and as a long-simmering war for hunting territory and supremacy between these two flared in 1763, they abandoned their villages and sought safety among the towns of the Choctaw. Triumphant Creeks laid claim to their lands by right of conquest, while the Choctaw, speaking for the Naniaba and Tomé, also claimed the territory.[75] In 1765, the Choctaw had ceded the Naniaba Island to West Florida. The Creeks had not.[76] The Creek towns also claimed the deserted village sites of the Taensa Indians.[77] These Indians, allies of the French, had moved into the area during the early part of the eighteenth century and served as a buffer for the settlement of Mobile. With the withdrawal of the French, the Taensa evacuated their settlements along the Mobile-Alabama-Tombigbee system and returned to their homeland.[78] West Florida now claimed Taensa land as part of the original French "lease," while the Creeks claimed the land by right of conquest. The second area of contention between the Creeks and West Florida was due to surveyor mistakes which had resulted in the West Florida government awarding grants on unceded lands. Settlers had actually established themselves beyond the agreed-upon boundary, which remained unmarked. A third area of concern, at least on the part of West Florida, was the closely circumscribed boundary around the capital at Pensacola. The land granted by the Creeks around Pensacola in 1765 had formerly been settled by the Yamasee, who evacuated with the Spanish.[79]

In 1771, the Creeks and British met in Pensacola to address these issues. Governor Peter Chester, who claimed the settlements beyond the 1765 boundary had been done without his knowledge, placated the Creeks by informing them he had successfully ordered that they be removed.[80] He then relentlessly pushed the Creeks to cede their "pretensions" to Naniaba Island as well as additional land along the Escambia River all the way to the fall line. The Upper Creek speaker, Emisteseguo of the Little Tallassee, rejected the Choctaw claim to the lands of the Naniaba above Mobile and staunchly maintained that the Tombigbee River was the western boundary of the Creek country.[81] As negotiations continued, the Creeks, hoping to compromise, offered to "lend" the British additional land around Pensacola as far as an abandoned Spanish cowpen. Emisteseguo pointed out that the Spanish, who had violated their boundary agreement with the Creeks, had been forced to abandon their settlement there long before 1763 by Creek warriors. Emisteseguo also asserted that Creek people intended to settle the area around the cowpen themselves, as soon as they concluded their war with the Choctaw.[82] Expansion into conquered territory was not new for the Creeks, who, as much as the British, saw themselves as colonizers of Florida.

Superintendent John Stuart, speaking for West Florida, rejected the land offered as "only four miles of very poor land ... it is not worth the trouble of altering the old lines and drawing a new treaty for such a trifle."[83] He then pressed them again for lands along the Conica and Escambia Rivers, casting his request as "moderate." The Creeks, rather than relent to the superintendent's condescending and excoriating pressure, retired for private deliberations and later sent word to Stuart and Chester that they had decided to leave the congress rather than continue offending their friends by their inability to give them what they so ardently desired.

The British pressed the Creeks to continue discussion on other matters, only to renew their request for more land the next day. Emisteseguo, again serving as spokesman, firmly reminded them of his responsibility to his own people and told them in no uncertain terms his position was unchanged: "I am still the same man I was and not like a child varying my opinion every instant."[84] Emisteseguo then reiterated the Creek position regarding their boundary. The Tombigbee River was the western boundary of the Creek people, and the Choctaw had no right to cede lands east of the river. The line between the Creeks and West Florida would remain at the Tensaw Old Fields. He enumerated treaty violations committed by British subjects: hunting on Indian lands, driving cattle beyond the boundary, and making settlements on the border and even in Creek towns. Trade regulations, agreed to in 1767, had now been laid aside on the king's order. In short, the headman lamented, "I have talked to no purpose and [find] that our agreements have fallen to the ground."[85] In assessing Creek medal chiefs as spokesmen for their people, Emisteseguo's determined discourse may well have been their finest hour.

But Stuart persisted, pointing out that the Naniaba and Tomé, as well as the French, had planted on the disputed territory before their removal. He asked the Creeks, "supposing the property of all the eastern side to be really yours, will you refuse us the same advantage you allowed the French and the same said tribes?"[86] Such heavy pressure from their allies—sweetened with promises of "valuable consideration in goods"—ultimately worked, and the Creeks ceded to West Florida the rights to the disputed lands of the Naniaba and Tomé.[87] The treaty description noted that the new boundary encompassed all the former settlements of the French as well. The award to the British was made by the authority of the headmen from the Alabama towns who were all present and who held claim to the land in question.[88]

Beyond the "island" of Naniaba the Creeks refused to budge, but they did offer to present West Florida's request for additional land to a general meeting of Upper towns.[89] In April 1772, the Upper Creeks met to deliberate and rejected further cessions. At the Little Tallassee, the speaker for the Abeika, Tallapoosa, and Alabama tribes declared: "We have been asked two or three times for the land . . . which we cannot nor will not give as we want that for our hunting land, the former boundary must stand but as far as the Old Spanish cowpen they may plant as land lent. The land is ours and we have given what we think we can spare and we hope there will be no difference between us about it, by too many demands of this kind may cause friends to lean one from another."[90]

John Stuart was convinced that Upper Creek reluctance to approve a boundary extension in West Florida was due to machinations in Georgia, where prominent traders were attempting to obtain a cession of land for that colony. Although the Upper Creeks were opposed to any further cession to Georgia, that land was controlled by the Lower Creek towns. After considerable turmoil, the Lower Creeks were persuaded to transfer 2.5 million acres of land to Georgia in 1773. The Georgia New Purchase, as the grant was styled, represented a departure from earlier land cessions. The cession was originally proposed by the Cherokee as payment for their trade debts. But much of the land they offered to Georgia was territory that the Creeks had wrested from them in a series of earlier wars for control of hunting territory along the Savannah River.[91] When the Creeks refused to cooperate, their traders threatened to withdraw from trade and leave the Creeks without guns and ammunition with which to fight their Choctaw enemies in West Florida. The threats alternated with free rum and promises of free goods as payment for the lands, in addition to abrogation of the entire Creek national debt. This boundary, they said, would be permanent. The pressure and rewards were too great to resist, and it was the Lower Creek headmen who assumed authority for the transfer, which proved to be the most divisive cession in the postwar period for the Creek people.[92]

At the congress, Creek warriors, still enraged at the Cherokee, excoriated that tribe for broaching the deal and presuming to alienate Creek lands. William Bartram, who attended the congress, recorded that an unnamed Creek headman "with an agitated and terrific countenance, frowning menaces and disdain, fixed his eyes on the Cherokee chiefs, asked them what right they had to give away their lands." Insults followed, and the Creeks, according to Bartram, threatened to walk away from the deal unless the Cherokee publicly withdrew their claim to the land. The Georgia scribe was instructed to acknowledge in the treaty that it was the Creek towns who possessed the "exclusive right of alienation."[93] In addition to the parcel along the Savannah River, in former Cherokee territory, the Creeks also ceded a sizeable tract along the Ogeechee River, once considered prime Creek hunting land.[94] The cession rankled many Creeks, particularly young warriors, who resented the loss of hunting lands. Matters came to a head in late December 1773 when Creek warriors committed a series of murders and other hostile acts on the ceded lands. In Creek towns, accommodationist headmen worked fervently to control the anti-cession dissidents and assuage Georgia's anger over the murders. In the end, they averted war, but dissent lingered on.[95]

Within these hard-won borders so carefully crafted by a coterie of Creek headmen, the Creeks, like all other southeastern tribes, harbored notions of infringement of sovereignty due to unwarranted trespass, whether it be a violation of hunting territory, unauthorized settlement within their borders, or the destruction of resources on that land, such as felling trees. Moreover, they sought to control traffic through their territory, called for limitations on the number of traders allowed into their towns, attempted to place restrictions on the amount of rum that traders could bring into their nation, placed prohibition on cattle drives by whites across their territory from Georgia to the Floridas, and pondered ways to deal with the growing problem of settlers moving along trading paths to territory on the Mississippi River.[96] At various conferences, Creeks declared they had a right to burn houses, stores, and huts built beyond the boundary line and to kill cattle that strayed onto their lands.[97] As for cattle kept by deerskin traders at their stores in the Creek towns, in disregard of Creek wishes and various treaty agreements, headmen asserted that should the traders' cattle commit "any mischief amongst the corn and get killed the owners must not expect to be paid for, or say anything about it."[98] And when negotiations with the British over the amount of rum that traders could legally bring into their towns proved impossible to enforce, headmen took matters into their own hands, seeking out and destroying kegs of rum carried by traders in excess of the established limits.[99] By mid-1771, they raided illegal settlements along the Georgia line and seized property. Lest the British conclude they were mere thieves, the Creeks sent a list of the property seized and claimed it was done to "assert our native rights."[100]

The boundary that emerged from the negotiation process was ideally meant to follow natural boundaries and geographical features: paths, rivers, distinctive outcroppings, and ponds. Not only did such natural boundaries reduce the labor and time spent in marking the boundary, they required less decision-making on the part of the boundary delegations and could not be "easily mistaken" by either surveyors or settlers.[101] Frequently, in running a line between points, the boundary also traversed swamps (including the Okefenokee in Georgia), cane breaks, and other formidable barriers. Where possible, trees were felled or marked along a fifty-foot wide corridor that would unmistakably signal the division of territory.[102]

If negotiating the boundary had proved difficult, marking it proved even more so. Portions of the West Florida line were left unmarked, as a series of governors perpetually hoped to obtain a larger cession before fixing a visible boundary line.[103] Continuing warfare between the Choctaw and Creeks likewise hampered efforts to mark the line. No part of the line was marked in East Florida, as governors there also perennially hoped for boundary extensions. And where delegations did sally forth to blaze trees, there were heated arguments. Along a section of the Georgia New Purchase line, the surveyor's "little wicked instrument," in this case a compass, was deemed a "liar" by the Creeks helping mark the line. Local iron ore deposits may have skewed the compass, or the instrument may have been purposefully misdirected by the surveyor. Whatever the reason for the deviation, the marking delegation proceeded without the compass at Creek insistence. In most cases, the boundary delegation included a mix of cartographers and surveyors, complete with their chains and other instruments. The best instruments accompanying the survey crews were the minds of the Creek delegates, for they carried with them mental maps, vivid topographical images they could disgorge as precise oral descriptions of the land they ceded and the land they intended to keep. Creeks displayed an astounding ability to walk a boundary, described orally at a congress, without error. When errors did creep in, it was usually the result of rum or bribery, which the Georgians, in particular, were adept at employing.[104]

Even where marked, the line was frequently ignored by colonials and colonial land officials. There was also trouble along the boundary, and incidents soared as Creek warriors visited tippling houses or taverns that sprang up at the border in order to trade rum for Creek horses. Vagabonds, farmers, and cattle keepers were problems as well. One Cusseta chief noted with disgust that almost immediately after a portion of the line was marked in Georgia, "the white people made a large step" over it and were settled "two days march" over the marked line.[105] To the very end, the British saw the line as a temporary expedient and Indian hunting grounds as opportunities. The Creeks, facing pressure from both Georgians and West Floridians for more land, increasingly cast descriptions of their boundary line in terms they believed the British would understand. A people who had no brick or stone walls now wished to erect them. Their boundary, they repeatedly said, should be "a great brick wall not to be passed." It should be "like a Stone Wall never to be Broke."[106]

The Creeks found that even brick and stone had limitations as a barrier, for gigantic "steps" over the boundary, as well as British demands for land in West Florida and Georgia, continued until the American Revolution focused diplomacy in different directions. For the colonies—soon to be states—the notion of a fixed boundary was ludicrous. American backcountrymen openly flaunted royal decrees, royal governors, and negotiated lines. The inability of the royal governors to control the backcountry was emblematic of larger woes. As far as the records relate, the British were never able to answer a question posed by the headmen of the Lower Creek towns in 1767: "Whenever the Virginia people (Back Settlers) are told by our people that they are over the Line & if they don't keep in the Bounds they will Burn their Houses, they make answer they will burn the Governors House over his Head. If the Governor cannot keep these Virginia People under [control], how can we keep our people under [control]?"[107]

Nor could the governor keep his own council members in check. One of them, Jonathan Bryan, in an attempt to circumvent the king's prohibition on private purchase of Indian land, attempted to lease tracts from the Creeks.[108] The American Revolution put a stop to the proceedings. Georgians, in fast retreat in the wake of Creek border hostilities that resulted from the New Purchase Cession, were too distracted by the threat of Indian war to send delegates to the First Continental Congress. But after the war, Georgians renewed with vigor their efforts to alienate Creek land claims.[109] The Creeks themselves did not abandon the concept of a marked and permanent border. In 1790, as headmen from the Creek divisions, led by Alexander McGillivray, started for New York to treat with President George Washington, knowledgeable reports asserted "they place great confidence in the united states; and wish to agree with them, upon a permanent boundary, over which the southern states shall not trespass."[110]

Though the boundary created by the Creek headmen between 1763 and 1773 was far from a "stone wall" that kept white settlements at bay, the efforts of the eighteenth-century leadership had forged a new sense of national identity, based not merely on town and tribal identity, but on territorial limits. Their efforts represented a triumph of consensus and traditional town leadership as well as innovation as ancient patterns of governing encountered new opportunities and perils while diverse and dispersed towns worked toward a single goal.

The Creeks conjured a variety of images to describe their relationship to the land. For the Mortar, the land represented fire, food, shelter, and medicine—the things necessary for life. In essence, the land *was* life itself. Most Creeks viewed their property in the same memorable way that the Cussita King saw the situation: "our land is like our flesh."[111] In early 1774, Emisteseguo held a lump of white clay—sacred soil—and declared it represented the square ground where the Abeika, Tallapoosa, and Alabama met. "This piece of chalk is the same as ourselves," he sent word to the British.[112] And so it was.

The author wishes to thank Kyle G. Braund, Robin F. A. Fabel, and Gregory A. Waselkov for their comments on an earlier version of this essay.

Carolinians Abroad

Cultivating English Identities from the Colonial Lower South

S. MAX EDELSON

"I am become a perfect Englishman," wrote Peter Manigault around 1750, "a Mug of Porter stands a poor Chance when I meet it, and I like red Wine better than Madeira."[1] For this young South Carolina law student abroad, an extended sojourn in London provided an education that reached beyond immersion in the scholastic traditions of the Inns of Court. Like his elite counterparts in Charlestown and its productive plantation countryside, Manigault invested in cultivating a viable English identity by immersing himself in English settings and consuming English things. Like others who idealized English culture, yet found themselves struggling against the grain of provincial habits and expectations when abroad, Manigault perceived a bridgeable but evident gulf separating those traveling from Britain's colonial periphery from those reared within its cultural core. Although descended from Huguenot immigrants, it was Manigault's status as a provincial Creole that made him aware that he was a less-than-perfect Englishman. Long exposure to the social, economic, and cultural environments of the South Carolina lowcountry had constituted his character in fundamental ways.

When eighteenth-century South Carolinians like Manigault ventured to England as absentee plantation owners, business travelers, students, and loyalist émigrés, they saw perhaps for the first time the tensions that set the practices of their adaptive colonial culture against those that prevailed in the metropolis. The cultural environment of the Lower South, shaped pervasively by the demands of plantation agriculture, inculcated expectations and behaviors that were cast in sharp relief by divergent English ways. Unstable commodity earnings encouraged lowcountry planters, during times of financial instability, to curtail spending on luxuries and depend on enslaved labor and plantation produce for their families' subsistence. Cut off from the fiscal shelter provided by their plantations while abroad, South Carolinians saw the status-affirming consumption of English elites as an extravagance they could rarely hope to match. Members of South Carolina's small, interdependent colonial elite cherished the informality of their social gatherings; in Britain they found signs everywhere of prohibitive social rigidity. Cultivating a vast plantation landscape during the prosperous twenty-year period preceding the American Revolutionary War generated high expectations for upward social mobility and wealth accumulation. In Britain, the scale of economic enterprise and the prospects for advancements seemed, by contrast, narrowly circumscribed. Colonists came to the mother country with the humility of cultural supplicants eager to refine colonial selves hewn roughly out of the materials at hand in a distant provincial backwater. Their unexpectedly negative encounters with English society tarnished both their visions of English social perfection and perceptions of themselves as English people. Although the affirmation of unique American identities awaited the rejection of British political authority in 1776, these critiques of Britain by colonial travelers reveal a pre-revolutionary cultural foundation for the construction of viable American identities.

By the middle decades of the eighteenth century, the planter-merchant elite increasingly invested plantation earnings in the consumption of English goods and the construction of rural and urban buildings designed after English architectural fashions. They diverted enslaved workers from the rice and indigo fields to enlarge gardens planted with English trees, vegetables, flowers, and ornamental plants. They founded organizations devoted to music, philosophy, and science that made Charlestown an American center for refined cultural pursuits. But however well-clothed and well-spoken these elites might appear, they were keenly aware that their Englishness was interleaved with the exotic contributions of a subtropical locale, from its Africanized population to its economy built on the production of agricultural commodities. Landscaping plantation grounds and building elegant townhouses provided little more than Anglicized oases within a cultural environment that diverged sharply from the metropolitan model. Members of the planter-merchant elite labored in their pursuits of refinement under the weight of a cultural inferiority complex that propelled them eastward across the Atlantic.[2] By transplanting themselves and their children to England, the merchants and planters of the Lower South sought to reconstitute colonial identities through sustained immersion in English society.

The emergence of distinctive Carolina foodways underscores how adaptation to the lowcountry altered colonists' most basic cultural practices and preferences. When seventeenth-century settlers saw that crops of wheat rotted in the fields, they were forced to plant maize, what they called "Indian corn." Having to make due without proper bread was a demoralizing discovery for those seeking to establish recognizably English lives in America. Eating African rice and Indian corn, some feared, might even unbalance English bodies and imperil health. When George Appleby, a successful Charlestown merchant who retired to the English countryside, attempted to donate supplies of Carolina rice to the poor of his parish in the 1770s, he was surprised when they rebuffed his largesse. These destitute English men and women feared that this "outlandish" meal might wreck havoc on English constitutions to the point of causing blindness.[3] Carolinians abroad, by contrast, yearned for familiar foods despite the lingering English prejudices against consuming them. Eliza Pinckney sent a barrel of rice to her sons' English headmaster with the instruction that the "children love it boiled dry to eat with their meat instead of bread." Elias Ball Jr. asked his Carolina relatives to "send us a small Cask of Corn grits" in the next Bristol-bound vessel.[4] Once in the mother country absentees viewed corn and rice with fondness, despite their status as emblems of a crude, exotic culture.

Just as colonists integrated Lower South foods into their diets as commonplace staples, experiences within plantation society insinuated a range of distinctive preferences into their working conceptions of social, economic, and environmental order. Because volatile transatlantic markets for their commodities jeopardized the incomes of plantation estates, South Carolina elites developed conservative views of family consumption and insisted that their children learn skills of some economic utility along with the habits of gentility in the course of their educations. The demands of rice agriculture even shaped their aesthetic impressions of landscapes. In the lowcountry, these were mundane, and thus unremarkable, values. In England, colonial cultural differences became palpable as travelers gauged their altered selves against elite English preferences that they found, to their surprise and sometimes dismay, they did not share. Carolinians abroad thus evaluated the metropolis, and the long cultural shadow it cast over the colonies, with new eyes.

The many centrifugal forces at work in the colonization of British America, by which settlers detached themselves from European societies and fanned out across New World landscapes, disrupted experiential connections with the home society. Colonists in the Lower South first established an institutional infrastructure modeled on metropolitan examples, then pursued fortunes and prestige that would have in all likelihood been denied them in Britain. They continued to regret, however, an inability to fulfill expectations for their societies that English men and women might take for granted as commonplace characteristics of their cultural environment. Such features were perhaps even more important than courts, churches, and legislative assemblies—institutions that anchored colonial practices self-consciously to English forms—to obtaining a sense of identification with and easy familiarity in the provincial places they inhabited.[5]

In the second half of the eighteenth century a largely Creole planter elite, many of whose members had never visited Britain, embraced the standards of metropolitan society as normative ideals and edifying contrasts to disordered agricultural landscapes, a social hierarchy distorted by planters' rapid accumulation of wealth, and a population composed chiefly of African slaves. The strength of this mimetic impulse was reflected in the extraordinary frequency with which planters sent their children to Britain for intellectual and cultural "improvement." Lowcountry elites abroad encountered English society in a series of actual experiences rather than as an idealized abstraction. These problematic homecomings featured unexpected moments of disenchantment with life in the metropolis. Carolinians abroad often found themselves coming to terms with a sense of their own cultural distinctiveness as a viable provincial variant rather than as a sign that they were falling away from the standards of the center. These encounters revealed a range of unique, self-defining preferences and exposed the ways in which economic experiences influenced distinctive habits and expectations.

Underpinning the cultural disorientation of colonists abroad were concerns for wealth: how to acquire it, how much of it to spend, and how it might serve to denote positions in a social hierarchy. Lowcountry planters chafed at times under the standards for conspicuous consumption in the metropolis, but not from a sense of insecurity that their estates were insufficient in comparison to those of other elites. By various measures, the value of real and personal property (including slaves) in the eighteenth-century lowcountry made the typical planter among the wealthiest inhabitants of the Anglo-American world.[6] Those among the more select subgroup that established residences overseas undoubtedly surpassed the mean. Lowcountry planters carried with them a conception of the relationships linking wealth, consumption, and estates that diverged from English understandings.

Experienced planters recognized that "the nature of our estates in this Country, being chiefly in negroes," impelled them to leverage the debt incurred to buy slaves against expected future commodity earnings. Under such fiscal constraints, the appearance of a plantation estate, in extent and amenities, bore little relationship to the real financial resources of its owner.[7] Yearly plantation income fluctuated with volatile commodity prices and unpredictable agricultural seasons. Such was the "Uncertainty of Carolina Estates" that planters tended to pay off debts and invest earnings in new slaves and more plantation acreage before determining what remainder could be earmarked for consumption.[8] More than merely a defensive, self-conscious reaction to English cultural superiority, the planters' critiques of English elite consumption were grounded in economic experiences with volatile estates.[9] As they promoted the virtues of thrift against excessively luxurious living, habits of reinvesting plantation returns to better weather unexpected downturns informed their responses.

In early South Carolina, promotional writers tempted potential immigrants by comparing plantation settlements to English agricultural estates in their ability to provide a stable annual income.[10] Over the course of the eighteenth century, planters learned that their capital investments in lowcountry tracts and enslaved workers could rarely fulfill English expectations for reliable income from land ownership. Plantation enterprises often enabled their owners to generate remarkable returns on their investments, however, as good harvests and favorable market conditions compensated for environmental disasters and periodic market downturns over a course of years. Under such constraints, bequeathing an augmented estate to one's heirs, rather than siphoning off spending money at the end of each season, became the means by which the colony's land- and slave-owning elite aspired to sustain its status. A planter's death was the moment of reckoning for assessing the real value of such estates and the success or failure of strategies of long-term accumulation, when the indebtedness that accompanied a working lifetime's capital acquisitions was tallied against an inventory of slaves, land, livestock, and produce. When John Martin came from England in the late 1780s to assume control of an inherited rice plantation on the Winyaw River, he imposed an English financial conception of an estate onto the shifting financial fortunes of a South Carolina plantation enterprise. His first impressions of Belvior plantation convinced him that his new estate was "capable of producing [£]1000 pr. Annum." Martin enjoyed a "very good" furnished house and a garden and vineyard that afforded "all sorts of Delicates," had "no servants wages" to pay, and presided over eight hundred acres and a labor force of close to sixty slaves. He hoped to pass on a handsome living to his son after clearing the estate's debts by divesting his property of superfluous tracts of land. But other heirs took possession of their portion of Belvior's slaves, and, after Martin's death, creditors liquidated the remaining assets, while the lands that he assumed would place the estate on a sound financial footing proved all but worthless.[11]

Some English absentees shared Martin's conception that the value of an estate inhered in its land's productive capacity. Just as an English landlord reckoned his income by the rents tenants were obliged to pay, they assumed their Lower South plantation estates entitled them to expect regular annual payments that could be devoted to consumption. John Channing attempted to make his Georgia plantation conform to the English model by proposing, somewhat implausibly, that the sale of hogs and other farm produce could be "sufficient to defray the current expenses, so that the whole of the Crop might be appropriated to my use." Other absentees, complained their resident plantation managers and agents, were "careless of . . . their estates . . . except the income," and "when that does not reach their expectations . . . and no allowance made for casualties, they are dissatisfied and too often make improper expressions of their displeasure."[12] In the lowcountry, curtailing unnecessary consumption and relying on plantations for subsistence helped planters endure dramatic drops in income. When facing regular outlays for living expenses in England, however, even experienced planters expected their Lower South estates to be "as secure as in England" in providing a reliable annual return. They joined other plantation owners, some of whom had never visited America, in complaining of "small Profits" from their "planting Interest."[13] As resources strained under the costs of displaying an elite status abroad, absentees struggled to reconcile divergent expectations for English and lowcountry estates.

After nearly two decades in South Carolina, Henry Gray sought to return to England with his family in 1764 to "fix in some cheap country in the West of England & to do a great many fine things in the farming way." Planter and merchant Henry Laurens estimated that the 10 to 12 percent return on his "money & Labours" Gray received in Carolina would bring but 3 or 4 percent in England. The "plain English of all which in my opinion is," Laurens wrote, "that he is leaving good Wheat Bread to take up with Rye."[14] Gray sought a more modest English future for his family than did wealthier absentees. Yet for all return migrants, England seemed to offer economic rewards incommensurate with what similar efforts would bring in the Lower South. Although increasing wealth enabled ever-larger numbers to journey to the metropolis, lowcountry elites weighed the social and economic costs that attended living there and measured unexpected realities against visions of a model society that had lured them across the Atlantic. "[W]e are in London, the center of knavery," wrote Louisa Wells in 1779 as she described her duties superintending the artisans who repaired the house that her father, loyalist newspaper publisher Robert Wells, had leased in the capital's Salisbury Square. English refinement, although admired as an ideal, tainted elite social life for many Carolinians who commented on needless extravagance, truculent and demanding servants, and uncomfortable formality.[15]

When not studying law at the Inner Temple, Peter Manigault spent more time with a Carolina family "than any where else." They "are very free and affable," he wrote to his mother, and "not stiff as most People are here." Although as the scion of a wealthy mercantile and planting family he mingled among elites on both sides of the Atlantic, he was "every day more and more surprized at the Extravagance that reigns every where."[16] He marveled at the expense of the country seat of a leading merchant in the Carolina trades and reckoned that "without I were Master of an Immense Fortune," it would be impossible to remain in London for very long, "for there are so many Ways of Spending Money that one never would have thought of."[17] Expected to justify his purchases to his father, Manigault excused his liberality by protesting that, rather than squandering his allowance in excessive consumption, he could "shew something, (either Knowledge or Effects) for the whole Money I have expended." Anticipating a reprimand after he bought a lace coat, he explained how he was "in a manner forced" to buy it. In contrast to the more relaxed social environment that prevailed in South Carolina, Manigault encountered unexpectedly stringent sartorial standards in Britain. When he attended church one Sunday with fellow Carolinian William Drayton he "was drest quite plain, my Friend had a Laced Waistcoat and hat, he, or rather his Laced Waistcoat, was introduced into a pew, while I, that is, my plain Clothes, were forced to stand up, during the whole time of divine Service, in the Isle." He hoped his father would think him "neither foppish nor extravagant" for the purchase.[18]

South Carolina's tightly knit, intermarried elite provided the social basis for uniquely harmonious provincial politics after 1730. Particularly in the small-scale environs of Charlestown, where one in three white residents resided officially by 1775, planters and merchants knew one another by sight. A loyalist returning to the state in 1784 was identified and challenged immediately by a patriot acquaintance at the wharf. He spent the next day walking "most all over the Town," and found that "some of my Acquaintance did take me by the hand & others would cast a sharp Eye on me."[19] Elites recognized one another personally in eighteenth-century Charlestown. Refined dress attested to their desire to emulate British fashions rather than to affirm to polite strangers that they belonged to the same social class. A planter accustomed to wearing the simple "Country Garb" of "Frock and Trousers" in the comparatively crude plantation countryside might opt for a more fashionable cape, wig, and sword before leaving his well-appointed town house.[20] Clothing was a subordinate, and sometimes misleading, status marker in this small-scale society composed of well-known personalities.

Seasonal mobility between country and town contributed to the informality of elite culture in other ways as well. Urban residences housed large extended families in the summer and fall malaria seasons, just as plantations became winter gathering places. Henry Laurens's Charlestown house was so "crouded with relations from the Country" one July, "that I had even two Beds set up in my dining room & another in a room always before reserv'd to myself." When cold weather eliminated the swarms of disease-bearing mosquitoes, elites migrated to the plantations, impoverishing social life in town and making it "as unfashionable to be" in Charlestown "at this Season, as in London in Summer."[21] Although this cycle of social visits between town and country mimicked the seasonal travel of wealthy English families, such mobility in the lowcountry was a direct response to the threat of malaria infection near plantation swamplands and complemented the role of Charlestown as the transatlantic marketplace for plantation produce. A visitor from New England was surprised that at a meeting of the Friday-Night Club, which he described as "consisting of the more elder substantial gentlemen," talk turned consistently toward "negroes, and the price of indigo and rice" rather than more refined topics of conversation. In the colonial lowcountry, the prosaic concerns of plantation production intervened in the enjoyment of refined lives and helped shape a distinctively casual colonial culture.[22]

When Thomas Pinckney traveled to Virginia in 1777, he informed his sister of the "abominable Custom which prevails every where I have been to the Northward of Charles Town . . . I mean that of the whole Company rising from Table immediately upon the Cloths being withdrawn after Meals, and the Ladies retiring to their Apartments; a Custom which spoils good Company, prevents that intercourse of the Sexes which serve to polish and improve both."[23] On the streets of New York, where the loyalist passengers of the *Providence* were detained en route to England in 1779, Louisa Wells confessed to feelings of social discomfort in part because her "dress was so different from the other Ladies." An indefinable sense of feeling and appearing out of place, which she attributed to "perhaps spleen, vapours, pride, &c.," soured Wells on "everything on the Continent of America to the Northward of Charlestown."[24] As South Carolina travelers ventured into the larger Anglo-Atlantic world, they rendered experiences of distinctiveness into a sense of cultural geography that set their society apart from English places to the north and across the ocean. South Carolinians relished the informality that governed elite social interaction and only realized that this relaxed sensibility marked them as unique when they perceived a heightened rigidity elsewhere.

Aside from supporting a family in England solely on the revenue from Lower South estates, lowcountry elites faced no more daunting financial challenge than educating their children abroad. At home, spending on clothing, furniture, coaches, books, and other signature possessions that proclaimed elite status could be halted and resumed to complement fluctuating plantation income. Carolinians' perception of themselves as a convivial, casual elite was perhaps predicated on the material shabbiness that such intermittent spending on items of display must have entailed. But parents often placed their young children in English boarding schools with the expectation that they would remain away from home until taking a degree from Oxford or Cambridge or being called before the Bar after serving at one of the

Inns of Court. John Fenwicke's debts mounted during the 1720s, despite steady remittances in rice and deerskins, largely due to the charges incurred by the education of his two sons in England.[25] Charles Cotesworth Pinckney's 1778 will referred to the debts of his father's estate which "have since increased on account of the Expence of the Education of my brother and myself" begun in England twenty years before. The "badness of many of the crops" since Pinckney's youth exacerbated the estate's financial troubles.[26] Other wills commonly provided that surviving children be provided with "the most liberal Education that can possibly be got."[27]

From 1760 until the close of the colonial period, South Carolina sent more of its young men to England to receive legal training than did all of the other southern colonies combined. In 1727, John Fenwicke favored a legal education for his son so that he might better defend his property rights in South Carolina when he came of age. Gabriel Manigault deeded his son close to twenty-five hundred acres of land after he returned from England a lawyer "in order to qualify & enable the said Peter Manigault to take his Seat in the Commons House of Assembly."[28] By paying for his legal training and then giving him land, the elder Manigault paved the way for his son, who later served as Speaker of the House, to become a prominent political leader in the colony. By the 1770s, lowcountry attorneys could commonly earn £2,000 to £3,000 sterling per year as executors of wills and plantation agents.[29] No other form of education offered so many opportunities to seek cultural improvement in the metropolis while also holding out the promise that money spent on learning would be, like capital invested in slaves, likely to offer handsome returns in the course of time.

Despite the costs, planters proved especially willing to invest in the refinement of their sons, and after 1760 South Carolinians outnumbered the children of other colonial elites at the English universities.[30] English educations intervened at a critical point in the constitution of lowcountry boys' identities. As one South Carolina tutor argued, "what we learn in our younger years sinks in to the memory, adheres to us till old age, and has a prevailing influence over all our conduct." Elite parents feared that growing up in the lowcountry made young sons ungovernable in ways that threatened to deform their adult characters with a diminished capacity to master themselves.[31] Venturing into the unrefined environments of the slave quarters and other savage places beyond the walls of plantation gardens exposed them to violence and wildness at an impressionable age. Such experiences might produce men unprepared to wield power over dependents and manage volatile economic enterprises with care and restraint. English educations, and the learning that took place in social interactions beyond the classroom, promised to chart a course for the development of genteel habits and proclivities suitable to masters, political leaders, and refined elites.

Forced by war to place their son in a Parisian academy, rather than an English school, Robert and Mary Cochran approved of a course of instruction in French, Latin, music, fencing, dancing, and drawing for their son. Such studies promised to make Charles Cochran "the most compleat young Gentleman that was ever born in Carolina—happy happy Mother, should I be, if you merit such a distinguish'd charactor."[32] Sarah Gibbes thought it "impossible to get a finish'd" education in South Carolina. She and other lowcountry elites desired for their children the comprehensive "improvement" that only an extended stay in Europe might provide. If "any thing tempts me to Cross the Atlantic Ocean," wrote Henry Laurens in 1762, "it will be to put the Boy to School in England."[33]

As an ornament of gentility, obtaining an English education for one's children served to distance them from a crude agricultural and commercial existence. Planters, however, could never stop tallying the costs of pursuing refinement on these terms. Those educating children abroad found it difficult to put to rest utilitarian concerns that the expense and effects of education might imperil the reproduction of a prosperous planter class. They wondered if classical studies unfitted a succeeding generation for the tasks of plantership and feared that children would fall away from the industrious sensibilities that could maintain painstakingly cultivated lowcountry fortunes. Schooled themselves in the vulnerability of plantation estates, they questioned whether expensive educations were sound investments in future prospects or, rather, ranked as enervating luxuries that dissipated family resources rather than shoring them up.

When deciding if his son William should serve a mercantile apprenticeship abroad, John Drayton wrote from South Carolina to make the case for a college education. In two years of studies, he proposed, he "may Improve, and that awkwardness wair off, and a Genteel behavior and carage in its Stead . . . if Billy can be Accomplished without going to the College, he need not go" as long as "he attains an easy Air, carage & Good behavior in Company." The experience of the older Charles Drayton, studying medicine halfheartedly in London after nearly eighteen years of English schooling, demonstrated the risks of deferring a return to Carolina for the sake of polishing a public persona. Convinced that Charles "will never make by his Profession the money I have spent on him," Drayton saw his son consuming like an English gentleman without due regard for the work that generated his liberal allowance. "Charles little knows that many hot Summers day I have been out in the field broiling my Head, while he is Spending with ease & pleasure what I so hard fatigued for." "I am his slave," Drayton brooded, "making money for him to spend at his ease, & suffering in a hot firey furnace to give him pleasure." At twenty-seven years of age, he was to be cut off from further support in hopes that he would come home to relearn the lessons that every planter knew about the precarious wealth generated by lowcountry estates. He "never knew the trouble of getting money," concluded Drayton, but he "is of full age & must bear the heat & Burden of the day." Drayton's younger son Thomas displayed the opposite tendency. He "absolutely" refused to study French, "alleging that it can be of no Service to him as a planter." The mixed results of educating three sons abroad exposed the ambivalent pursuit of an ideal state of attainment that Drayton described as becoming a "learned and sensible planter." Too little education, as well as too much, could create "a foolish planter or a foolish man."[34]

Henry Laurens wrote that a young Carolinian in his charge was "improving in his Person and his Book" under the supervision of an English schoolmaster, where he was to remain for several months before entering a university or preparing to "fix himself to the Business and Study of a Profession." He "is as much in earnest and as anxious to acquire Knowledge," Laurens wrote from Westminster, "as you Planters are in preparing your Rice Fields to secure large Crops." Although his own sons, John, Henry, and James stood to benefit from living in Britain, Laurens judged that "Not one in ten" English schools was "good for any Thing." The "vast Expense of Money" spent to educate children abroad "to learn ABC imperfectly enough" seemed to him to be a wasteful alternative to building good schools in Carolina. More disturbingly, he feared the "Loss of Morals and Constitution" that might attend growing up in the metropolis. Schools in England emphasized classical literature and languages to such an extent, he complained, that "hundreds of Men have their Mouths fill'd with jabbering Latin, while their Bellies are empty, whereas, if they had been taught to write good hands, and make perfect in Figures, they might every day meet with Employment which would give them Bread, and put them in a way to Affluence." While "my Child is wasting away his time to no purpose" at one school, he made urgent requests that "all the Produce of my Plantations which can possibly be spared, may be remitted to me" to pay the "very high Price" he was charged.[35] George Austin displayed the same impatience for the classical orientation of English secondary education when he planned to place his son "some where more to his advantage than to pore over Latin & Greek Authors of little utility to a young Man intended for Merchantile business."[36]

"Nothing has excited my wonder since I came to England," wrote Louisa Wells, "than the labour, toil, and expense which is bestowed on the plainest Education." Wells expressed relief at leaving the "dominion of Congress" as she and her loyalist compatriots aboard the *Providence* sailed out of Charlestown harbor in 1779. Wartime immigration presented an opportunity to fulfill a "wish, which I had, for so many years indulged, namely of coming to England," an act that renounced the role of colonist for that of English woman in no uncertain terms. Yet making good on long-standing cultural aspirations through migration did not force a rejection of character-constituting colonial practices that had shaped her own identity and distinguished South Carolina elites as capable "people of sense." Although Wells "could have kissed the gravel on the salt Beach" when she "first set my foot on British ground," she remained "thankful I was born and bred on the

Western shore of the Atlantic. I should have died under the horrors of a Boarding School."[37]

Expensive English educations promised to reconstitute the characters of rising generations of South Carolina planters and merchants. The lessons elite sons learned during their years abroad, however, carried costs that compounded the drain on shifting financial resources necessary to expose them to English culture. Manners polished in refined metropolitan society inculcated expectations for the self-conscious display of wealth that volatile plantation finances could rarely support with consistency. A pedagogy that urged students to shun the prosaic concerns of material gain in favor of erudition had the potential to unfit them for the mundane tasks, from balancing ledgers to brutalizing enslaved workers, that secured and advanced inherited fortunes. Yet even as planters critiqued English education for its impracticality, they appreciated English schooling as a way of insulating their children's developing characters from the obsessive regard for work and accumulation that dominated lowcountry society. Parents' utilitarian concerns were mocked in the *South-Carolina Gazette* by an anonymous author who proposed satirically that students could be fitted for a planter's life after instruction from a "Horn-book," or simple alphabet reader, because they could then distinguish the lettering on cattle brands and properly mark their rice barrels.[38] Only when lowcountry parents were determined to "procure the means of Knowledge for their Children" and were "half as careful to leave" their children "good examples as they are to bestow a large Inheritance," argued Mrs. Richard Capers from her Laurel Hill plantation, would a truly refined and moral society emerge in South Carolina.[39]

As South Carolinians abroad sought for their children the ingrained habits of gentility as a marker of English refinement, they also recoiled from a pedagogy designed to inculcate genteel behaviors at the expense of specialized knowledge and capabilities. This ambivalence launched a critique of metropolitan education animated by the unique demands of work in South Carolina's plantation economy. Such work called for a character constituted by a blend of virtue and expertise that English schooling seemed more likely to deform than develop. But far from demonstrating the precocious viability of colonial culture that stood as an alternative to metropolitan corruption, colonists avidly sought English educations as they deprecated them and framed their grievances within the terms of an ongoing English debate over the relationship between education and character. Joseph Priestly and other eighteenth-century reformers called for an end to rote learning, the abandonment of a narrowly classical curriculum, and favored the inclusion of subjects modern, scientific, commercial, and moral.[40] Carolinians' anxieties for their children's characters and prospects reflected the concerns of this dissenting tradition and adopted its language of critique. To speak ill of tutors, boarding schools, and university colleges in such terms was itself an English cultural activity, one that brought even the most disenchanted colonist into more intense engagement with metropolitan culture.

Loyalist émigrés, who had left friends and family and abandoned plantations in the Lower South to affirm their allegiance to crown and country, seemed prepared to relinquish provincial identities with the least compunction or ambiguity. During and after the Revolutionary War, the South Carolina Provincial Congress and the newly formed state Assembly passed a series of acts that forced absentees to declare their loyalties or face disenfranchisement and permanent banishment. Warfare exacerbated the typical difficulties in forwarding remittances to plantation owners abroad, providing financial incentives for all absentees, regardless of their political sensibilities, to return to South Carolina.[41] The chaotic state of much of the countryside during the war, compounded by a British invasion in 1780, also left absentee estates unsupervised, mismanaged, and especially vulnerable to unscrupulous overseers and predatory neighbors.[42] A 1777 act taxed absentee estates at twice the rate of resident holdings as a prelude to confiscating them outright. Once word of the law reached London, one absentee remarked: "In a short time I shall be almost the only Carolinian in London (except those who are banished) for the greatest part of them are going back as fast as they can."[43] Louisa Ojier reflected the initial enthusiasm of many loyalist refugees when she declared herself "much pleased with what I have seen of England and have no desire to return to Carolina."[44] It was said of another loyalist, so satisfied with his choice to remain in England that he nicknamed his newborn son "John Bull," that "it will be as much Impossible to purswade him to Carolina as to Fly."[45] For others who lost slaves and land and found themselves living among strangers on drastically reduced incomes, the American victory offered an opportunity to rebuild their fortunes, once again, as South Carolinians.[46]

Particularly for loyalists and other absentees who intended to make England a permanent home, the transition from colonial outsider to metropolitan insider meant overcoming the disorientation of inhabiting what seemed a foreign landscape. In letters to America, they drew contrasts between the Lower South and England that revealed how life in the lowcountry had altered their most basic expectations for topography, climate, and agricultural practices. Joseph Manigault, his body seasoned to the diseases of the coastal Lower South and accustomed to its temperatures, remarked that "when every body was complaining of the Heat of the weather, I found it rather cool than otherwise." So "great a Difference there is betwe[e]n our Climate and this," however, that he was left unprepared for "a Winter so severe as this had been." Another absentee confirmed that England was "a most agreeable summer Country."[47] Louisa Wells, by contrast, "laughed at the cold weather of this Country" and insisted that her family's carriage windows be kept down, during their initial trip to London, so that she might take in the sight of ploughed wheat fields, so rare in "our swampy county." "If the Almanack had not told me it was November," she recalled, "I should have declared it to be April or May" although other post chaises the party encountered on the road had their glasses up "and the people in them muffled as if the whole Island of Great Britain was covered with frost and snow." Carolinian bodies, seasoned by a lifetime's exposure to a subtropical climate, marked their bearers as modified English people, by turns hardier and more fragile than those around them who inhabited the same climate but experienced it differently.[48]

Some comparisons reflected the long-held conviction that British agricultural landscapes were models of refinement and careful husbandry. As one émigré said of the Irish scenery through which she traveled en route to England, "the land is all cultivated and looks like a Beautiful Garden." Elias Ball Jr., another wartime absentee, reported dairy cows that yielded twelve gallons of milk each day, some of which were "larger than our Working oxen." He remarked on pastures in which grasses of a "verdue & softness far surpassing any possible Imagination" grew to become fantastically lush. Ball's aspirations as a producer were much curtailed when compared to the standard of his vast Wambaw plantation. Just as planters aspired to emulate improved English farmsteads in their plantation gardens, he looked forward to inhabiting the genuine article and planned to rent "a House with garden & orchard & a little Grass Land to keep a Couple of cows."[49] Such a transition from the sprawling acres of a swamp plantation to a temporary retreat at a tidy English farm fulfilled a cultural aspiration but also represented a diminution of mastery and the contraction of the customary scale at which planters engaged in production.

The economic geography of the coastal Lower South—its combination of factor endowments that rendered land cheap and labor dear, its swampy topography well-suited for rice agriculture, and rising demand for its staple commodities, rice and indigo, in the Atlantic economy—encouraged sharp departures from English farming ideals. Metropolitan critics railed against stump-strewn fields, near-feral cattle that roamed wild, unfenced pastures, and planters' indifference to manuring, seeding, plowing, field rotation, and other hallmarks of improved farming practice.[50] The unkempt appearance of Carolina plantations to English eyes was made truly outlandish, a nightmarish reflection of a well-tended English farmstead, by its labor force of enslaved Africans who endured unrelenting toil in subtropical heat. Planters seem to have accepted the aesthetic standards that demeaned plantation landscapes in comparison to a model English countryside, yet they rejected the moral reproaches and calls for reform that came with such metropolitan judgments. As agricultural experts who adopted increasingly productive and sophisticated methods for making lowcountry land worked by African slaves pay, even those who had turned their backs on South Carolina and the new United States critiqued English agricultural spaces as cultural plaintiffs seeking redress.

When Elias Ball Jr. visited London's Hyde Park, a model of sculpted and refined space located in the heart of the metropolis, he judged it according to a planter's magnified sense of what constituted impressive dimensions for an altered, riverine landscape. The park's famed "Serpentine River . . . is nothing more than a Reservoir of Water Stopd with a Bank betwean two hills nothing like as large as your[s]," he wrote to his cousin, who presided over Comingtee plantation's 225 acres of rice fields, irrigated by a huge freshwater reserve.[51] Another Carolinian in Liverpool observed that, with the exception of the Thames, only the Mersey "deserves to be called a River," while "the river Avon . . . appears but a rivulet when compared to our Rivers." Louisa Wells, although impressed by a view of the Thames, crossed the "muddy stream of Medway" and was "surprised at the foulness of this famed River."[52]

England's storied waterways seem to have grown in the imaginations of Carolina travelers before their arrival. They looked askance at modest streams where they had expected majestic rivers. Experienced observers of the lowcountry's agricultural landscapes had long gauged productive planting lands by the rivers they adjoined. Plantation neighborhoods clustered and extended along rivers, which formed the region's most important commercial thoroughfares and encouraged constant water communication between Charlestown and its expansive plantation hinterland. By mid-century, planters sought out highly productive rice lands along massive, recently settled tidal rivers and, in the process, raised the standard for what constituted an admirable hydrographic landscape. The studied gaze of Carolinians abroad, attuned to discerning and evaluating riverine terrains, superimposed images of lowcountry topography onto the English rural scenery through which they passed. They had perhaps expected England's cultural preeminence to be echoed in the grandeur of its natural and agricultural resources, but found instead, in a direct comparison of colonial and metropolitan rivers, a surprising point of South Carolina's superiority.[53] Although Ball acknowledged that the "Cultivated parts" of the Devonshire countryside were "very Buty Full," he surprised himself and his correspondent by concluding that it contained "Large tracks of

Barren Lands in it." He advised his cousin "never to part with one inch of your Land if possible Eaven the most Barren spot is Fertile Compared to vast tracks in this Kingdom."[54]

Such dissonance between idealized expectations of England and the disappointment registered by planters abroad bore witness to the conflicting cultural stances that absentees assumed in their actual encounters with the metropolis. Loyalist absentees came to England as especially willing supplicants, eager to embrace a society they had been bred to admire. At the same time, their experiences as planters influenced the way they viewed and evaluated their surroundings. The adaptive criteria by which they determined the productive potential of lowcountry land, manipulated wetlands for the production of rice, and brought heterogeneous terrains together to form viable plantations became the hallmarks of an expertise at the core of their self-conceptions as producers. When scrutinized through the cultivated eyes of experienced planters, negative appraisals of vaunted English spaces brought two parallel modes of gauging identity into tension. This collision of conflicting standards inspired feelings of disorientation powerful enough to reveal the terms by which lowcountry planters might be a distinctive people who inhabited a place distinguished by achievement rather than defined by inferiority.

"[W]e never knew our own happiness in Carolina," wrote Ball, who found himself socially isolated and short of money while he remained in England during and after the Revolutionary War. Once a prominent planter, by the autumn of 1784 his shaky finances warranted a move "into sum Interior part of the Country to search for Cheap Living." Departing London meant leaving the thin ranks of the Carolina expatriate community where Ball might still depend on social connections forged in the colonies. Without "American Friends," he observed, "it is very difficult to Form any society in this Country."[55] During a trip through Devonshire he asked after "People of our Name & was told their was Several familys in good Sircumstanceis," but the decades of disconnection that separated the American and English branches of the Ball family limited any practical desire to impose on such tenuous relations or even to meet distant kinsmen out of genealogical curiosity.[56]

"I should like to have Cum to this Country Exceadingly on a party of pleasure but people who has bin usd to live in our Independant Manner in Carolina Can Never like to live hear," he concluded after two months abroad. Unable to describe fully the nature of "a Certain Independence & Fredom in Carolina" that he found wanting in England, Ball speculated that the sharp constraints on economic opportunity was "the Reason why you Find the Scotch Irish & Inglish men are so Exceading loth to Leave Carolina." It was possible to live comfortably in England, but only if one "can Retrench his desirs of ganeing wealth & retrench his way of Liveing into a small Compas."[57] This sense of confinement contained a social as well as an economic dimension. As he imagined the extended Ball family busily engaged in the rice harvest on their several plantations, he wished he could "Jump a mong you . . . & then leep Back a gain" and related dreams in which "I was in your Neighbourhood." A desire for social connection, difficult to recreate in England, gave rise to conscious and subconscious evocations of lost Carolina community for the banished loyalist.[58]

When they claimed allegiance to country, South Carolina elites struggled to force identities that oscillated between local experiences and English ideals into a stable category. At home and abroad, colonists attempted to reconcile affiliations with a colonial society in which their characters had been constituted with loyalties to the metropolitan society that guided their most profound cultural aspirations. Even when pushed to choose between conflicting identities, particularly during the Revolutionary era, they revealed a capacity to evade unequivocal patriotic stances in favor of composite self-perceptions.

Writing from his Crowfield plantation in 1732, "R.F." reflected on the state of cultural attainment in early eighteenth-century South Carolina in the *South-Carolina Gazette*. He urged his fellow planters to pursue more consciously lives of reason, religion, and virtue made possible by "the happy Influence of his *Majesty*'s auspicious Reign" as well as a material foundation of a "very prosperous and agreeable Situation" in Carolina. At question was the challenge of promoting individual "Attainment" and the "right *forming* of a Man" so that the "Capacities of our Youth" might elevate the moral stature of the colony as a whole.

Such a project sought to "excite us to a laudable Emulation" of models for ethical rectitude and dispassionate truth-seeking. "These Considerations, founded in a ardent Love of my Country (for I acknowledge myself a *Native* of *Carolina*)," were aimed at "seeing my Country rise, as much superiour in the *Abilities*, and *Merits* of *her Sons*, to those of her *Fellow-Subjects*, in the *British America*." To embrace lives of learning, he argued, was far more important than "to spend our time in laying Schemes, and forming Contrivances to amass Riches." R.F. affirmed his identity as a South Carolinian by holding out hopes that his country's rising generation would transform it into the most intellectually and morally accomplished province of British America.[59]

When British hostilities with France and Spain during the middle decades of the eighteenth century became transatlantic imperial conflicts, southeastern elites celebrated an amalgamated patriotism by conceiving of the Lower South as "a frontier to all the English Settlements." They shored up English identities in opposition to the despised characteristics of the enemy and understood South Carolina and Georgia to be vital strategic bulwarks that secured English society in North America.[60]

In 1779, historian Alexander Hewit played to the post-revolutionary sentiments of his American readers by asserting that such complex identities and divided loyalties had lost their cogency from the moment of colonization. The "first generation of emigrants retained some affection for Britain during their lives," he argued, "and gloried in calling her their home and their mother country; but this natural impression wears away from the second, and is entirely obliterated in the third."[61] Hewit underestimated the capacity for South Carolinians to identify with the place of their birth while retaining a broader allegiance to Britain. American patriot and absentee planter Ralph Izard justified military resistance to Britain in 1775 on the grounds that "my Countrymen have been driven to the necessity of defending themselves." When he departed England for France in 1777, however, Izard regretted "having quitted a Country which from my Infancy I have looked upon as my own, & for which I have had the most unbounded affection."[62] Izard's unwillingness to fully renounce a British identity in the midst of a war for independence reveals the steadfastness with which lowcountry planters sustained cultural loyalties to the metropolis. Throughout the colonial period, and even beyond it, lowcountry life bore the marks of increasing Anglicization despite the fact that English-born immigrants made up a progressively smaller proportion of the white population.[63]

Exiled loyalist Louisa Wells recalled the moment of her arrival in Britain in paradoxical terms. She thought of England as "my home: the Country which I had so long and so earnestly wished to see," but it was an imagined home she had never inhabited until she disembarked. When Wells recalled with fondness the view of Charlestown's Bay Street mansions from the harbor, she proclaimed that "there are few travelers who are not attached to their native place and are ever making comparisons with it."[64] Abroad again nearly a quarter century after his student days in London, Peter Manigault confessed to his mother in 1773 that his "whole Thoughts are so wrapped up in my Friends in Carolina that there is no Pleasure, no Satisfaction for me in England, And I am continually making Comparisons, which right or wrong, always end in Favour of my own Country."[65]

When they expressed uneasiness with and separateness from English society, Carolinians abroad targeted specific English practices and environments rather than leveling subversive critiques at English society as a whole. Their own self-conceptions as inhabitants of a British province in America rested on the assumption that their young "country" had the potential to acquire the English cultural characteristics that it lacked as it developed economically, socially, and politically. Sheer physical distance fostered the belief that such a trajectory might describe South Carolina's future. Atlantic exchange enabled colonists to idealize England as a cultural paragon without experiencing English life directly. They consumed English books, news, and goods; they integrated English ministers, government officials, and new settlers into elite society; and they emulated English judicial and legislative procedures. Under the influences of constant infusions such as these, even the most divergent practices could be perceived Jack P. Greene has argued as "well within the parameters—and logical extension—of English behaviors." Amassing "social and cultural capital" in colonial British

America meant tailoring English forms to local circumstances and discarding, simplifying, and modifying "everything from economic practices and social organization to law, and even language" that did not answer to the demands of colonization.[66] South Carolina travelers in England saw firsthand what this long-term process of transatlantic adaptation had concealed: that their pursuit of Englishness in America had shaped their colonial society in distinctive ways and molded their own preferences and perceptions as members of that society.

South Carolinians' idealization of English society rendered unrealistic expectations vulnerable to contradiction in encounters that colored the content and tone of their correspondence home. Disquieting experiences abroad disabused them of the presumption that England was "a Second Eden, especially [in comparison] to Carolina, which . . . would bear more Assimilation, to the Libyan Dessarts."[67] As they engaged in constant comparisons between Carolina and England that often led to new appreciations of lowcountry society, they were hardly less subjective in their revised appraisals. Planters abroad felt out of place. They longed for family and friends and lashed out defensively against the strain of attempting to enter the ranks of elite society in England and making plantation estates pay the substantial costs of living abroad. The trying contexts that complicated these journeys "home" encouraged criticisms of English values and practices and strengthened identifications with South Carolina, which uprooted travelers imbued with virtues they had seldom recognized before leaving. As the wife of a prominent merchant revealed over tea in her London lodgings, "she longed to be in Carolina now as much as she wished to come to England when she was there."[68] During moments of cultural disorientation, unexpected nostalgia for home had the power to temporarily reverse the polarity of the cultural imperative that had long drawn colonial settlers to emulate and revere English society.

South Carolina elites, conscious of their own society's rudeness, adhered to the proposition that contemporary Britain stood at the apex of human civilization, a refined, commercial society to which their own simplified and distorted version stood as patently inferior. Such admissions of inferiority, however, floated on the surface of character-shaping economic and social experiences. Deeper engagements with the material conditions of lowcountry life encouraged defenses of provincial culture and critiques of metropolitan social formalism, excessive consumption, and the confined scope for economic enterprise.

Plantation agriculture composed a material foundation that permeated South Carolina elites' cultural environment. The dining tables laden with African and American foods, the informality that prevailed at elite social gatherings, the domestic spaces and rural landscapes that blended the work of plantation management with family life—these were the forums in which the commonplace identities of lowcountry whites were constituted. This was a society that celebrated English culture, and increasingly invested the earnings from plantation agriculture in emulating English ways, but it was also one that had unwittingly veered away from some of that model society's basic tenets. When South Carolinians forged direct connections with England as travelers abroad, these encounters exposed differences in outlook, behavior, and expectation that made the home country seem a foreign place. Such experiences gauging English life against Carolina expectations revealed areas understood to have particular bearing on the constitution of early modern selves: the ways in which inhabiting places shaped personal character, the connections between eating, bodies, and personality, and the role of formal education and informal social participation in shaping the economic and social roles of children. These material encounters between Carolinians and England reveal a process of collective identity formation on the colonial periphery. As stakeholders in colonial cultures abroad, Lower South elites sought to claim their provincial identity as an adaptive variation on British cultural standards that was justified by the unique demands of Carolina conditions. Transformed by the work required to assemble fortunes on the periphery, planters began to perceive the distance between the values they had acquired and those to which they aspired when encountering metropolitan society firsthand.

The American South and English Print Satire, 1760–1865

MARCUS WOOD

The American South follows the pattern of North America generally as only registering in the British popular graphic consciousness periodically, in bursts. What instigated these bursts was primarily war, or the fantasies generated around war. The great spawning grounds for English visual satire about the American colonies, and then the United States, were the American War of Independence and the American Civil War.[1] Obviously these events are separated by enormous cultural shifts, and as importantly for the perspective of this essay, by vast changes in graphic technology. During the period of the War of Independence, English graphic satire was in its infancy, and the stiff and laborious process of copper plate engraving still vied with single-sheet etching as the preferred medium. Personal caricature hardly existed as a form, and most prints were crudely emblematic.[2] In many ways the War of Independence was an historical force which developed the political etching into the major form it was to become in English print satire from the late 1780s until 1820. Arguably, (the argument being with Francisco Goya), the greatest print satirist of all time, James Gillray, developed his unique stylistic range and cut his satiric teeth on the American Revolution.[3]

Yet, by the time English print satirists were dealing with the buildup to the Civil War in the 1850's the forms of graphic production were utterly changed. The single-sheet etching was dead, and the woodcut and then the lithograph came to dominate illustrated periodical journalism. Single-sheet satires no longer existed as a fashionable form with mass distribution. Also the complicated metaphorical, narrative, and semiotic codes of the period 1790–1820, generally and quite correctly designated the "golden age of English print satire," had devolved into something much closer to what we are now familiar with as the political cartoon. In other words, both technically and in its content, print satire had devolved and degenerated as an art in England by the period of the American Civil War. The most violent and conceptually revolutionary print satire was being produced in France.[4]

Having said that, it might, however, be useful to add that this decay of form and content does not have any huge implications for the representation of the American South. The southern states and the southern people—male, female, adult, juvenile, black, white, European immigrant, imported slave, Native American—did not at any point from 1760 to 1865 have a detailed or clearly developed set of imaginative identities for the English. America in general is treated and narrativised as a social, political, and geographical entity in monolithic terms. The increasingly ungainly metaphorics demanded by the British public for the personification of America reflect a general trend in nineteenth-century English graphic satire. The following analysis defines some of these processes of mass stereotypification, attempts to explain how they work and why they happened, and explores why England imaginatively constructed America the way it did.

The form of this discussion is dictated by two wars, and is consequently a bit of a chronological see-saw. I'll begin by sketching out a general picture of the ways in which America, and the South in particular, had been stereotyped, iconified, and symbolized before, and during, the period of the War of Independence. This work was the primary visual archive to which subsequent representations of the United States returned. Having provided this condensed context as an analytical backdrop, I will then consider the more varied and particularized representations of the South which were generated in England during the period of the Civil War.

I will concentrate the study of the latter period on a single English publication, *Punch*. I have chosen *Punch* because it became, soon after its appearance in 1841, far and away the most widely circulated and influential forum for the production of graphic satire in Great Britain. *Punch* was also the only mass circulation illustrated periodical devoted to graphic satire which spans the entire period.[5] While English illustrated periodical literature was exploding in terms of circulation from 1840 to 1865, visual satire was not a popular, sophisticated, or hard-hitting form, as it had been fifty years before. There was not a big market for political print satire anymore, and that which did appear bore no resemblance to the great works which had flooded England from the Storming of the Bastille to the Peterloo Massacre in 1819. After the mid-1820s the single-sheet etched-print satire died completely. This was the form in which all the great artists of the golden age worked: James Gillray, Thomas Rowlandson, George Cruikshank, and Richard Newton were almost exclusively single sheet draftsmen and etchers.[6] Not only did this form of print satire die, but the entire formal vocabulary, and what one might term "the satiric spirit of the age," died too. The political radicalism, and the sexual and social libertinism of the Regency, was buried and forgotten; suddenly what is now seen as an emergent Victorian bourgeois liberalism came to dominate, and there were new stringent rules governing what could and could not be said in graphic satire. Bodily functions, nudity (with the modest exception of the occasional statuesque female breast), and sexuality were excised from the satiric vocabulary of all periodicals.[7] The British imperial agenda dictated an increasingly normalizing and paternalistic set of assumptions regarding the construction of the National OTHER, whether European, Russian, Chinese, African, South American, or North American. *Punch* is of particular importance as marking a graphic center which defined how the new phenomenon of "middle" Britain wanted to represent itself, its colonies, and its colonial rivals, through dominant modes of nationalism.

What was the graphic inheritance of *Punch* in terms of the representation of the American South? During the second half of the eighteenth century, when print satire really developed as a mature form in England, America was hardly represented at all until the mid-1760s. During the two decades leading up to the War of Independence, English political prints show little awareness of any sort of geographical or political differences within the American colonies. Herbert Atherton's still classic study *Political Prints in the Age of Hogarth* quite correctly finds hardly a

Fig. 1. *The Great Financier or British Economy for the Years 1763, 1764, 1765.* Etching, 1765, BMC 4128. British Museum Department of Prints and Drawings.

reference to America, and only one print where America in presented in the generalized icon of an "Indian."[8] Print satire was driven by a broad-based domestic political radicalism that incorporated the American colonies in the role of victim of an unfair and unrepresentative tax system. American colonials across North and South were seen as extensions of English victimhood, as brothers in oppression. So the first prints tend to personify America in highly vulnerable and sympathetic guise as an obedient and yet abused noble savage or young woman.[9] The first full-fledged assault on the stamp tax imposed on the colonies is a typical example. The anonymous *The Great Financier or British Economy for the Years 1763, 1764, 1765* (fig. 1) shows America, North and South—indeed all the extant English colonies—as a kneeling Indian, holding a large sack marked dollars, and around its neck is a yoke, like an African slave yoke, marked "taxed without representation."[10] America appears as just one small element within a disastrous and imperial economic landscape created by ministerial corruption and Pitt the elder's warmongering. As discontent in the colonies

Fig. 2. *The Able Doctor or America Swallowing the Bitter Draft.* Etching, 1774, BMC 5226. British Museum Department of Prints and Drawings.

mounted, America gained a more central iconic position, and personifications of victimhood extended out from the image of the Indian to that of Columbia as a young woman abused by corrupt British cabinet ministers. Yet again there is no notion of an American North and South. The most renowned development of this theme of abused female innocence was *The Able Doctor, or America Swallowing the Bitter Draft* (fig. 2). Here, rape is metaphorically introduced to attack the Boston Port Bill of 1774. Lord Mansfield pinions the young woman's arms and she is stripped to the waist, while Lord Sandwich kneels at her feet, grips her left ankle to separate her legs, and lifts up her skirt, gazing lasciviously at her face, which is torn back as Lord North force-feeds her tea.[11]

It was in the context of the depiction of extreme violence against a woman that the first print to introduce individual American colonies into English print satire occurred. This was, however, in its initial manifestation, an American print originated by Ben Franklin in 1766 as part of his lobbying campaign against the stamp tax. *Magna Britannia— Her Colonies Reduced* (fig. 3) was sent as a card to English politicians in

Fig. 3. *Magna Britannia-Her Colonies Reduced.* Engraving, 1776, BMC 4183. British Museum Department of Prints and Drawings.

the colonies and the mother country. The print was then reproduced anonymously in England in 1768, testifying to the sympathy with Franklin's stand and the fluid transatlantic exchange of prints at this point. The abused female here is Britannia, not Columbia, and each of her limbs is an American Colony, viciously severed by the effect of taxation. Her dress has been cut off at the navel, her lower torso naked, and her right leg, inscribed Virginia, has been tossed onto the ground at right. This discarded human fragment is in fact the first representation of the South or part of what was to become the South in a visual satire printed in England. Yet its graphic lineage is complicated and ultimately leads back to England via Franklin. The image of the butchered female as a metaphor for the effect of bad colonial policy on Britannia was first fully (and a deal more brutally) worked through in an earlier English print. In *The Conduct of two B*****rs* (fig. 4), the two Lord Pelhams are shown butchering and mutilating the figure of Britannia, her guts drawn out on a winch, her severed arms lying on the ground and inscribed with the colonial tags Gibraltar and

Fig. 4. *The Conduct of two B*****rs.* Engraving, 1745, *BMC* 3069. British Museum Department of Prints and Drawings.

Cape Breton, a key strategic point in the French wars in Canada which had fallen into French possession.[12] Franklin's development of this print in *The Colonies Reduced* lacks the brutal realism of the source, but gains in terms of the stark economy with which the central iconic figure of the ruined female body is isolated.

From the mid-1760s almost all the prints opposed English policy in the colonies and, when it started, the war. These works did not treat the Americans, at least until their alliance with France, as foreigners. Most of the prints did not concern the representation of America directly, but were directed against the unpopular figures associated with the war's management—or rather mismanagement—in England.[13] The prints are firstly anti-state, then anti-military, and finally even attack members of the royal family, ending with the king himself.[14]

Fig. 5. *The Curious Zebra Alive From America*. Engraving, 1788, BMC 5487. British Museum Department of Prints and Drawings.

Generally throughout the war America is homogenized and presented in a number of inclusive symbolic guises: as a hot air balloon, a young woman, an old woman, a young Indian maiden, groups of Indian cannibals, a menagerie of beasts, a slaughtered goose, a dish of sprats, and so on.[15] Collective emblems completely predominate, and prints which do try to present distinct colonies usually do so by a process of reductive collectivization. In some of these Virginia and the two Carolinas get a mention. Yet attempts to isolate the colonies often say more about English ignorance than they do about American political reality. For example *State Cooks, or the Downfall of the Fish Kettle* is a response to the English disaster at Yorktown. The print shows thirteen English colonies, including Virginia, the Carolinas, and Georgia—and also among them the Floridas, Quebec, and Nova Scotia. Wishful thinking no doubt. Other prints represent South and North alike through such labeling of animal forms. So one of the most popular parodic forms, the menagerie advertisement, is used in *The Curious Zebra Alive From America* (fig. 5). The colonies are shown as a desirable curiosity which English Ministers, and the French, try to seize while Washington

Marcus Wood

Fig. 6. The *American Rattlesnake*. James Gillray, etching, 1781. Ashforth Collection.

firmly grasps its tail.[16] Again in metaphoric terms the effect is to show all colonies as a seemlessly united part of a single America, a victim of a variety of European colonial ambitions. There is also of course the possibility that the unusual importation of a black and white-striped African animal could be an early encoded reference to the presence of African slaves within the American colonies—in the design the black stripes hover anonymously between the white stripes, each of which is described with the name of a colony.

British prints did develop something of an indigenous iconography for describing America during the war, and some of these emblems were developed out of American prints and had a special relationship to the South. For example, there are many prints depicting America when at war as a rattlesnake.[17] In August of 1781, with Lord Cornwallis deciding to dig in with his army in Yorktown, the American troops closing in on him, and final British capitulation looking more and more probable, Gillray produced *The American Rattlesnake* (fig. 6), a print which brilliantly took up and developed probably the first and certainly the most pungent print satire produced in the American

Fig. 7. *Join or Die*. Woodcut, *Pennsylvania Gazette*, 1754. Library Company of Philadelphia.

press, *Join or Die* (fig. 7). This superbly economic and justly influential image was conceived and printed very early on, again by Franklin, in the *Pennsylvania Gazette* in 1754 and concerned the urgency of uniting against both the French and Native Americans. It was immediately printed in every leading East Coast paper.[18] The fragmented snake then re-appeared in the mid-1760s in the anti-stamp tax propaganda, and made its way to England. It showed America as a rattlesnake, the white rattle at the end of the mutilated tail clearly visible. Each segment of its mutilated body is given the initial of a colony, and the South is represented by Virginia and North and South Carolina, which constitute the snake's tail sections. During the war the rattlesnake came to have strong associations with the South. In the early stages of the war each colony designed its own flag, and many individual companies of soldiers did the same. South Carolina took up on the specific inheritance of Franklin's print and adopted the rattlesnake, with the slogan, "Don't tread on Me," and it appeared in a square in all the military flags of the colony. When we return to Gillray's serpent, it is not, however, exclusively southern, but showed Franklin's serpent now formidably (and with the exception of its jaws quite naturalistically) reconstituted. Within its coils lie the doomed squares of two British armies, while the empty third space on the left encircled by the snake's tail, the space originally given to the South by Franklin's print, is announced for rent in a placard attached to the snake's tail. "Two British Armies I have thus Burgoyned, and Room for more I've got behind." The implication is that the British did very little in their attempts to invade the deeper southern colonies, and are welcome to have a go again at the Carolinas and Georgia. At the same time as giving the South a special place in the war, this snake in its healthy completeness implicitly represents the three southern colonies as fully united with the North.[19]

Yet in terms of geographical or occasional specifics, very few prints are actually set in the South. Instead, it is unsurprisingly Massachusetts and New England that dominate the prints dealing with specific events and places during the campaigns. There are a few exceptions, however, and some of these are significant in pointing the way for the subsequent representation of the South. The British military and naval setbacks in South Carolina in the early Autumn of 1776 led the opportunistic Mathew Darley to develop his social satire into a political context.[20] Darley made his name with work focusing largely on ridiculing the excesses of contemporary French and English fashion, male and female. The massive coiffures which had become highly fashionable amongst ladies in Paris and London are used as the imagistic base. South Carolina is presented as a young woman sporting a huge headpiece which supports the tents of a military garrison, a series of well-fortified cannon positions, and flags showing an eagle's head, a cap of liberty, a sword, and a leaping lioness or leopardess. Miss Carolina Sullivan is described as "one of the obstinate daughters of America."[21]

It was, in fact, in the context of the reluctance of the colonies, and some southern merchants in particular, to give up their lucrative trading arrangements with the British, that the South began to appear exclusively in several print satires. Merchants in the provincial capital of Virginia, Williamsburg, proved particularly refractory over the matter. In the *London Chronicle* there was an article that provided the narrative

Fig. 8. *The Alternative of Williamsburg.* Phillip Dawe, mezzotint, 1774. Ashforth Collection.

context for Phillip Dawe's mezzotint *The Alternative of Williamsburg* (fig. 8): "They erected at the principal avenue to the town a very high gibbet, upon the one side of which they hung a barrel of tar and on the other side a bag of feathers, and on each of them the following inscription: A CURE FOR THE REFRACTORY. In a very short time the deed bore testimony that there was not one who had not experienced the salutary effect of so healing a medicine."[22] In Dawe's print the gibbet with inscription is dutifully shown, and an armed and threatening mob—including women and children—force the well-dressed merchants to sign the petition, on a barrel marked "Tobacco a present for John Wilkes esquire, Lord Mayor of London." Wilkes, the notorious hell-raiser and popular radical maverick, had been a longstanding supporter of the rights of the colonies. It is difficult to know what the cultural agenda is here. The merchants appear dignified, frightened, and pitiful. The mob violent, mocking, coarse. The tar and feathers are a barbaric symbol of a punishment which mob rule over the stamp tax had already made its own in Boston. (Several prints in England and America showed excisemen undergoing this torture.) Wilkes, especially after he decided to become Lord Mayor, had a less than clear-cut profile in England.[23] The print is finally impossible to "place" politically. The suggestion here might well be that the southern merchant gentleman are being stupidly forced into agreeing to a policy which hurts both colonists and mother country, and that the southern trading aristocracy are dignified friends of England in a way that the northerners are not. Then again, it might be saying that these overdressed and greedy traders are betraying the principles of a rebellion with which many English citizens completely sympathize. Given his satiric track record, it is likely that Phillip Dawe himself was not that clear about what he was trying to say.

And yet it was Dawe, and not Gillray or Rowlandson, who produced probably the most penetrating print satire made in England about the colonies and slavery during the course of the war. This was another fine mezzotint specifically directed at considering the effects of the Non-Importation Agreement on southern life. Southern females appear as the central subject in *A Society of Patriotic Ladies at Edenton North Carolina* (fig. 9). In adopting what was basically a set of trade sanctions against Briton, the Non-Importation societies allowed colonial women, and especially wealthy and fashionable ones, to become both actively and martyrologically involved in the war effort. The London papers carried often-amused reports of how ladies, especially in the North, were prepared to give up all luxuries to help the war effort. They are reported abandoning ribbons and appearing in society in homespun gowns rather than in gorgeous imported textiles. Dawe's title is self-explanatory, *A Society of Patriotic Ladies at Edenton North Carolina*, but there is a lot more to this print than first meets the eye. It has a claim to be the first print satire produced in England to critique southern slave holding. The women on the face of it are represented like any group of English ladies in one of Dawe's more common mezzotints dealing with social satire. The women destroy tea and colonial produce

Fig. 9. *A Society of Patriotic Ladies in Edenton South Carolina*. Phillip Dawe, mezzotint, 1774. Ashforth Collection.

and sign a petition. The wording is highly significant: "We the ladies of Edenton do hereby solemnly engage not to conform to the pernicious custom of tea drinking, or that we the aforesaid ladys will not promote & wear of any manufactures from England until such time as all acts which tend to Enslave this our Native Country shall be repealed." Here in a print set in the South is a very rare yet bitterly ironic mention of slavery. The slavery seems to be the imagined slavery of the colonies to English tyranny, but things are not that simple. While the ladies fill in their petition, the figure of a black female slave, in white headdress, gazes laughingly out of the picture, holding the ink pot and quills with which the white women sign the petition. She has a very different relation to this declaration of independence, and to "this our native country." The print holds the seeds of what is to become a primary thrust of English anti-southern print satire during the Civil War. This stance of amused irony at white American hypocrisy over its intended ideals of liberty, while supporting a slave economy in the South, is almost obsessively, and for the most part much more crudely, developed in the pages of *Punch*.

This is the point at which I shift from the explosion of prints generated by the War of Independence to the prints generated in England around the time of the American Civil War. Two historical facts tend to underpin most of this material. The first is that England lost the War of Independence and never, in graphic terms anyway, forgave the ex-colonies for the defeat. The second is that just as the War of Independence ended, abolition as an international propaganda movement took off. England abolished the slave trade in 1807, and officially at least colonial slavery in 1833. If you combine these facts with the continuation of a slave-based plantation economy in the American South, you have the raw materials and the recipe for the majority of English print satires directed against the United States from 1840 to 1865.

Punch, or the London Charivari, as it was titled, appeared in Britain in 1841 and rapidly became the flagship journal of the new order. The two graphic stalwarts of the journal during the period 1841–1865 were John Leech and John Tenniel, who epitomized the slick draftsmanship and satirically anodyne stance of the journal. *Punch*'s subtitle might have claimed the inheritance of the great French satiric journal *Le Charivari*, but it existed in a different political and theoretical climate and space.[24] Complacency, assumed national superiority, and narrative crudity are the qualities which dominate the political prints. And they saturate the presentation of the American South as thoroughly as any other subject.[25]

When we come to the slow resurgence of interest in America as a subject for print satire, in England, first in the 1840s and more concentratedly in the 1850s, many of the stereotypes from the American War remain in place. America is still represented sometimes as an Indian, and sometimes as Columbia, who can be a young or old woman. Yet a monolithic division in the representation of North and South has evolved, the North is presented as a Yankee, with pretensions to sophistication and obsessed with the dollar, and the South as a violent planter figure obsessed with slavery, tobacco, and alcohol. Overall the major new development is the introduction of the figure of the black slave. The slave appears as an increasingly difficult, contradictory, and open metaphoric site as the war progresses and tends to occupy a problematic middle ground between North and South. So, I will organize this discussion of *Punch's* representation of America and the South thematically, considering the shifts which occur in extant stereotypes and the introduction of new figures and tropes.

The figure of the Native American still permeates the prints, but has become more complicated as a result of the familiarization of a European readership with Indians via travel literature and the effect of touring groups of Native Americans, in circuses and freak shows. The most celebrated Indian troop to visit England were the Ojjobeway, who feature in a number of prints and articles, including a series of unpleasant mock advertisements where Indian males are presented advertising in ludicrous terms for English wives.[26] Yet the old figure of the Indian in feather skirt and headdress as representative of all America still flourishes. Now, however, these symbolic amalgamations of the whole of America invariably incorporate the South purely in terms of symbolic references to slavery. So for example very near the beginning of its career *Punch* remains quite close to the earlier prints in showing in *Fair Rosamond or the Ashuburton Treaty* (fig. 10) an emblematic figure of the stout and middle-aged Britannia handed a poisoned chalice marked "Treaty" by a fierce female Indian who carries a dagger in the other hand. Puffing on a cigar, she bears a skirt marked with the stars and stripes. A new addition, however, is the slave driver's scourge, and around her waist she wears a large metal belt marked in capital letters, "SLAVERY." This is typical of several prints showing emblematic Indians where the presence of the South is given simply in terms of violent symbols of the slave power, most commonly a knotted scourge. This print has a particular concern with the diplomatic construction of slavery between England and the United States. The Webster Ashburton treaty of August 9, 1842, was organized to settle various diplomatic gray spots, including a push for the final suppression of the

Fig. 10. *Fair Rosamond or the Ashuburton Treaty.* Wood engraving, *Punch* 3 (1842), 203. Sussex University Library.

slave trade. While America was officially bound to support abolition of the trade, the presence of the slave colonies was seen by English commentators to render the treaty absurd.[27] Consequently, the print shows the former Noble Savage as a degenerate extortionist. The only earlier prints to present the Indian in extreme guises of savagery related to English use of Native American forces against the colonists in the War of Independence. These anti-English prints produced in England to support the colonists had presented Indians as cannibals or murderers.

This theme of American degeneration into utter savagery as manifested in the figure of the Native American was far more fully exploited at various points during the Civil War. The most flamboyant example is the representation of America reneging on its debts to England during the Charleston harbor blockade in the print *RETROGRESSION (A VERY SAD PICTURE) War-Dance of the I.O.U. Indian* (fig. 11). In the accompanying

Fig. 11. *RETROGRESSION (A VERY SAD PICTURE) War-Dance of the I.O.U Indian.* Wood engraving, *Punch* 42 (1862), 45. Sussex University Library.

commentary to the print I.O.U. Indian is depicted as an anthropological curiosity: "Of his religion not much seems to be known, except that he swears a good deal, never laughs and refers to something which he calls Dollar as the Great First Cause of all his actions. He has a strange hatred for the black man who he ill treats either morally or physically as much as he can . . . we find that he has lost nearly all traces of his English descent, and has acquired the propensities but not the savage virtues of the Indian aborigines." This is England having its cake and eating it, too: the Americans are not just behaving like savages, they are worse than savages.

Another of the devices of eighteenth-century satire that translated directly into the nineteenth-century depiction of America was the angry or discontented child.[28] Given the almost obsessive patriarchal and matriarchal constructions of England as John Bull and Britannia respectively, America appears repeatedly as one of the gallery of national children which the British symbolic parental powers must bring to heel. Only a few pro-British prints during the War of Independence had used this device, most notably *Poor Old England Endeavouring to reclaim his wicked Children*, where the colonies are a group of angry urchins, each hooked through the nose. Yet this theme is dominant in subsequent set piece prints concerning diplomatic relations between England and America in *Punch*. Consequently, America as an infant Yankee-Noodle in *What? You Young Yankee Noodle, Strike Your Own Father?* is a pugilistic little boy squaring up to a massively condescending John Bull. However, the guise, costume, and accouterments of the figure are again specifically representative of southern slave-holding. The figure wears a broad-brimmed planter hat and white trousers, and the leaded thongs of the ubiquitous slave driver's scourge hang from his pocket.[29]

The joke is repeated tediously again and again, but increasingly in terms which set the North and South against each other as warring urchins in the playground who must be protected by Father Bull and Mother Britannia. *JOHN BULL'S NEUTRALITY* is typical. John Bull stands in his shop door, while two shame-faced urchins, the North and South, furtively drop the stones they are carrying. Bull announces sternly "Look here boys, I don't care twopence for your noise, but if you throw stones at my window, I must *thrash you both*." The announcement here in the late 1850s would seem to be supporting English intervention if Anglo-American trade interests are seriously threatened.[30]

Despite the myth that England was in sympathy with the South, partly as an heroic manifestation of pastorally upheld chivalric fiction, and more meaningfully because it supplied the raw materials for a large part of the massive British textile industry, *Punch* treats the South predominantly with hostility, and secondarily with neutrality, as the equal of two evils. Many big prints treat the South as the place which focuses all that is abhorrent about the United States. Increasingly the South is invariably seen as the home of "slavery, lynch law, the annexation of Texas and tobacco chewing." A spectacular whole page print satire, with the bludgeoningly ironic title *THE LAND OF LIBERTY, recommended to the consideration of Brother Jonathan* (fig. 12) essentializes the common targets. It shows a southern planter in white trousers and

Fig. 12. *THE LAND OF LIBERTY, recommended to the consideration of Brother Jonathan.* Wood engraving, *Punch* 13 (1852), 215. Sussex University Library.

a broad brimmed white hat, with a six shooter stuck in his belt and a scourge hanging from his pocket. He lounges in a rocking chair with a rum punch, and his boot on the head of a toppled bust of Washington. He blows out a vast cloud of tobacco from his cheroot, which expands into a series of narrative vignettes representing scenes from southern life and recent history. At the top of the print the devil watches over a representation of the brutal annexation of Texas. There is also an extended scene of slaves landed from a ship and driven to sale by a planter, intimating the continuation of an illegal slave trade into the southern states. Above this is a scene inscribed "lynch law" showing a stripped black slave led by a mob to a noose on a tree. Above this two southern gentleman fight the inevitable duel.

Almost all of these elements have been grafted wholesale from American abolition propaganda produced in the Northern cities. They

Fig. 13. *Our Peculiar Domestic Institutions.* Wood engraving, *The Anti-Slavery Almanac,* 1840. American Antiquarian Society.

can be found in the whole-page print satire *Our Peculiar Domestic Institutions* (fig. 13), which the New York Anti-Slavery almanac of 1840 carried. The charges which the North brings against the South have become blurred in the eyes of an English readership, and now are seen to contaminate the whole of the United States.

Through the mid-1840s the South, personified as the brute planter, became a more and more dominant icon used to thump home the theme of American hypocrisy over the slave issue. The crudity of these prints can hardly be exaggerated. *Liberty Equality and Fraternity Dedicated to the Smartest Nation in all Creation* gives a tripartite representation of the United States, in which the figure of Liberty, with a black face but holding a white mask in front of it, holds the planter's scourge aloft and is about to beat a cowering black boy stripped to the waist and tied to a whipping post. A planter with gun and rum punch looks on and pronounces "O ain't we a deal better than other people! I guess We're a most splendid example to them thunderin' old Monarchies!"[31]

Although North and South are ruthlessly categorized in terms of antagonistic essentials, *Punch* dealt more leniently with the North and increasingly presented the South as irrational, cruel, and belligerent.

Fig. 14. *THE AMERICAN TWINS, OR NORTH AND SOUTH.* Wood engraving, *Punch* 31 (1856), 125. Sussex University Library.

For example, *THE AMERICAN TWINS, OR NORTH AND SOUTH* (fig. 14) shows North and South as youthful embattled males. Joined like Siamese twins at the stomach by a large label inscribed Union, two slender, muscular young men fight. The South however is shown as the more brutal and irrational aggressor. Decked out with a large hunting knife in one hand and a revolver in the other, and with a large scourge stuck in his belt, the South attempts to murder the North. The North stands unarmed, gripping the South firmly, but not murderously, by the throat, staring determinedly in the eyes of his outraged adversary. The face of the South is shown darkened. Whether this is anger, the effect of strangulation, or the result of miscegenation is not clear. By 1862 these stock characters of North and South remain virtually unchanged, although in *THE SENSATION STRUGGLE IN AMERICA* they are more evenly matched aggressors, locked in a deadly knife fight and

Fig. 15. KING COTTON BOUND; Or, The Modern Prometheus. Wood engraving, Punch 41 (1861), 176. Sussex University Library.

suspended over a black chasm labeled "Bankruptcy," probably in objective terms the main concern of *Punch's* readers. The left hand of the North has a precarious grip on a shattering tree branch inscribed "Union."[32] The final print to deal with the war in *Punch* sticks to these simple emblems of the North and South as embattled males. THE RE-UNITED STATES shows two war-battered figures, the North with a slash on its nose, the South with a plaster on its nose and its arm in a sling, shaking hands and sharing a glass of punch.[33]

Overall, virtually none of these crude couplings of personalized North and South present the South as manifesting any dignity or admirable qualities. When there are positive constructions of the South, they iconographically isolate the South and relate to the South's trade relations with Britain. The most complicated example is *KING COTTON BOUND; Or, The Modern Prometheus* (fig. 15). Referring to the effect of the North's blockade of Southern ports, this image shows the cotton interest as a Promethean Monarch made of a patchwork of textiles and wearing a crown. He is stapled to a huge block, with an iron band marked blockade. An eagle with the union flag on its wings tears at his liver. Yet it is very much the aristocratic, patriarchal white South which is metaphorically portrayed here. The slaves are not included in the process of martyrology. This comes out clearly in the poem opposite, which carries the same title and also carries a sophisticated commentary on the blockade's effects on the English textile industry. It is very revealing of the nationalistic and self-serving attitudes toward the war which typify English print satires that the victims of King Cotton's Promethean torments under the cotton blockade are presented not as Americans, let alone as black slaves, but as English factory workers.[34] Prometheus, who as in the classical myth is shown suffering for mankind, does not hear the screaming of the American Eagle which tortures him, but the sounds of starvation from England:

And another thought is pressing,
Like hot iron on is brain—
Millions that would fain be blessing,
Ban e'en now, King cotton's name.
O that here these those hands are bound,
That should scatter wealth around.

Noth this Eagle's screaming smothers
That sad sound across the sea—
Wailing babes and weeping mothers,
Wailing, weeping, wanting me.
Hands that I would fain employ,
Hearts that I would fill with joy.

I must writhe—a giant fettered,—
While those millions peak and pine;
By my wealth their lot unbettered,
And their suffering worse than mine[35]

In the final section the poem moves on to conclude that English military intervention in breaking the blockade would be a blessing. Intriguingly all moral issues relating to slavery and the war are suspended: when English suffering is the subject it seems as ever that the normal moral rules do not apply.

Yet *KING COTTON BOUND* is an exceptional print, and in future issues *Punch* continues to harp on slavery—and the South's blindness to its moral failing over this issue—as the only cause of war. Indeed, the very same issue carries a quotation from the *New Orleans Delta*, in which the paper insists that "the African *slave trade* and African slavery conducted on humane principles, and regulated by law, must have the preference over every other form of compulsory labour. When Humanity has quite settled itself as a slave-dealer, of course we shall have Philanthropy beginning business as a housebreaker, and Rectitude making its way through a crowd as a pickpocket."

Punch continued throughout the course of the war to introduce ironic quotations from the southern press, and prints using the already violent southern stereotypes to illustrate them. Yet by far the most significant shift in the presentation of the South from the War of Independence to the Civil War relates to the introduction of the black slave. I want to end by considering this feature.

Blacks emerge primarily as a satiric vehicle for attacking America, North and South, and not as a socio-political reality. The predetermined graphic status of the slave is nowhere better exhibited than in *THE DIS-UNITED STATES—A BLACK BUSINESS* (fig. 16). The print shows the South as a skinny, shabbily dressed white, holding a long-barreled rifle in one hand and a revolver in the other, and wearing the customary planter's hat and smoking a cheroot. The North is a taller figure, dressed elegantly in urban attire, complete with top hat and kid gloves. The South glowers, the North strokes its chin contemplatively. The Southerner's face is caricatured, the Northerner's is not. Yet both appear recognizably human, as opposed to the figure of the black burly field slave who stands with an imbecilic expression of hilarity as he tears a map marked North and South in half. The black here is presented as a figure with no political agenda, but simply a figure who enjoys

132   The American South and English Print Satire, 1760–1865

Fig. 16. *THE DIS-UNITED STATES–A BLACK BUSINESS.* Wood engraving, *Punch* 31 (1856), 185. Sussex University Library.

malicious delight in witnessing the process of mutual destruction that the unionists and secessionists are going to begin. While on one level this is an extension of the argument that slavery is the only thing dividing North and South, in this print the slave himself seems mischievous and the active ingredient fomenting the war.

While the black slave comes to be one of the central symbols for representing the American South and its maintenance of chattel slavery, the forms of representation for the blacks bleed out into some extreme graphic contexts within *Punch*. Both the caricatured representation of the planter and the representation of the freed slave relate closely to graphic traditions which had been worked out in the context of English abolition and emancipation propaganda in the period 1780–1830.[36] The ex-slave in the British colonies is fairly frequently treated, and emerges as a comic hold-all for British color-based prejudice, which is then transferred to the American black. I haven't got time to discuss in detail the extent to which the constructions of the American slave grow out of the demeaning rhetorics developed to describe the emancipated

Fig. 17. *Running through his estate.* Wood engraving, *Punch* 3 (1842), 218. Sussex University Library.

English colonial slave, but will give some quick indications of how this crude rhetoric deluges the pages of Punch.[37]

During its first ten years *Punch* carried a medley of small, black silhouette caricatures as head and tail pieces to articles. Much of the basic anti-black humor in *Punch* is essentialized in these frivolous but nonetheless vicious little prints. *Running through his estate* (fig. 17) shows a Caribbean or American planter with a whip chasing a black through a cane field. *Levying Black Mail* shows a python lifting up and swallowing a black slave. There are literally hundreds of such prints scattered through the publication. What I want to highlight is how an unthinking anti-black stereotyping permeates *Punch*. This element in the journal illustrates the extent to which by 1840, and right through the ensuing half century, an assumed negrophobia operates as the backdrop for the representation of southern slavery, and comes to saturate representations of the American South in European graphic satire.[38]

Overall *Punch* has what now appears a strange race agenda. It certainly joined in the generally held sentiments that slavery was in principle a bad thing, while using the continuation of American slavery as a weapon to attack American democratic pretensions. Influential pro-slavery texts produced in England which had widespread circulation within the United States are attacked. The most notorious negrophobe tract to come out of England in the 1840–1860 period (it was printed in the late 1830s and reissued in revised form as a counter attack to

Uncle Tom's Cabin in 1853) was Thomas Carlyle's *On the Nigger Question*, and *Punch* singled this out for attack in a parodic police report supposedly detailing the activities of Carlyle.[39] The article was "Punch's Police: A Very Melancholy Case":

> *Thomas Carlyle was brought before Mr. Punch charged with not being able to take care of his literary reputation . . . witness did not believe the reputation of the accused in any positive danger, until some three or four months back, when he detected him running wildly up and down the pages of "Fraser's Magazine," pelting all sorts of gibberish at the head of the Jamaica niggars—fantastically reproaching them for being "up to the ears content in pumpkins when they should work for sugar and spices" for their white masters—threatening them with the whip, in a word dealing in language only dear to the heart—witness mean pockets—of Yankee slave-owners and Brazilian planters.*[40]

Here a piece of pro-slavery propaganda published by one of the most prominent English literary and social theoreticians of the Victorian era is presented as an anomaly. Its only supporters are seen as the slave powers of America and Brazil, despite the fact that the tract had a wide following in English society.

The Great Exhibition at the Crystal Palace provided a new, mid-century opening to attack America over slavery and to slip into a generalizing picture of how slavery dominated the whole of the deep South. The article "America in Crystal" opens with a sarcastic reference to the enormous crystal eagle that dominated the American contribution. It then goes on to comment on what was without doubt the most sensational success story of the American exhibit, Hiram Powers's erotic "The Greek Slave."[41] The satire continues: "A very little consideration might have given us the American Eagle, with the treasures of America gathered below its hovering wings. Why not have sent some choice specimens of slaves? We have the Greek Captive in dead stone, why not the Virginian slave in living ebony?" The next issue of *Punch* took up the hint, producing the suggested sculpture in woodcut. *The Virginian Slave Intended as a Companion to Powers's "Greek Slave"* (fig. 18)

Fig. 18. *The Virginian Slave Intended as a Companion to Power's "Greek Slave."* Wood engraving, *Punch* 20 (1852), 236. Sussex University Library.

took the form more of a mock monument than a statue. The base of the pedestal carries the *"E Pluribus Unum"* motto, while the pedestal itself is ornamented with scourges, ropes, and chains. A topless black woman slave leans against a whipping post draped in the stars and stripes. She is manacled at her wrists and ankles, and stares out with an expression of exaggerated and passive hopelessness.

The earlier article continues its attack on slave holding in the American South by quoting from a recent travel book by Lady Emmeline Wortley. The attack is significant in that it makes an implicit connection between the attitudes of the English aristocracy and the southern slaveholders of Virginia. In proposing an exhibit of slaves for the American contribution to the Crystal Palace, Lady Wortley is suggested as a likely "commissioner." We are told that "her ladyship is invited to the slave estate—a sort of black Arcadia—the property of the late President's son." The dwellings were "very nice," many of them "ornamented with prints," doubtless the Declaration of Independence. Her Ladyship is shown the rising generation of slaves—from slavery at the breast to slavery just running alone: "Such a congregation of little smiling, good-natured raven rolypolies, I never saw collected together before. One *perfect duck* [why not blackbird?] of a child was only about three weeks old, but it comported itself quite as orderly as the rest.... It was as black as a little image carved in ebony, and *as plump as a partridge (in mourning)*." The piece concludes with a small print satire, again a parodic exhibit intended for the Crystal Palace under the title *Sample of American Manufacture*. A figure representing the slave power, with scourge and planter costume but with the face of an eagle, stands above a group of cowering chained black children in silhouette.

The black child as victim continues to appear in prints up to and during the Civil War, while female personifications of America, and of certain slave states, allow for the graphic accusation that the slave power behaves like an abusive mother to its black children. A concise example of such an exploitation of familial metaphor is: *DIVORCE À VINCULO Mrs. Carolina Asserts her Right to "Larrup" her Nigger*. Here a muscular white woman with ferocious profile, and wearing a madras turban, carries the knotted scourge in her right hand and raises her left fist. The North appears as a stern protective father, while the slaves are embodied in the figure of an imploring black child in field hand costume, who begs the North to protect it. This print perfectly encapsulates the manner in which *Punch* is only prepared to sympathize with the slave when embodied within an image of total vulnerability, innocence, and passivity. A more fanciful variation on this theme appears in *OBERON AND TITANIA*. There the North is presented as Lincoln/Oberon confronting the South/Titania with the original cause of their falling out. Shakespeare's original has Oberon argue, "I do but beg a little changeling boy, To be my henchman," to which Titania replies, "Set your heart at rest; The fairy land buys not the child of me." In recasting the dialogue, with Lincoln announcing, "I do but beg a little nigger boy to be my henchman," and the South replying, "Set your hand at

Fig. 19. THE AMERICAN DIFFICULTY. "President Abe: 'WHAT A NICE WHITE HOUSE IT WOULD BE, IF IT WERE NOT FOR THE BLACKS.'" Wood engraving, Punch 40 (1861), 193. Sussex University Library.

rest, the Northern land buys not the child of me," the black is again a passive bone of contention.[42]

As the war progressed, blacks would continue to be presented either as an infantilized victim or, when in adult form, as irresponsible rogues.[43] Other prints present blacks as an almost entirely abstract problem, which the North is impotent to solve. Maybe the most powerful print to move the representation of the black in this context toward the realms of a visual abstraction is the remarkable THE AMERICAN DIFFICULTY (fig. 19). Here a disconsolate Lincoln stirs up the grate with a poker, while a black smoke billows out of the fire. Within the smoke are a myriad of little black stick figures, only barely decipherable as human forms. The subcaption reads *"President Abe: 'WHAT*

Fig. 20. *ABE LINCOLN'S LAST CARD OR, ROUGE-ET-NOIR*. Wood engraving, Punch 43 (1862), 161. Sussex University Library.

A NICE WHITE HOUSE IT WOULD BE, IF IT WERE NOT FOR THE BLACKS.'" This is a clever print, the war itself is metaphorised as a domestic fire burning out of control, the fragments of soot, or smuts, known colloquially as "blacks," become the slaves. The blacks have no individuality or personality but exist as a collective darkness, thrown up by the destructive fire of war, and polluting and obscuring the domestic space of America, symbolized by the presidential "white house" itself. This is a peculiar metaphor presenting blacks as a form of incendiary filth which in its invasive intensity has saturated the very metaphoric home of American Democracy itself.

There is another print that is equally abstract and equally negative in its construction of the Southern black. Here the racist term "spade" for black is literalized in a representation of the war as a game of cards, *rouge et noir*, between North and South. Jefferson and Lincoln play on a board which has been placed on a barrel of gunpowder. The title reads *ABE LINCOLN'S LAST CARD OR, ROUGE-ET-NOIR* (fig. 20). Lincoln's controversial decision to allow black troops to fight for the North is reduced to his grim raising of the ace of spades above the card table. The black spade at the card's center carries a tiny grinning face, a significant face because it represents nothing less than the English construction of the heroic activities of the black troops in fighting for the North and emancipation.

From this point on the black slave increasingly enters center stage in the big set-piece prints on the Civil War. Increasingly blacks are not presented as tragic and homeless victims of the turmoil of the war, but as a comic conundrum the North cannot solve. With the decision to let blacks fight as regular troops for the North, *Punch* increasingly saw an opportunity to present blacks themselves as the symbolic representatives of both North and South, but when granted such semiotic centrality their roles are invariably absurd and belittling. THE BLACK CONSCRIPTION shows a capering black Confederate shaking hands with a smiling Union soldier, also black. They say "Dat you sambo, yeah, yeah . . . Bress my heart how am you Jim," with a main caption reading "When black meets black then comes the end of war," the implication being that blacks will not want to fight each other on any grounds. There is a similarly insulting elaboration of the same theme in a print called THE BLACK DRAFT.[44] This shows Lincoln and a Confederate officer each trying to force medicine, placed in a mug marked conscription, down the throats of two comically terrified black soldiers. What comes out increasingly is the obsessive denigration of blacks and a sense that America is of no importance until it finishes the war and clarifies its trade policies.

In summary, English print satire invariably brought some pretty blunt ideological tools to bear on the construction of the American South. In many ways the prints which came out the War of Independence are more complicated, uncertain, and visually ambitious than those which followed. It seems that the British graphic satiric psyche when it responded to the Civil War operated almost neurotically out of two main areas. The first was an inability to deal with the *fact* of American independence, let alone the remarkably complex socio-economic developments occurring across a vast land mass. Consequently America was boiled down to a set of lowest common denominators, a greedy North and a barbaric South, both presented most commonly as angry men, or spoilt children. The second area was a bitter-sweet self righteousness over the issue of slavery which could only lead English print satirists to abstract the issue. From the perspective of mid-nineteenth-century London, American slavery was a vicious evil which placed England on the moral high ground. Yet the slaves themselves are consistently denigrated. They are shown as debased and risible, represented purely according to the stereotypes not of so-called scientific racism, but of a brute racism which was rapidly gaining the ascendancy when English printmakers, satiric or otherwise, represented blacks of any type on any issue. The groundwork for this brutally reductionist construction of the black slave and ex slave had been formed in a variety of publishing areas within Britain for over fifty years.

British Views of the Confederacy

R. J. M. BLACKETT

Booths selling a wide array of goods donated by supporters of the Confederacy in Britain lined the ornate walls of St. George's hall, Liverpool, in October 1864. An estimated ten thousand people attended the three-day bazaar. The crush was so great that the organizers were forced to turn away two thousand on the final day. No one, least of all the organizers, had anticipated such a response. All who mattered seemed to have attended. Even Thomas Dudley of the American consulate in Liverpool was impressed: "[a]ll the elite and Fashion of the town has been there," he wrote home, "indeed one may say it has been patronized generally by the whole people." It was, he observed, the most highly patronized bazaar in the history of the country, with proceeds of close to £24,000. Much of the money raised was earmarked for Southern prisoners incarcerated in Federal prisons. Ever since the beginning of the Civil War, Confederate supporters in Liverpool had been collecting and remitting funds to what James Mason, the Confederate commissioner in England, called "confidential agencies at the North." Those in attendance took time to view a flag that was to be presented to Captain Semmes of the Confederate navy, and a sword and bible gifts to Robert E. Lee from admirers in Britain. It was an event replete with cultural and political symbolism.[1]

The driving force behind the event, like so much else associated with the Confederacy in Britain, was James Spence, the Liverpool tin-plate merchant and principal propagandist for the secessionists. Spence's substantial business connections with the United States had fallen prey to the economic downturn of 1857. By the outbreak of the war he was only just beginning to recover. Largely self taught, Spence was a man of considerable ability. He was, Mason observed, "full of enterprise . . . an able and experienced merchant . . . a man of large research, liberal and expanded views and great labor." Spence put his considerable talents at the disposal of the Confederacy. His book, *The American Union*, which appeared in the fall of 1861, at a time when many in Britain were still searching for a usable explanation of why the two sides had come to blows, was the clearest and most sustained argument in favor of independence for the Southern states. Written in just fourteen weeks, the work went through four editions in as many months and was later translated into French, German, Italian, and Spanish. Early in the war, Spence had been instrumental in the formation of the Liverpool Southern Club, the first of its kind in the country. By 1863, as the contest to influence British public opinion heated up, he was at the center of the many national organizations formed to promote the Confederate cause. His forty-five articles written for the *London Times* between February 1862 and January 1865 were a sustained argument in favor of recognition of the Confederacy. Spence was also intimately involved in the effort to raise money for the Confederacy through the sale of bonds in the financial markets of Britain and Europe.[2]

Not surprisingly, Spence's indispensability to the cause bred suspicion and some jealousy. Confederate agent Henry Hotze found him a little too mercurial and unpredictable. Having agreed to work with Hotze on the *Index*, a newspaper promoting the cause of secession, Spence found the rigor of publishing too onerous and ceased his contributions after only a few editions. Charles Prioleau, the Liverpool representative of the Charleston, South Carolina, firm Fraser Trenholm, and a major figure in the effort to win recognition for the Confederacy, had nothing but "personal respect and regard and admiration" for Spence's talents as a writer and speaker. Nor could he find flaws in Spence's character. But the fact that Spence had failed in business "once or twice" bothered Prioleau. Although Prioleau knew that Spence had repaid his creditors in full, the suspicion lingered that these failures reflected badly on Spence's business if not his political acumen. Hotze also worried that Spence was too willing to concede to British antislavery traditions and to publicly pledge that Confederate independence would lead to eventual emancipation. In fact, many of his allies suspected Spence of harboring an emancipationist agenda. What they did not realize was that Spence was fully aware of the fact that public support and political recognition of the Confederacy was unlikely without some commitment to future emancipation. His argument for emancipation, he insisted, "commits no one, but is very valuable as a means of turning the flank of the enemy and I have reason to say has done good service."[3]

Such tensions did not deter Spence from throwing himself fully into the organization of the Bazaar in Aid of the Southern Prisoner's Relief Fund, as it was officially known. Like so many other bazaars of its kind, much of the work fell to women. But Spence was astute enough to recognize that the impact on the public of a bazaar of this sort would be enhanced considerably should it adhere to established British social traditions. As a result, he enlisted the support of twenty-three patronesses, including the Marchioness of Bath and the Marchioness of Lothian, Lady Mildred Beresford-Hope, Lady Wharncliffe, and Lady DeHoghton, the wives of prominent figures in the Confederate cause. Each of the patronesses was coupled with the wife of a prominent Confederate exile as representatives of one of the seceded states. Lady Wharncliffe and Mrs. Prioleau, for example, represented South Carolina, and the Countess of Chesterfield and Mrs. Slidell, Mississippi. Each couple manned a stall selling goods produced by one of the seceded states. Others walked the hall raffling goods to patrons who attended piano recitals and the performances of an operetta company. In such settings of Victorian splendor, the coupling of aristocratic and Confederate women seemed to confirm a natural alliance between British aristocracy and Southern chivalry.[4]

Such an alliance seemed only natural to the supporters of the Confederacy. No unbiased observer, Hotze declared: "Southern America, in manners, forms of speech, and habits of thought and business, resembled more old England, while Young England resembled more Northern America." For generations the South had been "proud of its closer affinity of blood to the British parent stock, than the North, with its mongrel compound of the surplus population of all the world could boast of." Lord Wolseley concurred. The South, he told readers of *Blackwood's*, the conservative journal, comprised "the descendants of our banished cavaliers." The North, on the other hand, was "descended from the offscourings of every European nation." The result was a Southern political tradition in which reasoned paternalism reigned as compared to Northern democracy with an "imbecile executive above, a restless, purposeless multitude below, linked together like a kite tied to a balloon...."[5] Spence and others thought the present conflict had its origins in the struggle for American independence almost a century earlier. The War of Independence and the failure of Britain to hold on to its colony, was attributable in part to the divided nationalities of the people who had settled America. Compared to rowdy Massachusetts, filled as it was with Celts and Germans, British-originated Virginia had stayed loyal to the crown during the Revolutionary War. The people of these two states were more opposed to one another than any two people in Europe. Massachusetts and the rest of the North were "from their birth turbulent, arrogant, and seditious. An intense and selfish fanaticism marked that people from the first, as it does this day. In the South, with the exception of Louisiana, in which there is a population of French origin, the people are almost of purely British descent."

Percy Greg, a journalist, historian, and major propagandist for the Confederacy, saw things similarly. In a book written after the war, he insisted that the people of Virginia and Maryland "preserved visible traces of the loyalty, moderation, and English patriotism which were the proudest traditions of our cavalier ancestry." Unbridled democracy ruled elsewhere. Not surprisingly, the Revolution had its origins among the disloyal in New England where the Puritan leaven had encouraged rebels and regicides and had "mutilated the national ensign." Not surprisingly, true Englishmen felt an affinity for those who had stood with them during the Revolution.[6]

How one viewed the war depended in large measure on the stand one took on the demands for political reform at home. In that sense, the Civil War became a platform on which the more parochial struggles over reform were played out, one in which views of American democracy played a pivotal role. The war, the editors of the *Times* maintained, was the inevitable outcome of a society governed by the majority—that is, "the less wise, less practised, less considerate, less circumspect, less adroit, and less informed part of the population...." In any system where the preponderance of popular will is allowed to operate without checks or limits, political upheavals are almost inevitable. The view from the editors' desk was of a country drifting inevitably toward anarchy and the possibility of military dictatorship. Those "extreme liberals" who have been clamoring for an enlargement of British democracy should take note of the collapse of a system that has proven to be utterly destitute. "When we see that unlimited democracy conveys not the slightest security against the worst of wars and the most reckless extravagance," the editors concluded, "we may apply the moral at home, and congratulate ourselves that the old British Constitution has not been precipitately remodeled after the Manchester design."[7]

Most of those opposed to political reform, conservatives and liberals alike, the majority of whom threw their support to the Confederacy, could see political degeneracy brought on by expanding democracy. To Spence and others, the Founding Fathers of the United States of America, those natural leaders of men, schooled as they were in British political traditions, had been replaced by men of limited talent. Democracy, whether in France or the United States, replaced skilled, natural leadership and talent with mediocrity. "It is the inevitable result of Democracy," Spence told his *Times* readers, "when attempted on so large a scale, that the minority becomes abject, the majority despotic. The essence of freedom, its completeness in the individual man, becomes extinguished, and men moved no longer by the guidance of reason and choice, but as fish move in a shoal, by the volition of the mass." How else, the editors of the *Times* insisted with their accustomed acerbity, could one explain the results of the 1860 election that produced a "rural attorney for Sovereign and a city attorney for Prime Minister."[8]

Underlying much of this opposition to American democracy was an abiding belief in the superiority of British political institutions and traditions. Even among those who were opposed to the Confederacy there existed a profound national pride in Britain's mixed constitution, with its balance between the monarchy, executive, and Commons. This was a system that ought to be emulated and not be imposed upon or jettisoned as some political reformers were attempting to do. Other countries, both in Europe and across the Atlantic, would guarantee their citizens political liberty and stability should they adopt the "progressive character" of British institutions.[9] Not surprisingly, much of what was said about the upheaval across the Atlantic was tinged with a sense of British superiority. Even old allies in the abolitionist movement grew testy over this tendency of British colleagues to be dictatorial and patronizing. The English think they are superior to all others, the American Charles Fairbanks observed after a brief visit in the early years of the war, and so "assume a lofty tone" when addressing others "and toward America especially, since she is a young nation, they carry themselves with the bearing of a very high superiority." The *Times* marveled at this tendency to take umbrage. The "gasconading spirits of the North," the editors declared, made it impossible for Union supporters to take well-meaning advice or accept the intent of British neutrality.[10] The fact that their advice recommended the breaking up of the union never seemed to have caused the editors much concern.

For some, especially radicals who had gone into exile in America following the failure of the Chartist uprisings, and those who had emigrated in search of better opportunities, this belief in the superiority of the British system was based on the failure of America to live up to their expectations. John B. Horsfall, a leader in the movement for improved working conditions in Lancashire in the early 1850s, was disillusioned by his experiences in America. "Her citizens have all got the vote," he wrote home, "but that does not prevent her roughs and her rowdies from exercising the right to carry and use bowie knives and revolvers." Many of the more than thirty-six thousand British immigrants who returned from the United States between 1858 and 1860, Wilbur Shepperson has argued, were "irritated by the nationalism of Americans, by the confidence, which verged on arrogance, and particularly by the constant demand that all Englishmen offer unqualified praise of the new order."[11]

Horsfall's views did not go unchallenged. For many, especially those committed to political reform, the United States set the standard to which all democrats should aspire. The existence of a liberal constitution, the lack of a religious establishment, the availability of cheap land, and high wages became the standard by which radicals measured

Britain's shortcomings. The Union and Emancipation Society saw no reason to destroy what was the most "magnificent development of human activity and constitutional liberty." To Ernest Jones, the old Chartist, the United States was "the noblest republic the world has ever known." And while Henry Vincent, Jones's Chartist colleague, conceded that the country had attracted some rapscallions and outcasts, he maintained that "the brightest and best portion of the American people—... the early American people—represented ... the industry, the energy, the faith, the perseverance, and the progressive instincts of the Old World."[12] In comparison, they agreed with William Lloyd Garrison that the Confederacy was "playing the traitor in order to establish the dominion of the devil, and to enlarge the boundaries of hell." W. E. Adams, a radical newspaperman, declared that no one committed to the struggle for expanded liberty in Europe or anywhere else could turn their backs on the oppressed slaves and support those who were fighting to maintain slavery, "to beat, bruise, and brutalise a poor and friendless race." A country that had provided refuge for European political exiles, who had "welcomed Kossuth, who [had] sheltered Worcell, who [had] applauded Garibaldi—we who [had] sympatised with every effort however desperate, and rejoiced over every victory however small, on behalf of human freedom—shall we of all the peoples in the world be the means of re-uniting the already broken chains of slavery?"[13]

Such views put Spence and other supporters of the Confederacy at a distinct disadvantage in the public debate over the war. Why, given Britain's abolitionist tradition, their opponents insisted, should anyone support a movement whose aim was a reaffirmation of the legitimacy of slavery. The editors of the *Times* suggested a number of reasons why the secessionists should be supported, all the while skirting the issue of slavery. They insisted that the Confederacy had beaten the odds and seemed well on the way to achieving independence; that the demand for independence was "natural"; that secession was an accomplished fact and was irreversible; that it was impossible to conquer so vast a territory, and even if it were, the cost would be too prohibitive; and that Britain should maintain its cherished tradition of supporting the underdog. Others added to the list of possible grounds for support the argument that an independent Confederacy would destroy protectionism and enhance free trade. Some even suggested that a reunited Union would grow much stronger and far more inimical to British commercial and other interests.[14]

While many were willing to concede that these arguments had some merit, supporters of the Confederacy could not escape the fact that at the heart of the new country lay the institution of slavery. A few advocates, such as the Reverend William W. Malet, vicar of the Hertfordshire village of Ardeley, chose to make a virtue out of a necessity. Following a visit to South Carolina, he took pains to paint an idyllic picture of slave life, insisting that work routines were not onerous and that slaves had ample time to indulge their literary and religious tastes. Conditions were so pleasant that a group of freed slaves from Virginia had chosen to return home after experiencing conditions in the free North. For Malet and others the issue turned on whether slavery had been and continued to be a boon to the African. Those committed to the notion that it was thought they found confirmation in the failure of emancipation in Jamaica. Ever since the publication of Thomas Carlyle's scurrilous attack on the Jamaican freedmen a decade earlier, many were convinced that the freedman had shown a lack of enterprise. Carlyle's contention that black labor had to be ordered by their white superiors resonated among those who had serious reservations about the freedman's ability to survive away from the plantation. Anthony Trollope suggested that the West Indian freedman had not kept their part of the bargain when they abandoned the plantations, a clear indication that they were not fit for freedom. The laws of nature, he declared, had made the Negro inferior to the European.[15] Even among supporters of the Union there were some who questioned the slave's ability to enjoy the fruits of freedom. After much agonizing, Richard Cobden thought the future of the Negro "all over the world" depended on how they performed as soldiers in the war. He was willing to concede that they did possess the physical abilities. In India, he wrote Charles Sumner, the Sepoys were largely responsible for capturing territory from the British "although they are a very inferior race physically to the

Negroes. Whoever heard of a Hindoo offering to fight a picked Englishman in the prize ring? He would hardly have a better chance than a woman. But we have black men doing this in England. Tom Cribb had to fight a severe battle for the champions belt with the Negro Molyneaux."[16]

In spite of Cobden's curious mixture of race, ethnicity, and gender, his views on the future of the Negro were not uncommon. George Odger of the shoemakers' union and a Union supporter, saw things only slightly differently, and like Cobden was optimistic about the impact of the Negroes' participation in the war. People, he insisted, generally did not fraternize with their social inferiors. While most in the audience would be upset if their sister were to marry a Negro, they would not be if she married a black prince. It is this sense of social superiority that has fueled Northern dislike of the Negro. But, he predicted, the commitment to emancipation will raise the Negro in the social scale. Northern treatment of the Negro was similar to the way the English treated the Irish. He anticipated that the collapse of Negro slavery would lead to political and social equality for the Irish. Some wondered about the merits of such subtle distinctions. After all, God had made all men equal "as it regarded their powers of body, and their susceptibilities of instruction, improvement, and enlargement of mind." The Negro had demonstrated this fact even under slavery. With an eye on those like "Another Southern Sympathiser" who had condemned abolitionists for trying to persuade the working class that the Negro was his equal when they knew full well that all "the Negro prodigies we have heard of are a mixture," one editor rejected the "sneer and the smile about amalgamation." Put quite simply, the "black man was his brother, and . . . was entitled to his sympathy as much as Jefferson Davis was."[17] The issue of race, as Douglas Lorimer has argued, was central to the debate over the war. The founders of the London Anthropological Society made the connection explicit when they invited Hotze to join the organization. The society aimed, Hotze admitted, to question the "heresies that have gained currency in science and politics, of the equality of the races of men."[18]

Confederate supporters found themselves in a bind: if Carlyle and Trollope were right about the disastrous outcome of West Indian emancipation, why and on what grounds would one advocate freeing the slaves in the Confederacy. Their options were further constrained by the fact that few in Britain in the 1860s would have dared to oppose emancipation. It had to all intents and purposes become part and parcel of the national patrimony. West Indian emancipation, the ultimate in disinterested philanthropy, showed Britain at her best. No British advocate of the Confederacy could ignore this reality. While it grated on their sensibilities, Southerners in Britain also realized that they stood little chance of success in their struggle for recognition if they failed to address the question of emancipation. Their task was made more difficult, of course, by the Confederate government's refusal to entertain any form of emancipation. The question then became: how best to satisfy British antislavery traditions and at the same time not undermine the foundation on which the Confederacy rested. Satisfying both needs caused considerable tension between British supporters and representatives of the Confederacy. Hotze, for instance, thought Spence and others were too quick to promise emancipation in their efforts to win public support even while he conceded that the widespread "instinctive aversion" to slavery could not be ignored. Ironically, with nothing else to draw on than the West Indian experience, British supporters called for a form of gradual abolition. Alexander J. Beresford-Hope, a leading proponent of the Confederacy, condemned calls for immediate emancipation, which he insisted would cause the "greatest misery," for the freedmen would be thrown onto their own resources unprepared. It would result in "bloodshed, outrage, destruction of property, and perpetual starvation over the South, by the letting loose of a race half-savage, [and] half-childish." He proposed instead a gradual abolition that would occur over a number of years. Once the South had been brought into "intimate relations with Europe," relying as it would have to on the continent's "manufacturers, education and literature," and aware of the general aversion to slavery, it will be compelled to "change its course in regards to slavery." Members of the Manchester Southern Club concurred in this approach. They called for gradual abolition, "not abruptly or without due consideration, but by a system such as has prevailed in the West Indies; not, however, to degenerate into "squatting and idleness, such as have cursed emancipation in the British colonies." To do otherwise could result in a situation where "bereft of a home, employment, friend, and a paternal oversight" the freedman "would sink and fall backwards as the race has elsewhere done, when left suddenly to care for itself." But opponents gave no quarter. Beresford-Hope was accused of opposing slavery in the abstract but defending it in the concrete, and others demanded to be shown where "speedy emancipation" had been a failure.[19]

These differences were an integral part of the public debate over the merits of the contending sides of the war. In the small town of Todmorden, which straddles Yorkshire and Lancashire, for example, R. Bell, a Union supporter and his opponent, "A Factory Operative," carried on a sustained debate in the local paper lasting five months until the editor stepped in to call a halt to the dispute. "A Factory Operative" led the charge, with Bell snipping away at his facts and logic. While he found slavery to be repugnant, "A Factory Operative" called on the British to be sympathetic, considering that slavery had existed in its territories until only recently. He went further: slavery had been a positive good, doing more to civilize the African "than any other means hitherto tried." Facts proved, he argued, that so long as "the Negro remains at home, no influence can be brought to bear upon him which will sufficiently counteract the attractions of his barbarous customs; and . . . history does not record one single instance of such a race being civilized by the efforts of the missionary or by those of the colonist." Wherever two races have come into contact, the inferior have had to retreat or run the risk of being exterminated. When Bell wondered how one could condemn slavery and support a system whose sole purpose was to keep blacks in slavery, "A Factory Operative" changed the topic. The Confederacy ought to be supported because they were a people struggling against superior odds. What he admired in the South was their "fortitude, their endurance, their courage, and the display of those manly qualities generally under suffering the most intense." The South was also dissatisfied with the Union and so should be allowed to leave. Bell rejected such arguments as "foolish." How can any form of government be held together under these conditions? England, he pointed out, had made short work of rebels at home and abroad even when they were in their own country and when "they were governed contrary to and quite against their will." Finally, "A Factory Operative" pointed to shortcomings in republican forms of government, especially their tendency to become repressive once consent had been abandoned. Given the American experience, he predicted that republicanism had run its course and that the country would evolve into "some superior order of government more suitable to its growing wants." When Bell shifted the debate to the contending merits of free and slave labor, his opponent was put on the defensive. Northern farms, Bell argued, were more productive; there were more schools, more libraries, and more newspapers in the North. "This proves to a demonstration that where the labour is free all encouragement is given to the spread of knowledge, but where it is slave labour all is done to keep not only the poor slave ignorant, but his white brother-labourer as well."[20]

The debate over the contending merits of free and slave labor was central to the efforts of Union supporters to undermine plans by their opponents to win working-class support for the Confederacy. Early in the war Spence had laid out a strategy that he hoped would win recognition for the Confederacy. It rested on continued Confederate successes on the battlefield that, he predicted, would raise serious questions about the continued legitimacy of the Union, and exploiting disruptions in the critical textile industry, caused by the shortage of cotton, through public agitation that together would bring pressure on the government to recognize the Confederacy. As the cotton famine caused by the shortage of cotton began to take hold in the principal textile towns of Lancashire and Cheshire in early 1862, Spence got together with a small group of working-class figures partial to the Confederacy to plan a series of public meetings and lectures. The group included William Aitken, Mortimer Grimshaw, John Matthews, Thomas Rhodes, and Kinder Smith, all of whom had been active in the struggle to improve working conditions for textile workers in the previous decade. The money to finance these efforts seems to have come from the coffers of the Liverpool Southern Club and from Hotze's discretionary funds. Within days of the meeting with Spence, Aitken and others organized a massive meeting in Ashton attended by an estimated six thousand. The organizers called for lifting the blockade and recognition of the Confederacy. But opponents had gotten wind of the meeting and did all they could to mute its impact. Posters condemning the meeting were plastered throughout the town, warning that a group of agitators had been hired by the "enemies of liberty, the advocates of slavery, and paid by the agents of the rebels in South America, in order to get the accent of the people of Lancashire in favour of breaking the blockade, and thus acknowledge the rebel government." A resolution in support of the Confederacy was countered with an amendment from the floor calling on the government to continue its policy of neutrality, to do all that it could to encourage the destruction of those who promoted slavery and oppression, for, it declared, America was "the most liberal government in the world." Although it is not certain if either the resolution or the amendment was carried, the opposition could claim victory for preventing a declaration of support for the secessionists.[21]

Charles Francis Adams's concern that these "insurgent emissaries" could exploit the effects of the cotton famine to win recognition for the Confederacy was not unfounded. Over the next few months Aitken and the others organized a series of meetings throughout Lancashire. They had promised Spence that they could guarantee crowds of thirty thousand at some of their meetings. Support for the Confederacy from such large meetings during a time of rising unemployment could not be ignored, nor could anyone miss the fact that they were organized to coincide with motions in Parliament calling for recognition. Under these circumstances, such "pressure from without" could not fail to have an impact on government policy. The public meetings and lectures were reinforced by frequent letters to editors, pamphlets, and books, Spence's very popular articles for the *London Times*, and memorials and petitions to the government. But what Spence and his supporters could do, so could the opposition. As a result, a sustained public debate ensued which lasted for the rest of the war and which touched all corners of the country, from the major cities to small remote villages and towns. The debate in Todmorden between Bell and

"A Factory Operative" was replicated in Newmilns, Scotland, Butleigh, Somerset, and Penmark, Wales, and many other small towns. By the middle of 1864 much of the fire had gone out of the activities of Spence and other supporters of the Confederacy. The opposition had carried the day, sustained by more effective organization, supported by a cast of talented African-American lecturers, including Andrew Jackson, Jefferson Davis' former coachman, financed by wealthy supporters and the resources of the American consulates in Britain, especially those in Liverpool and London, and endorsed by radicals and political reformers, such as W. E. Adams, prominent political figures such as John Bright and Peter A. Taylor, and a working-class population that, by and large, gave their support to the Union.

At the heart of this pro-Union alliance lay a call for international working-class solidarity. The positivist Professor Edward S. Beesly of University College, London, insisted that cheap and unpaid labor in one place cheapens labor everywhere. At the core of opposition to the Union and its emancipation policies in Britain, he maintained, was the recognition of this link and the acknowledgment that freedom for the slave in America will lead to the improvement of conditions for workers in Britain. W. E. Adams writing under the pseudonym "Caractacus" concurred: it was not color alone that distinguished slaves from owners, "it was poverty also." If the South succeeded, all the "horrors" of Europe will be reproduced in America. "The logic of slavery is inexorable," he concluded, "it does not recognize colour, only condition."[22] These links were a common feature of pro-Union working-class meetings especially after Lincoln's Emancipation Proclamation went into effect in January 1863. John Turner, a gardener and secretary of the Ashton branch of the Union and Emancipation Society, insisted that emancipation was a working man's question, for "if it was right for slavery in one part it was right in another; and it behooved the working classes to give no help to scoundrels who wanted their work done for nothing." To support the Confederacy, his fellow townsman Jonathan Biltcliffe pointed out, was only to add another link to the chains of 4 million slaves and in so doing "help in their own enslavement." In spite of the dislocations caused by the cotton famine,

"A Factory Operative" of Bamber Bridge rejected the call of those who insisted that self-interest should determine their views on the war. "I regard the future peace and prosperity of a great people, the emancipation or consigning to hopeless bondage of four million human beings as questions of greater moment than those which relate to the removal of any temporary suffering from amongst ourselves," he wrote his local newspaper. He was also aware that the cornerstone of the Confederacy was the "enslavement of the working man white as well as black." In America they say blacks are inferior, and only whites can enjoy freedom, a Mr. Johnson told a Leicester meeting. In Britain workingmen were told they "were the scum, and were machines, or were ignorant and requiring to be better educated." In the near future, he predicted, both slavery in America and their own "political slavery" would be abolished.[23]

It was, among other things, this positive link between the rights of workers at home and slaves in America that supporters of the Confederacy—most of them conservative and generally opposed to political reform—tried to decouple. While they all paid homage to British abolitionist traditions, they cast a wary eye on the domestic political consequences of the war and emancipation. As the war drew to a close, many radical supporters of the Union tried to make these links even more explicit. A country that had twice elected a man of Lincoln's background, the second time in the midst of a war, was an inspiration to all those committed to political reform. As the war drew to a close, "A Working Man" of Ashton made the links most explicit: "We have a general impression amongst us that the once despised and enthralled African will not only be free, but enfranchised, and in spite of his master; and when the slave ceases to be, and becomes enfranchised free men, then the British workman's claim may be listened to."[24] Spence and others had tried unsuccessfully to prevent this eventuality. Had the Confederacy cooperated and proposed some form of gradual emancipation as Beresford-Hope suggested, their supporters thought they stood a good chance of winning recognition and at the same time forestalling political reform at home. Spence poured scorn on those who argued that the Republican Party's plan to contain the slave states within existing borders would lead to emancipation. "I would like someone to explain this process of dying out," he told a Glasgow meeting. "These slave states are twenty times as large as England—that is not a very small or narrow space." The only way to guarantee emancipation was through the break up of the Union and the independence of the Confederacy. An independent South, squeezed between a powerful and free North and the civilizing influence of Europe, would do what Britain did in the West Indies. If the war continued emancipation would be jeopardized, for the North ran the risk of further fragmentation. Spence made it abundantly clear that his was not the traditional abolitionist drivel but a practical solution to a difficult problem. He was opposed to slavery not because of any idea that all men are created equal—for those who do usually call for freedom without preparation—but because a man should not be a chattel. One editor dismissed these ideas as mere subterfuge, an impractical call for "emancipation by escapement."[25]

Much of the steam had gone out of the pro-Confederate agitation by the fall of 1864. Although many still hoped that the armies of the South could turn the tide of the war, it was clear to most impartial observers that the North had gained a permanent upper hand. Always the optimist, Spence found something to cheer about in such reversals: the more compact the size of the country, he had long maintained, the more difficult it would be for the Union to defeat their opponent. But Spence's logic escaped most observers: one could not transform military defeats into political successes. By the last summer of the war almost all of the pro-Confederate organizations were moribund. The Southern Independence Association, formed when the Manchester Southern Club and the Central Association for the Recognition of the Confederate States merged in October 1863, had ceased much of its public agitation one year later. Much of the work was now taken up by the Society for Promoting the Cessation of Hostilities in America, whose secretary, the Reverend Francis William Tremlett, rector of St. Peter's Church, Belsize Park, London, had a close working relationship with Matthew Maury, one of the Confederacy's commissioners to England. Public agitation was now limited to infrequent lectures and meetings addressed by Spence, the Reverend Edward A. Verity, incumbent of Habergam Eaves, near Burnley, and T. B. Kershaw, an overseer at a mill in Manchester.

With the approach of the 1864 presidential elections, Confederate supporters searched for ways to throw their support behind what they saw as a rising peace movement in the North. If Lincoln could be defeated, they reasoned, there was a greater likelihood that George McClelland, the Democratic candidate, would call for a cessation of hostilities. They settled on a two-pronged approach: calling for an armistice in America, and another attempt to persuade the British government to reverse its policy of neutrality and recognize the Confederacy. The Peace Address, as it came to be known, was the brainchild of Kershaw. By mid-summer 1864 the *London Times* reported that the Address had been signed by three hundred thousand people, over half of them from Ireland. Organizers planned to have Joseph Parker, one of the secretaries of the Southern Independence Association, deliver the Address to Horatio Seymour, governor of New York and one of the leaders of the peace party, in time, they hoped, to affect the outcome of the election. In spite of Spence's opposition to the plan, which he thought was ill advised, Parker sailed for America carrying the Address. As Spence had predicted, Seymour considered the Address an unwarranted interference in American affairs and refused to accept it. Parker then set out for Washington, D.C., where he hoped to deliver the Address to Secretary of State William Seward. Parker was kept waiting until he could prove to Seward that he was an official emissary from the British government. Unable to do so, Parker returned to England embarrassed by his rejections in New York and Washington, and ridiculed by opponents at home.[26]

The Peace Address was backed up at home by a flurry of petitions to Parliament in the first half of 1864. An estimated eighty-one were either submitted directly to the House of Commons or to Lord John Russell, the foreign secretary. The petition to Russell contained ninety thousand names and was submitted in July 1864 by a deputation of workingmen.[27] Although these activities were driven by the hope that the government could still be pressured to recognize the Confederacy, by the end of the year even the staunchest advocate had to conclude that all was lost.

The sense of euphoria surrounding the success of the Liverpool bazaar in October 1864 is understandable in the context of such failures. The size of the attendance and the amount raised suggested continued strong support for the embattled Confederacy. This was not the first time that the public had responded so generously to efforts on behalf of the secessionists. In a matter of weeks following the death of Stonewall Jackson in May 1863, Beresford-Hope had managed to raise a substantial sum of money to have a statue executed in honor of the slain general. The commission went to John Henry Foley, possibly Britain's foremost sculptor, but illness prevented Foley from completing the work before the defeat of the Confederacy. It was not until the collapse of Reconstruction in Virginia and the election as governor of a former Confederate general that the statue was shipped to Richmond, where it was unveiled in October 1875 in ceremonies attended by over thirty thousand.[28]

The success of the bazaar provided Confederate supporters with an opportunity to embarrass the newly reelected government in Washington by showing how callous they were to enemy prisoners. Ever since the start of the war, British supporters had managed to get aid to soldiers imprisoned in the North. Much of the money raised through the bazaar could have been disbursed through traditional channels without much fanfare. In fact, by January 1865 £18,000 was remitted to agents in New York by Charles Prioleau. In addition, supporters sent "five thousand flannel shirts, five thousand pairs of flannel drawers, ten thousand pairs of wool socks, and two thousand blankets." But organizers saw an opportunity to tweak the nose of the Federal government. Lord Wharncliffe, president of the Southern Independence Association, applied to Charles Francis Adams for permission to employ an agent to visit and distribute funds to prisoners. Seward rejected the application on the grounds that the Union was providing for its prisoners, who were being well treated and therefore needed no charity, and because most of the money had been raised by those who had profited directly from illegal trade with the insurgents.[29]

Seward's response only confirmed to the faithful the callousness of the Federal government. It may have eased the wounded pride of Confederate supporters, but it did little for the cause they espoused. Increasingly, Spence, Wharncliffe, Beresford-Hope, and the others turned their attention to supporting exiled Southerners. Ever since the beginning of the war, there had been fairly substantial exile communities in London, Liverpool, Manchester, and smaller provincial towns such as Leamington Spa. The communities worked closely and socialized with their British supporters. Confederate commissioners and other prominent Southerners living in London were frequently and sometimes lavishly entertained. Tremlett's home in Belsize Park was fondly referred to as the "Rebel's Roost." Mason was a regular guest at Beresford-Hope's manor, Bedgebury Park, in Kent and at Beresford-Hope's London home. Confederate soldiers who had escaped to Britain drew on funds held by the Distribution Committee of the Liverpool Southern Club. During a visit to England and the continent by George W. Randolph, the former Confederate secretary of war, in November 1864, he was warmly received by Spence. When the end of the war cut him off from family, and the bank in which he had deposited most of his money collapsed, supporters came to Randolph's aid until he was able to return in September 1866. When Confederate secretary of state Judah Benjamin fled the country, he found a warm welcome among friends and was admitted, he reported, to the "splendor and comfort of an English gentleman's country seat, and with a crowd of titled and fashionable guests." Jefferson Davis had a similar experience when he temporarily settled in Britain following his release from prison. As Spence's son recalled, their home in Liverpool became a temporary home for many Confederate exiles after the war.[30]

To Spence the Confederacy was made up of gallant people fighting a war of independence against a militarily superior foe. "Here is a people shut out from the world," he wrote at the end of the first year of the war, "deprived of all the comforts of life, starting without tools, money, credit, ships or soldiers, disappointed in their political calculations, their commerce annihilated, the value of their property extinguished, over-matched in men and means of warfare, assailed with torrents of abuse, and depressed by a long course of adverse events."[31] In light of these facts, to support the Union was to discredit the British sense of fairness and concern for the underdog. Such lofty views may have hidden the fact that Spence's support was driven by his business failures in 1857 and the fact that he was deeply invested in blockade running activities out of Liverpool. Whatever the personal reasons for his support for the Confederacy, Spence's views resonated among some textile workers in Lancashire, Cheshire, and Derbyshire who had been thrown out of work because of the cotton famine. As far as they were concerned, support should be given to the side that would guarantee a supply of cotton to the mills. But how could one take such a position, opponents wondered, when the Confederacy had deliberately refused to release cotton, or alternatively burned stores of cotton it held, in an attempt to pressure Britain and Europe to recognize its independence. In light of the resulting economic dislocations, the policy of preventing the export of cotton seemed particularly callous. Others viewed the protagonists differently. How could one support the Confederacy, they asked, and not do violence to British abolitionist traditions. More significantly, the majority of those involved in the struggle for political reform were concerned that the experiment in American democracy that they hoped would be emulated in some fashion in Britain was under siege from secession.

Who, then, were the supporters of the Confederacy? J. Sella Martin, an American fugitive slave who spent most of the war years ministering to a working-class congregation in the East End of London, insisted that the Confederacy drew most of its supporters from among the ignorant, who knew little about the true causes of the war; those with financial interests in the South, many of whom had invested heavily in blockade running; those opposed to the extension of the franchise; those who believed that the South had a right to secede; and those who were angered by the North's refusal to openly commit to the emancipation of the slaves. The evidence suggests that Martin was not far off the mark. To this group could be added those Moncure D. Conway, a Virginian exile in London, labeled the "magnates of English literature," men like Carlyle and Charles Kingsley, who were not, he contended, original thinkers. For many in this group the failure of West Indian emancipation was a clear indication of the inability of blacks to function effectively outside the order and discipline of plantation slavery. While few were willing to argue for a continuation of slavery, and all were openly proud of Britain's decision to free its slaves, the freedmen's insistence on a life away from the plantation confirmed for many the race's inability to function effectively without the guiding hand of the European. Support for the Confederacy would ensure that the same mistakes were not repeated in America. Finally, there were those for whom nationalism was an important feature in the debate over the war. For those committed to political reform, America offered an alternative to the restrictive franchise at home. But even while arguing for the adoption of the American model of voting rights, there were few who were willing to abandon what they considered to be Britain's superior system of government.[32] Yet the fact remains that in spite of the range of support the Confederacy attracted, it was singularly unsuccessful in stamping its view of the war on the British public.

The South and the British Left, 1930–1960

HUGH WILFORD

During a symposium on William Faulkner's place in world literature held in 1973 at Texas Tech University, the distinguished southern literary critic Cleanth Brooks analyzed the reception of Faulkner's work in Britain. According to Brooks, who as a former Rhodes Scholar at Oxford University and cultural attaché at the American embassy in London was well qualified to pronounce on the subject, the British critical response to Faulkner was characterized by literary snobbery and an alarming ignorance of even the most basic facts about the American South. A review in the *London Evening News*, for example, misidentified the hero of *Sartoris* as a Virginian; a contributor to *The Sphere* wrongly located the setting of the *Light in August* as Alabama. One British reviewer even placed Faulkner's Oxford in the state of Missouri. "From the viewpoint of the British Isles," Brooks fulminated, "Mississippi is evidently interchangeable with Missouri or Alabama or even Virginia." The cause of this sorry state of affairs, the southern critic concluded, was a combination of amateurish reviewing practices and British intellectuals' habit of deriving their impressions of southern life from biased reports by hostile commentators in the northeastern states. Hence "the British conception of the South is usually not only incomplete but unwittingly prejudiced," with "all the bad features of any second-hand report."[1]

Although Brooks was not writing specifically about left-wing critics, much of what he had to say did apply to the British left's perceptions of the South. "America" had long functioned as a potent but ambiguous symbol in the imagination of British leftists. For nineteenth-century radicals the "Great Republic" had served as an inspiring model of the sort of egalitarian society they hoped to create in the Old World.

By the early 1900s the United States had been transformed before the fascinated British gaze into the most advanced industrial economy in the world, with all the good and bad consequences that entailed. The South, however, with its "peculiar institution" of slavery and predominantly agrarian economy, fitted neither of these images of social and industrial progress. The result was that many British leftists tended either simply to leave it out of their imaginative constructions of "America," or to accept hostile northern descriptions of it as a "benighted region" condemned to social—particularly racial—inequality and economic stagnation. This view was especially popular amongst members of the British communist movement, who nonetheless pinned the blame for southern backwardness on northern capitalism.

This, however, is not the whole story. As I hope to show in a survey of the three decades between 1930 and 1960, the British non-communist left—a category I define broadly to include Labour Party politicians, trade unionists, and literary intellectuals—exhibited a surprisingly complex set of attitudes toward the South. True, the region's economic and social problems tended to be the main concern of most leftists, segregation in particular being a focus of criticism and protest (much, of course, as slavery had preoccupied British abolitionists a century earlier). However, it is not quite accurate to say that this was due to overreliance on secondhand sources of information: the British left produced its own commentators on American affairs in this period, many of whom possessed firsthand experience of the southern states. These observers were not solely interested in race relations, moreover, commenting on other aspects of the region, such as its party politics, industry, and literary culture. Furthermore, when they did write about race, the opinions they expressed did not merely reproduce those of northerners, but reflected British values and experiences as well as other extraneous factors peculiar to the period. Nor was there only one viewpoint on the South: internal doctrinal, social, and cultural divisions within the British left meant that there was a range of often mutually contradictory perspectives. The "South," then, was no more stable or unproblematic a category in the British leftist imagination than "America" itself.

Labour politicians were present in the South throughout this period, and behaved there much as one would expect foreign socialists to behave: that is, they protested social inequality, forged links with white liberals, and agitated the race issue. During a trip to Kentucky in 1932, the young leftist firebrand and Member of Parliament for North Lanark Jennie Lee visited an encampment of striking miners and was detained by the local police. Apparently undeterred by this experience, Lee returned to the South, more precisely Marked Tree, Arkansas, in February 1935 and led a column of sharecroppers on a march through the town singing "We Shall Not Be Moved."[2] Visiting Atlanta, Georgia, in the winter of 1949 during a speaking tour of the United States arranged by Americans for Democratic Action, the MP for Coventry East and maverick socialist intellectual Richard Crossman met with "liberal and Labor organizers" who told him about the "terrible difficulties" they faced: the racism of the white industrial workforce, the "self-segregation" of blacks, and the "peonage" of agricultural workers.[3] In 1952 the flamboyant journalist and Labour MP Woodrow Wyatt shocked his white hosts in Natchez, Mississippi (a town which reminded him of "a tropical Cheltenham"), by addressing a meeting of black citizens and "urging them not to be afraid to use their votes to advance themselves." How his audience received this speech is unfortunately not recorded, but Wyatt believed that the Natchez whites forgave him his "English eccentricity." Evidently Labour politicians' privileged status as foreign guests, combined perhaps with the South's historic Anglophilia, gave them latitude to flout the racial etiquette of Jim Crow in ways which might otherwise have provoked violent retaliation. Certainly there is little sense in Wyatt's recollections of his having run any personal risk in taking the action he did.[4]

Still, it would not do to exaggerate the British Labour presence in the South. During this period the overall number of transatlantic trips by Labour MPs probably increased: in addition to the American lecture circuit, on which European leftists were surprisingly popular, there were the official exchange programs instituted during the early years of the Cold War, which tended to target members of the non-communist left (Wyatt, for example, was in Mississippi on a Smith-Mundt "Leader

Specialist" award). However, British Labourites tended to steer clear of the South or, if they did visit the region, stick to the same well-worn itinerary, that is, Charleston, New Orleans, Atlanta, and, at a pinch, Montgomery or Birmingham. Why this should have been is not entirely clear: either the lecture invitations were not forthcoming—performances such as Wyatt's can hardly have endeared Labour MPs as a class to southern white elites—or the visitors themselves elected to go to parts of the United States where the American labor movement was better developed. In any case, the result was that while a sizeable minority of Labour MPs did have firsthand personal experience of the South, the majority had to resort to other sources of information about the region, such as the observations of London School of Economics professor and party chairman Harold Laski.

If any individual personified the British left's ambivalent fascination with America, it was Laski. A regular visitor to America since a spell during the 1920s spent teaching at Harvard, a personal friend of a number of prominent American liberals, including Franklin D. Roosevelt himself, and an unabashed admirer of America's egalitarian political ideals, he was also a rigid Marxist whose outspoken criticism of U.S. capitalism earned him the sobriquet "the Lenin of the British Reds."[5] Both these impulses were evident in *The American Democracy*, a massive study of U.S. civilization published in 1949 that courted comparisons with earlier American commentaries by such European observers as Tocqueville and Bryce. It was, however, the book's Marxist theoretical framework that caught the attention of contemporary reviewers. Arthur M. Schlesinger Jr., for example, dismissed the work as an anti-American polemic by a British fellow-traveler; according to Alistair Cooke, Laski's portrayal of America "had the subtlety of a Diego Rivera painting."[6] Despite such barbs, *The American Democracy* was widely read in Britain and exercised a strong influence in Labour Party circles.

The passages on the South in Laski's tome are predictably critical and clearly informed by the author's Marxist convictions. The region is constantly portrayed as an economic colony of the industrial North, and its racial problems as basically class phenomena. Racism amongst "poor whites," for example, is depicted as an ideological instrument used by capitalist elites to prevent the emergence of interracial, working-class solidarity.[7] As long as northern capitalists and their allies in the South continued to exploit the region and its workers, so Laski's Marxist logic went, Jim Crow and other forms of racial inequality would remain. This is not to say, however, that the portrait of the South contained in *The American Democracy* is altogether lacking in complexity or nuance. Indeed, it is arguable that Laski's Marxist approach combined with his undoubted knowledge of American affairs to give him an unusual and valuable perspective on southern life. In one section he engages in an incisive critique of the group of conservative writers and literary critics known variously as the "Fugitives," "Agrarians," or "New Critics" (although he does not identify them as such, he refers by name to John Crowe Ransom, Allen Tate, R. P. Blackmur, and Yvor Winters). While perhaps unduly harsh in some of his declarations—"they are actors in a dead play, performed in a theater where there is no audience"—Laski is highly astute in ascribing to the apparently asocial New Criticism a political motivation—that is, a "profound abhorrence of contemporary America" not dissimilar to that felt by U.S. Marxists.[8] In another lengthy passage inquiring into the causes of the "victimization" of the southern black, which draws extensively on Gunnar Myrdal's *An American Dilemma,* Laski repeatedly rejects arguments based on racist assumptions about "a biological inferiority in the Negro as compared with the white man," seeking his explanation instead in environmental and historical circumstances. Nor, despite his fundamental pessimism about the South's future, did Laski fail to detect signs of positive change, such as the presence in the region of white liberals (he names as examples the journalists Virginius Dabney and Jonathan Daniels) and, more important, recent advances by blacks themselves. "The Negro, in spite of all handicaps . . . is more conscious of his powers, more confident of his achievements, less willing to accept the relation of servility than at any previous time."[9] In an era of growing world-wide resistance to racial oppression, the South would, Laski predicted, be hard put to preserve its racial regime forever.

Despite the prescience of these observations, the most impressive passages about the South in *The American Democracy* concern not its future but its past development. In these Laski, perhaps because of (rather than in spite of) his preoccupation with economic and social factors, displays a surprisingly good grasp of new directions in southern historical scholarship. For example, in a paragraph about the antebellum period, he contests Ulrich B. Phillips's claim—still influential in the 1940s—that slavery was a benign institution that commanded the loyalty of southern blacks, drawing on the recent work by Herbert Aptheker, *Negro Slave Revolts in the United States,* to portray instead a region constantly troubled by slave resistance. A similar awareness of changing historiographical fashion is demonstrated when the discussion turns to the Reconstruction era. A 1939 *Journal of Southern History* article by the racial liberal and proto-"revisionist" historian Francis B. Simkins, "New Viewpoints of Southern Reconstruction," is cited in order to disprove the "Dunning School's" contention that the Republican governments established in the South immediately after the Civil War were unusually incompetent, vindictive, and corrupt. "Few of them even approached the Ferguson standard in Texas, or the Huey Long standard in Louisiana, or the Talmadge standard in Georgia," Laski points out. Finally, in considering the post-Reconstruction period of southern history, Laski draws on C. Vann Woodward's *Tom Watson, Agrarian Rebel* to illustrate his argument that poor white racism was deliberately encouraged by "the old ruling class and the 'robber barons' of the Gilded Age."[10] Laski ends his survey of southern history by praising the continuing determination of the region's black inhabitants to improve their position despite the barriers erected against them. In short, however much Laski's Marxian mindset might have vitiated his appreciation of other aspects of American society and culture, the analysis of the South's past presented in *The American Democracy* positively benefited from it.

This is not to say that Labour observers of the South always achieved such understanding and insight. Stereotypical notions of the region and its inhabitants derived from literature- and film-clouded British perceptions: as a youthful Tony Benn admitted on arriving in Austin, Texas, in 1947, "one's first day in the real South presents a temptation to look round for a type." Even a racial liberal such as Bryan Magee, who was so disturbed by segregation that he had difficulty sleeping while he was in the South, could write of meeting a "jet black" cook on a plantation outside Charleston who "rolled her eyes."[11] This susceptibility to racist images of southern blacks might also have had something to do with Britain's own history of imperialism and colonialism, in which the Labour Party was thoroughly implicated. While the late 1940s witnessed a historic wave of decolonization presided over by the Attlee government, prominent Labour politicians, such as Foreign Secretary Ernest Bevin and, for that matter, several on the party's left wing, remained captivated by Britain's imperial past and paternalistic attitudes toward "colored" peoples. Indeed, the American left was often highly critical of Labour foreign policy on this score, particularly with regard to the Middle East. One cannot escape the suspicion that some of the attacks on Jim Crow issuing from Britain in this period were prompted, in part at least, by a desire to respond in kind to such criticisms. "Are you not a bit out of date in bothering so much about British imperialism, which is in retreat even in India, Burma and Indonesia?" Kingsley Martin, editor of the influential left-wing British news magazine *The New Statesman and Nation,* asked American liberal Max Lerner in 1946, with perhaps excessive defensiveness. "What about your own racialism?"[12]

Another factor complicating Labour perceptions of the South's race problems was the growing size during the 1950s of Britain's own black population, which increased from almost nothing at the beginning of the decade to over two hundred thousand by its end. Although at first slow to come to terms with the implications for Britain of this development, Labour politicians were forced by the race riots which erupted in London's Notting Hill district in 1957 to acknowledge the existence of racial inequality at home as well as abroad. In May 1959 the *New Statesman* carried a report on a tour of Notting Hill by the labor secretary of the National Association for the Advancement of Colored People (NAACP), Herbert Hill, who painted an extremely grim picture of race relations in the area, noting *inter alia* the high incidence of police brutality toward black residents, the poor living conditions endured by immigrants, and the inaction of local white liberals.[13] The realization that Britain itself was not immune from racial conflict prompted a more complex, modulated understanding of America's problems amongst British Labourites.

Labour impressions of the South also need to be viewed in the context of internal party conflicts in which "America" played a vital symbolic role. Hitherto the focus has been mainly on the Labour left: Lee and Crossman, for example, were both members of the left-wing group known as the "Bevanites," named for its leader during the 1950s, Aneurin Bevan (indeed, Lee was married to Bevan). Typically, the Bevanites tended to be critical of the United States generally, partly because of their conviction that the Attlee government had been too quick to accept American leadership in the Cold War, and partly because they perceived America to be hostile to the kind of socialist institutions they were seeking to create at home in Britain.[14] However, Bevanism was not the only doctrinal impulse within the Labour Party. More powerful because it enjoyed the support of the leadership and the unions, and more vigorous intellectually, was the group of young intellectuals known either as the "revisionists," due to their desire to modernize party doctrine, or the "Gaitskellites," after their leader, Hugh Gaitskell.[15] In contrast with the Bevanites, the Gaitskellites were ardent supporters of the Atlantic alliance in the Cold War and looked to America as a source of inspiration for British socialism (both tendencies for which, incidentally, they received discreet support from U.S. government agencies, about which more below). Hence they were less inclined to draw attention to the racial problems of the southern states and more optimistic about the region's future than the Labour left.[16]

If Harold Laski was the chief interpreter of American affairs to the Labour left, that role was performed for the Gaitskellite wing of the party by its leading theoretician, the former Oxford don and future foreign secretary Anthony Crosland. Throughout the 1950s, Crosland constantly cited the writings of American social scientists and the example of U.S. society itself as he strove to bend the Labour program away from its traditional concern with economic nationalization (Crosland was persuaded by the arguments of A. A. Berle and John Kenneth Galbraith that economic ownership was now less of an issue than managerial control) and toward a greater emphasis on social equality.[17] This project, whose origins can be traced back to the 1930s and the work of revisionist Labour intellectual Evan Durbin, culminated in 1956 with the seminal Gaitskellite text, *The Future of Socialism*. In this Crosland invoked America "as a test-case of the factors affecting social equality," noting in particular the country's lack of a hereditary ruling-class, the absence of proletarian consciousness, and the generally "natural and unrestrained" atmosphere (all points which implicitly contradicted Laski's class-based analysis of American development). Although contemporary Bevanite allegations that Crosland was uncritically pro-American were unfair—he was at pains to point out that "social equality can quite well be combined with a reckless foreign policy, . . . social intolerance, and all manner of reprehensible things"— nonetheless his admiration for the United States, and concomitant reluctance to dwell on its bad points, shines through. Hence there is no acknowledgment of the existence of segregation in the southern states, only a throw-away reference to "Negro emancipation" as if it were an historical inevitability that had already been largely accomplished.[18] Jim Crow simply did not fit with the image of "America" Crosland was seeking to present to British socialists.

This is not to say that Crosland lacked firsthand experience of the South. During a lengthy visit to the United States in 1954, he toured several southern states and recorded his impressions of them in an unpublished diary. The diary is unusual in the Labour literature on the region in that it barely mentions segregation, concentrating instead on aspects of southern society often ignored by British observers. Thus Crosland was extremely interested in southern party politics, remarking on the historic regional hegemony of the Democrats and their current electoral impregnability, but predicting that the situation could not last indefinitely because the "rapid rate of industrial growth" and corresponding increase in the strength of organized labour would drive conservative businessmen out of the party and into the arms of the Republicans. Another feature of southern politics which attracted Crosland's attention was the impact on the region of McCarthyism (a major concern for all European observers of the United States in this period, admittedly), or rather the lack of it. "South v. good—virtually untouched by hysteria," he noted in his diary. "Press and politicians solidly anti-McC., . . . little loyalty activity." Finally, Crosland wrote of the southern states' diverse architectural and natural attractions, the "lovely ironwork" and "exquisite patios" of New Orleans's French Quarter, for example, and the "tropical flora and fauna" of Florida "in a complete American setting."[19] Read next to other Labour writing about the South, this interest in aspects of the region other than its race relations is distinctly refreshing. Crosland's freedom from Marxist dogma and the anti-American tendencies of the Labour left made him receptive to impressions usually unavailable to British Labourites. On the other hand, considering his commitment to social equality and the timing of his visit, which coincided with the Supreme Court's *Brown* decision, his lack of concern about Jim Crow and the campaign against it is equally striking.[20]

The Gaitskellites' noninterventionist approach to the South's race problems was shared by their principal allies in their fight against Bevanism, the leaders of the British trade union movement. Take, for example, the attitude of Walter Citrine, general secretary of the Trades Union Congress (TUC) from 1926 to 1946, as revealed in a diary he kept while touring the United States in 1940. Arriving in New Orleans, where he was due to address the annual convention of the American Federation of Labor (AFL), Citrine was immediately struck by evidence of racial discrimination: certain drug stores' refusal to serve black customers, the whites-only guest policy of the convention hotel, the segregation of audiences at public meetings. However, apart from a passage in which he refers with obvious distaste to a display of early nineteenth-century posters advertising a slave sale, Citrine appears not to have been particularly bothered by New Orleans's racial regime, reporting it in the same detached, wry, faintly condescending tone he used to describe the city's architecture and transport system.[21]

This attitude—which, as will be discussed shortly, carried on into the 1950s—was produced by a number of factors. In spite of its association with socialist ideals, the British trade union movement was not especially interested in the welfare of racial minorities. Indeed, in the past it had tended to perform what labor historian Kevin Morgan has described as an "imperial role," assisting the British state in the administration of Empire, even helping colonial officials curb the militancy of "colored" workers.[22] Moreover, the TUC had a warm fraternal relationship with the AFL, which dated back to the previous century. Although this cooled somewhat during the early years of the Cold War, a reluctance remained amongst senior British unionists to raise issues which might embarrass their American comrades. There was also the tactical consideration that mention of segregation might provoke counter-criticism of the TUC's role in the Commonwealth countries, an issue about which the British felt increasingly sensitive during the 1950s.[23] Finally, the fact that both the American and British communist movements had been so outspoken in support of racial equality tended to discredit that cause in the eyes of the TUC's strongly anti-communist leadership. Again, the rise of the Cold War in the 1940s and 1950s, and the growing salience of segregation as a theme of communist propaganda, reinforced this tendency. More often than not, when labor leaders in Britain did bring up Jim Crow, it was to express their misgivings about the damage it was doing to the anti-communist cause in the Cold War.[24]

When one turns away from the leadership to the rank-and-file of the British trade union movement, however, a different picture emerges. Several historians have remarked on the generally sympathetic welcome given by working-class men and women to black GIs stationed in Britain during the Second World War. While the authorities attempted to impose their own version of segregation on the U.S. armed forces and British civilians, the latter objected to the discriminatory treatment suffered by African-American troops and even on occasion intervened to defend them from violent attacks by whites.[25] It is possible to interpret these incidents as belonging to a tradition of working-class British opposition to American racial injustice which predated the war and carried on after it. The files of the TUC contain a number of communications from member unions and trades councils urging the organization to protest what were perceived as racially motivated miscarriages of justice in the United States. In 1935, for example, the organizing secretary of the Association of Women Clerks and Secretaries wrote to Walter Citrine urging that the TUC general council petition the governor of Alabama to exercise clemency in the case of the Scottsboro boys and donate money to the defense fund organized by the NAACP.[26] (Significantly, the TUC, which had never heard of the NAACP, turned down both of these requests, arguing that the matter was best left to the AFL.[27]) Similar letters were sent throughout the 1950s, for example about the acquittal of the white men accused of murdering the Chicago boy Emmett Till in Money, Mississippi, the death sentence passed on Jimmy Wilson for stealing less than two dollars from an elderly white woman in Marion, Alabama, and the arrest and imprisonment of steelworker and NAACP official Ashbury Howard in Bessemer, Alabama, after he had organized a local voter registration drive.[28] (Again, the TUC either declined or hesitated to take a position in all of these cases.[29]) One case that attracted particular attention in Britain, as in other European countries, because of its apparent combination of racism and McCarthyism, was that of Paul Robeson, the black singer, actor, and radical denied a passport by the U.S. government. Trades councils in Croydon, Birmingham, and Manchester exhorted the TUC to intervene on Robeson's behalf so that "he should be free to travel and so provide pleasure to thousands of people with his songs."[30] Congress officials, however, suspected communist agitation of the issue—the secretary of the Organization Department implied as much when he sought assurances from the secretary of the Birmingham council that his "delegates, in being critical of the 'mote' in the eye of the USA, are not unmindful of the 'beam' still in the eye of the USSR"[31]—and responded, predictably, in the negative: "It is not the policy of the General Council in such matters to interfere with whatever action the American Trade Union Movement might consider it appropriate to take."[32]

If the TUC leadership found working-class British criticism of American racial injustice a minor irritant, for U.S. government officials engaged in a global contest with Soviet propagandists for "hearts and minds" it was a major embarrassment. In her recent, valuable study of

Cold War civil rights, Mary L. Dudziak shows how much importance the State Department and other interested government agencies attached to monitoring and combating negative foreign perceptions of American race relations in the early Cold War period. For U.S. officials in Britain there seem to have been at least three separate moments during the 1940s and 1950s when this issue appeared particularly worrisome. The first of these occurred immediately after the Second World War, when, against a background of growing British resentment of America's all-too-evident postwar political and economic superiority, the sentencing to death of two fourteen-year-old boys, Charles Trudell and James Lewis Jr., in Jackson, Mississippi, for the murder of their white boss provoked a flood of protests to the U.S. embassy in London. (Despite calls for him to intervene, Labour foreign secretary—and former trade union leader—Ernest Bevin refused to involve himself.)[33] Although British anti-Americanism died down somewhat during the late 1940s, it revived after 1950 as a result of the outbreak of the Korean War, the rise of McCarthyism, and the emergence of the Bevanites as a distinct political faction. In March 1951 the British Communist Party attempted to harness these various developments to its cause by publishing a pamphlet written by the *Daily Worker*'s foreign editor, Derek Kartun, entitled *America Go Home*. "We don't want you here," exclaimed Kartun. "We can get along in our quiet way without Coca-Cola, American admirals and American GIs.... Defense of freedom? What squalid hypocrisy from the butchers of Korea and the Negro-baiting rulers of the Southern States! ... So get out, America! ... Take your bankers and industrialists home to Detroit and New York. And there, in good time, the American working class will know how to deal with them."[34]

The atmosphere was ripe for communist exploitation of the race issue. According to a report home by a London embassy official, communist "front" groups "went to town" over two egregious cases involving black male defendants accused of raping white women, Willie McGee and the Martinsville seven. The embassy responded by reproducing handouts which were sent to individuals and groups who had written in protest and playing host to delegations of students and other demonstrators who had gathered in Grosvenor Square.[35] Again the furor died down, probably more as a result of the dissipation of the forces generating anti-Americanism in the early 1950s and advances for black civil rights in the United States such as the 1954 *Brown* decision than the efforts of the embassy officials. In any event, the next crisis did not occur until 1957, when Governor Orval E. Faubus's attempt to prevent the desegregation of Central High School in Little Rock, Arkansas, heavily reported in the European press, "struck hard at American prestige in Britain" and "heightened British condemnation of American discrimination against the Negro" (as the London embassy's public affairs officer put it).[36] According to the results of extensive polling of European public opinion commissioned by the United States Information Agency's Office of Research and Intelligence in the wake of Little Rock, 66 percent of British respondents had a "bad" or "very bad" opinion of the way in which the United States treated its black citizens, the second worst result in Europe after Norway.[37]

An apt illustration of both rank-and-file British anti-racism and official U.S. concern about it is provided by an incident that occurred in south Wales shortly before the Little Rock crisis. In June 1956 a junior official by the name of Neil M. Ruge was dispatched by the American consulate in Wales to report on a miners' gala in Cardiff. Although he did not attend the main meeting due to fears his presence might arouse anti-American feeling, Ruge did witness the gala parade of six thousand miners led by, amongst others, the communist general secretary of the National Union of Mineworkers, Arthur Horner, and Aneurin Bevan himself. The main theme of the parade, Ruge soon realized, was Paul Robeson's victimization by the U.S. government. This was evident not only in placards—the only ones carried in the parade—proclaiming, "This great voice must not be stilled," and, "Let Robeson sing in Wales," but also a "float repeating the Robeson theme."

> A man with face blackened, representing Robeson, stood in front of a table around which were seated several persons labelled "Congress" and "anti-progressives." Robeson would make pleading gestures to these persons who

would shake their heads negatively and make contemptuous gestures with their hands. One of the men around the table was wearing a Ku-Klux-Klan hood and had a hangman's rope in his hands.

It is open to question whether this *tableau*, with its politically subversive use of black-face and ingenious symbolic conflation of anti-capitalism, anti-McCarthyism, and anti-racism, was a spontaneous creation of the Welsh miners. A local police officer with whom Ruge spoke after the gala suspected that communists had imposed the Robeson theme on the parade "through the apathy of the rank and file." The American consular official was also struck by the float's failure to evoke the enthusiasm of the spectators it was passing. "The float received a faint smattering of applause from one group of women," he reported, "but they had applauded everything else indiscriminately. I think many spectators were a bit puzzled about the significance of the float."[38]

Ruge, of course, was predisposed to suspect a communist hand in anti-American activities. It is also possible that the spectators' appearance of political disengagement might have had something to do with the presence a few yards away of someone probably trying hard not to look like a U.S. government official. Robeson was, after all, a well-known and highly regarded figure in the mining communities of south Wales, where he had lived briefly during the late 1930s while making the film *Proud Valley*.[39] Nevertheless, Ruge's report does point toward an important truth about the popular British response to American racial problems. It was not a simple case of labor leaders acquiescing in Jim Crow while the rank-and-file opposed it. To begin with, one has to take account of the undoubted existence of working-class racism in Britain. Outside of the port towns, whose inhabitants had some personal contact with people of color, popular attitudes on racial matters tended to be based on ignorance and prejudice. White women who formed relationships with black immigrants were ghettoized, becoming for all intents and purposes "black" themselves; the mothers of babies fathered by black GIs suffered even greater ostracism.[40] After several years spent working in Britain as the London correspondent of *Newsweek*, American journalist Fred Vanderschmidt concluded that while the British "are not very color-conscious" generally, "in individual cases, they 'draw the line' as effectively as does a citizen of the American South." The support shown for eminent African Americans such as Robeson was, Vanderschmidt suspected, in part at least "conscious company manners, for our [that is, white Americans'] benefit."[41] Working-class ignorance about non-whites was dispelled to a certain extent by the black immigration of the 1950s. However, this phenomenon also led to increased racism amongst those in competition with the immigrants for jobs, housing, and other resources, as was evidenced by the rise of "nationalist" political organizations in the poorer neighborhoods of London during the latter part of the decade.[42] Moreover, as one U.S. embassy official put it, "unfortunate racial incidents in Britain itself" (a veiled reference to the Notting Hill riots) had the effect of "making the British less prone to criticize America" on the same score.[43] Finally, although difficult to measure precisely, one should not discount the effect on British popular opinion of official American propaganda designed to paint a flattering image of U.S. race relations, such as lectures, publications, and the kind of face-to-face meetings mentioned above.

Most effective of all in improving foreign perceptions of America was that central tool of cultural diplomacy, the exchange visit. Although the best-known U.S. exchange programs targeted elite academic opinion, this period saw the launch of several schemes designed to dispel popular misconceptions about American society and culture by bringing trade unionists and industrial workers to the United States. The reports filed by these visitors at the end of their awards offer one of the few means available of gauging the reactions of ordinary Britons to firsthand experience of Cold War America. In particular, they reveal a surprising variety of responses to the southern states. As ever, race was a major preoccupation. During a visit to the headquarters of the Tennessee Valley Authority at Knoxville—for obvious reasons, a popular destination for British socialists[44]—Derek Gladwin, a worker in the "Grimsby fish industry" who had received a travel grant from the English-Speaking Union, witnessed "obvious discrimination against the Negro" for what he claimed was "the first time in [his] life." He also noticed signs of growing white resistance to desegregation, such as the spread of the White Citizens' Councils—"the infamous Ku Klux Klan . . . under another guise"—and predicted that "the position of the Negro in the South is going to get worse before it gets better." Nonetheless, he was basically optimistic about the long-term future of southern race relations, noting that "great strides are now being made to integrate the races" and that "the very great majority of the American people abhor the color bar as much as we do in this country."[45] This optimism was shared by other exchange visitors, such as Scottish unionist and recipient of a Smith-Mundt Leader Specialist award John Lang, who emerged from talks with "Negro and trade union leaders" convinced that, "although racial discrimination still exists in most areas, much has been accomplished in recent years."[46] Even Woodrow Wyatt, the Labour MP and Smith-Mundt grantee who had urged blacks in Natchez to exercise their voting rights, was struck by "the substantial advance which the Negroes had made in the United States in recent years."[47]

However, racial equality was not the sole criterion representatives of the British labor movement used to judge southern progress. For the workers who visited the region as members of one or another of the "Productivity Teams" organized by the Anglo-American Council on Productivity (a Marshall Plan initiative intended to spread U.S. industrial practices in Europe), it was rather the economic success of the "New South," measured specifically in terms of wage levels and factory working conditions, that was their main concern. On the whole, the Productivity Teams liked what they were shown. "We never saw any workers who seemed to be overloaded with their system of work assignment," reported Martha MacCormack, a member of the cotton spinning team from Ashton-under-Lyne, near Manchester, after having visited mills in Greensboro, North Carolina, Charlotte, North Carolina, and Birmingham, Alabama.[48] The cotton yarn doubling team, whose itinerary took in Gastonia, North Carolina, Clover, South Carolina, and Sylacauga, Alabama, formed a similarly positive impression of the southern textile industry, observing that although the workforce was not unionized in any of the factories it toured, nonetheless pay and conditions were "at least equal to those in the Northern mills."[49]

Judging by the reports they filed, the workers on the Productivity Teams do not appear to have been much interested in questions of race. One report that did refer to the racial composition of the southern industrial workforce, that of the fertilizer production team, described black factory-hands as "willing workers with a simple childlike outlook on life" who were only employed on skilled processes after they "had been reduced to the simplest possible rule of thumb instructions."[50] In other words, while many rank-and-file members of the British labor movement opposed American racism and viewed the South almost exclusively in terms of its racial regime, others shared paternalistic assumptions about black inferiority or placed other concerns, more immediately relevant to their own personal interests, above the race issue.

Finally, what of leftist British intellectuals and their responses to the American South? Once again, it was the region's race problems that drew the most comment, and once again that comment was predominantly negative. Touring the United States at the beginning of the twentieth century, H. G. Wells was dismayed by the treatment of blacks he witnessed in the southern states, comparing it with the "brutal and stupid aggressions" perpetrated by white colonists in South Africa. At the same time, he was impressed, not to say moved, by the quiet determination of Booker T. Washington, whom he met over lunch in Boston, and the black Chicagoans, with whom he attended a meeting at Jane Addams's Hull House, to lead decent, civilized lives despite the obstacles placed in their path. "The tragedy of colour," Wells predicted, in words reminiscent of W. E. B. Du Bois (whose *The Souls of Black Folk* he read during his visit), would play "a by no means small part in the working out of America's destinies."[51] George Orwell, whose fascination with the United States and readiness to write about it were not diminished by the fact he never actually visited the place, was similarly critical of Jim Crow and sympathetic with the plight of southern blacks. He summarized the cases of racial injustice described in a *New Republic* supplement, *The Negro: His Future in America*, for the benefit of readers of his *Tribune* column, "As I Please," and chastised the leading British academic expert on American affairs, D. W. Brogan, in an *Observer* review of his book *The American Problem*, for having "lightly skated over" the fact that "millions of Negroes are both half-starved and disenfranchised."[52]

Most outspoken, though, in his condemnation of American race relations and advocacy of the black freedom struggle was Bertrand Russell. In a lecture delivered at New York's Rand School in 1942, the grand old man of British philosophy—whose authority to pronounce on such matters was perhaps slightly greater than that of other British observers on account of the fact that he had resided in America for a large part of the 1930s—claimed that "the Negroes" constituted "the greatest failure of democracy in the United States" and explicitly denounced such practices as sharecropping, segregation, and lynching.[53] Later, during the 1960s, Russell would achieve widespread notoriety in the United States for issuing such inflammatory statements as his message to the 1963 March on Washington, in which he likened America's oppression of its black population to Hitler's persecution of the Jews, publicly endorsing the views of such black revolutionaries as James Boggs, and linking his support of the African-American cause with his opposition to "imperialist" U.S. foreign policies. When Martin Luther King Jr. protested against American actions in Vietnam, the *Los Angeles Times* characterized him as "in danger of becoming the Bertrand Russell of the United States."[54]

Moving away from race, British reactions to southern culture, particularly southern literature, do not appear, at least at first sight, to have been much more favorable. The best documented case—Cleanth Brooks's essay on the subject has already been cited—is the adverse critical reception accorded the fiction of William Faulkner. The Oxford writer's first novel, *Soldier's Pay*, published in 1926, received generally positive reviews in Britain. Later works, however, were either ignored or criticized for alleged stylistic obscurity, technical incompetence, or moral depravity. Here, for example, is George Orwell on *The Hamlet* in 1940: "After a careful reading . . . I must record that I have quite failed to discover the plot of the story. All I can say is that it is about some people somewhere in the southern States of America, people with supremely hideous names—names like Flem Snopes and Eck Snopes—who sit about on the steps of village stores, chewing tobacco, swindling one another in small business deals, and from time to time committing a rape or a murder. A second reading... might extract something more definite, but it is my honest opinion that it would not be worthwhile."[55] Similar opinions were voiced by other *literati* on the British non-communist left, among them Cyril Connolly (whose position as editor of the foremost British literary review of 1940s, *Horizon*, gave his critical judgement considerable clout), C. Day Lewis, and J. B. Priestley.[56] The latter, whose critiques of U.S. "mass culture"—or, as he called it, "Admass"—earned him the journalistic reputation of being "the man who hates America," was equally critical of nineteenth-century southern literature, airily dismissing it as "a doubtful legend of romantic gestures and lazy living."[57]

This is not the only evidence to support Brooks's allegations of British literary snobbishness and over-reliance on secondhand judgements. Witness, for example, the contents of a special 1947 issue of *Horizon* on the American cultural scene, which were drawn overwhelmingly from the group of critics known as the "New York Intellectuals."[58] However, Brooks's critique omits certain intrinsic features of intellectual life in Britain which complicated and, to a certain extent, mitigated literary leftists' attitudes toward the South. Reverting to the perennial question of race, the same passages in which H. G. Wells criticized southern treatment of African Americans were loaded with references to "these gentle, human, dark-skinned people" and other expressions of paternalistic British racism. Indeed, Wells seems not to have felt much sympathy for the plight of the majority of American blacks—"a pleasant, smiling, acquiescent folk" who appeared to him "fairly content with their inferiority"—reserving it instead for the "tainted white... who is perhaps as English as you or I, with just a touch of color."[59] Bertrand Russell had to overcome a set of similar attitudes—"It seems on the whole fair to regard negroes as on the average inferior to white men," he had written during the 1920s—before arriving at the position he laid out at the Rand School in 1942.[60] Nor, despite his radical public stance, did Russell feel altogether at ease with the militant direction taken by the African-American freedom struggle in the 1960s, for example disagreeing with James Boggs over the question of whether the movement should abandon nonviolence, a suggestion which conflicted with his much-cherished pacifism.[61]

For George Orwell (whose own racial attitudes have been the subject of recent intellectual controversy), the oppression of blacks in the American South could be understood properly only if viewed through a socialist prism, "as a single facet of the world-wide problem of color" which had been produced by "the capitalist system." As the situation currently stood, white workers were prevented by "nationalism and race-hatred" from realizing the extent to which their own fate was bound up with that of "colored labor."[62] Orwell therefore urged his readers to rid themselves of racial prejudice and guard against the imposition on Britain of a "color bar" by a minority of "color snobs."[63] This also helps explain why he was irritated by the tendency of British socialists noted later by journalist Fred Vanderschmidt to criticize American race relations while failing to acknowledge similar problems closer to home. "People in Britain vy high-minded abt American treatment of Negroes, but cf. conditions in South Africa," reads an entry in his political notebook. "Meanwhile we profit indirectly from what happens in S. Africa, in Jamaica, in Malaya etc. But these places are separated from us *by water*. On this last fact the essential hypocrisy of the British labor movement is based."[64]

Similarly, the British response to southern literary culture was not merely one of resistance and rejection. As Mick Gidley has pointed out, there were "British voices raised in appreciation" of Faulkner's fiction (those belonging to Arnold Bennett and V. S. Pritchett, for example) from the beginning, while the novelist's reputation gained growing academic recognition in Britain from the mid-1960s.[65] However, it is in the realm of literary criticism that the British encounter with the South proved to be at its most complex and, arguably, consequential. Harold Laski's opinion of the New Critics might have been low, but not all British responses to southern intellectual life were so negative. During the 1930s Allen Tate brokered an alliance between the Agrarians and the Distributists, a group of conservative English intellectuals led by G. K. Chesterton and Hilaire Belloc, that culminated in the symposium *Who Owns America?*[66] In the postwar period the New Critics enjoyed equally cordial relations with members of the Bloomsbury literary establishment, which had been left-leaning during the Depression but was now apolitical or, as in the case of Stephen Spender, editor of the CIA-financed *Encounter,* supportive of the American cause in the Cold War. Again, it was Tate who was the main link (just as he was between the New Critics and the leftist New York Intellectuals), befriending Spender (who briefly hoped that the southerner might become his American co-editor at *Encounter*) and such younger critics as Frank Kermode (who later succeeded Spender as *Encounter*'s British editor).[67] Along with one or two New York Intellectuals, the New Critics were recognized in 1950s Britain as the "leading practitioners" of literary criticism in America.[68]

In the surprising absence of any studies of this subject by literary scholars, I would like to close by making a few tentative suggestions from a historical perspective as to the reasons for the New Criticism's prestige in early Cold War Britain. The first is that there were clear resemblances between the theory and methods of the New Critics and the school of literary criticism then gaining ascendancy in Britain, that associated with F. R. Leavis and the magazine *Scrutiny.* Both prioritized the "close reading" of isolated, decontextualized literary texts; both constructed literature as a saving remnant of civilization or receptacle of humane values in a hostile modern world; both even looked back to a prelapsarian moment of cultural wholeness before the onset of modernity—the antebellum South in the case of the New Critics and the "organic community" in the case of the Leavisites. This last feature in particular can perhaps be traced back to the two schools' common origins in the criticism of T. S. Eliot.[69]

Second, the New Criticism's privileging of Modernist over other literary texts fit well with the tastes of such Bloomsbury writers as Stephen Spender, which during the 1950s were being challenged by new anti-Modernist literary impulses originating in the British provinces, namely the "Movement" poets and the "Angry Young Men." Indeed, it has been argued by British cultural historian Alan Sinfield that the New Criticism was enlisted by Spender and other Bloomsburyites in an effort to reassert their cultural authority in the face of this challenge. Even if one does not accept Sinfield's argument, it is hard to deny that the revival enjoyed by Modernism in Britain after the late 1950s—and the resulting canonization of Modernist texts in the curricula of the rapidly expanding British universities—was underpinned to some extent by New Critical ideas and practices.[70] The irony was that a body of criticism which had originated as a provincial literary movement in America was now helping to defeat a provincial literary movement in Britain.

Finally, as with other exchanges between the South and the British non-communist left in this period, the effect of the Cold War must be taken into account. Lawrence H. Schwartz has already shown that the dramatic improvement of William Faulkner's literary reputation which occurred in the late 1940s and early 1950s was produced partly by Cold War conditions.[71] More recently, Frances Stonor Saunders has documented the links between John Crowe Ransom, *Kenyon Review*, and the CIA's effort in the "Cultural Cold War."[72] Again, it would not do to overstate the significance of these factors: to do so is to risk underestimating the autonomous power of intellectual discourse and lapsing into a kind of Cold War determinism. Nonetheless, it is difficult to deny that there were correspondences between the New Criticism and the aesthetic requirements of the U.S. effort in the Cultural Cold War—the common insistence on the formal demands of culture, for example, and the valorization of certain American Modernists, such as Faulkner— just as two of the principal "conductors" (to use Sinfield's helpful term) of Modernist American texts and New Critical ideas into Britain, Spender and Kermode, were linked to the CIA's cultural apparatus in the shape of *Encounter*.

Whatever the reasons for it, the high standing of the New Criticism in early Cold War Britain represents the only instance known to the author of southerners exerting a significant influence on the British non-communist left—and this of course is exercising a very broad definition of the category non-communist left—in this period. It was not until after 1960 that the example of the civil rights movement and, in particular, Martin Luther King Jr., began to have an effect on various

British protest movements, including not only anti-racism but also the Campaign for Nuclear Disarmament and even nationalist groups in Wales, Scotland, and Northern Ireland.[73] This is not to say, however, that there were no "encounters and exchanges" between the British left and the South prior to 1960. As this study has attempted to show, members of the "Old Left" generation in Britain evinced a lively interest in the South, not just its racial problems—although that was, admittedly, their primary concern—but other aspects as well. Not only that, the British response to southern affairs was far from straightforward, conditioned—perhaps "over-determined"—as it was by a variety of extraneous factors, including the British imperial experience, immigration, and, above all, the Cold War. Nor, for that matter, was it monolithic or univocal: rather it reflected a number of internal divisions within the British left, between different Labour factions (the Bevanites and Gaitskellites), elements of the trade union movement (leadership and rank-and-file), and literary groups (Bloomsbury and the Movement). Historian Mike Sewell has already hinted that the reactions to the African-American freedom struggle in the 1960s were similarly complicated: the Anti-Apartheid Movement in South Africa was a competing influence, as were indigenous forms of protest within, for example, the Irish nationalist movement.[74] When a historian comes to write the full history of the British New Left's response to the South after 1960, an important but strangely neglected topic, she or he would do well to bear these considerations in mind.

My thanks to the following, who provided advice and encouragement during the research stage of this paper: Lawrence Black, Robert Cook, Nina Fishman, Brandon High, Richard King, Michael O'Brien, Robert Taylor, Nick Tiratsoo, and Christine Woodland.

"By Elvis and All the Saints"

Images of the American South in the World of 1950s British Popular Music

BRIAN WARD

> *"The South appears in British culture through a number of stereotypes: there is the simple South of comical accents and mountain people or small-town folk asleep on front porches; the romantic antebellum South of courtly beaux and beauteous belles; and most familiar in recent years, the violent or gothic South of evil stirrings behind the magnolia in moonlight, usually some terrible racial or sexual sin or secret."*
>
> –HELEN TAYLOR, Circling Dixie

In September 1956, Betty Hurstfield began her teaching career in a large comprehensive school in northwest London. Years later she recalled how rock and roll from the American South had first intruded upon her working day: "I shall never forget the elderly senior mistress coming into the staff room one morning and saying sternly, 'I must speak to a boy called Elvis Presley because he has carved his name on every desk in the school.' "[1] While Hurstfield's senior colleague may have been oblivious to Presley's impact, his early popularity among British youths could be measured not only by the countless times his name was scratched lovingly into wood but also by the more prosaic evidence of enormous record sales and huge box office receipts. By the end of 1956, British branches of Woolworths already stocked Selcol's four-string plastic "Elvis Presley Guitar"—complete with auto-chord device, naturally, and available for a mere 79 shillings.[2] Two years later, Presley ranked behind only Winston Churchill as the best-known public figure among Scottish schoolchildren.[3] And lest Grady McWhiney should try to claim this as evidence of some kind of special Caledonian link to the South, a similar poll of thirty fourteen-year-olds in Bridgewater, Somerset, revealed that while only twelve students knew the name of Eisenhower, seven of Khrushchev, and four of Nehru, "everyone was on Christian name terms with a Mr. Presley."[4]

British youths' enthusiasm for Presley and for rock and roll more generally was but one example of a longstanding interest in the music of the American South—a musical culture which, of course, had its own historic indebtedness to British, as well as other European and African, influences. Indeed, rock and roll was not the only British musical vogue of the decade with close musical and emotional ties to the region. Before Elvis's first chart hit in the spring of 1956, the British traditional ("trad" or Dixieland) jazz revival and the skiffle craze which grew out of it had also betrayed a deep fascination with the real and imagined South.

Rather than simply cataloguing the enormous stylistic debts that British artists in each of these idioms owed to southern music, the focus here is more on how British fans, practitioners, and critics of first trad, then skiffle, and finally rock and roll harbored a set of preconceived, often highly romanticized and stereotypical, ideas about the region. The most important of these images was the perception of southerners, black and white, as, well frankly, rebels. In one corner of the British popular imagination, southerners always existed as outsiders, free spirits engaged in some kind of perpetual hedonistic struggle with restrictive codes of behavior and against the bonds of suffocating authority. It was certainly no coincidence that future Beatle George Harrison should call his first skiffle group the Rebels—a band that, in keeping with the do-it-yourself ethic of the skiffle craze, initially dedicated itself to recreating the sounds of southern country, blues, and rockabilly music on cheap guitars and sundry kitchen utensils.[5]

If at one level the South and its music were permanently available to British fans and performers as symbols of counter-cultural defiance, independence, and nonconformity, at another level they also conjured up images of solidity, stability, and rootedness. Sometimes these images of continuity and heritage merged with notions of southern reactionary conservatism, backwardness, intolerance, and insularity. More positively, however, they promoted a sense that southern music was literally well grounded, that it was linked to a particular place—often expressed in terms of a passionate veneration of the land itself—and that it exhibited a laudable respect for its own traditions. Thus, although rock and roll was sometimes dismissed as simply the latest frothy and disposable product of an avaricious American mass culture industry, relatively few critics leveled the same accusations against either trad or skiffle, both of which were preoccupied with ideas of authenticity and imbued with a deep reverence for their versions of the South's musical past.

The second major theme of the essay concerns how during the second half of the 1950s stock British ideas about the South underwent something of a transformation, becoming more complex, ambiguous, and ultimately less unequivocally positive toward the region. From the mid-1950s, extensive news coverage of the emerging southern civil rights movement and of the desperate white resistance that often greeted it forced British fans of southern-derived music to reexamine their attitudes about the South. It was a contradictory period during which the South was largely defined in the British media in terms of racial intolerance and a predilection for sudden violence and lawlessness and yet remained for many the source of a vibrant and utterly beguiling popular culture.

The trad jazz revival first stirred in Britain during the Second World War and flourished during the subsequent decade before reaching its commercial peak between the mid-1950s and early 1960s. Initially spearheaded by a coterie of enthusiastic amateurs who were variously bored by what remained of swing, bewildered by the esoteric experiments of bebop, and indifferent to the cool cerebral sounds of Miles Davis and his West Coast disciples, the revivalists attempted to turn back the clock and revisit the music of the New Orleans jazz pioneers of the early twentieth century. Part of an international phenomenon, the British trad boom was encouraged by the rediscovery in wartime America of one of those Crescent City veterans, Bunk Johnson, who had begun performing and recording again with much fanfare. Even more significant for the British Dixieland revival was a November 1949 appearance in London by the great Creole saxophonist and clarinetist Sidney Bechet. Making his first appearance in the country since 1920, Bechet performed with Humphrey Lyttleton's band, defying a musicians' union ban on foreign acts playing in Britain.[6]

The British jazz revivalists wore their admiration for the American South literally on their sleeves. Bobby Mickelburgh's combo took to the stage in the garb of Confederate troops, while Dave Hunt led a London group called the Confederate Jazz Band. Presumably both men saw the roots of the music as much in the grays as in the blues. Bob Wallis and his band routinely dressed as Mississippi gamblers, while George Webb succinctly dubbed his group the Dixielanders.[7] By 1956, even Luton could boast its own Delta Jazz Club at the Cresta Ballroom featuring trumpeter Steve Mason's Delta Jazz Band—this despite there being no obvious sign of a river, let alone a delta in that Bedfordshire town.[8] By the end of the decade Liverpool, which could at least claim a river—the Mersey—also boasted the services of its own Merseyssippi Jazz Band.[9]

Ken Colyer and his onetime trombonist Chris Barber were the two most influential figures in establishing trad as a significant force in British popular music. Both exhibited a deep fascination with the American South. Colyer was a genuinely gifted trumpeter and an evangelical enthusiast for early jazz. Too poor to pay for his own pilgrimage to New Orleans, he had joined the merchant navy hoping to make land there at some point. A docking at Mobile, Alabama, proved close enough, and Colyer hitched his way to New Orleans, where he effectively replaced the recently deceased Bunk Johnson in the group taken over by George Lewis. After a spell with Kid Ory's legendary band, Colyer was deported. In England, he formed his seminal Dixieland band, whose hit single "Isle of Capri" began to transform trad from an underground cult to a mass phenomenon. Chris Barber, who left Colyer in the early 1950s, completed that process. Barber played a smoother, somewhat less frenetic and collectively improvised style of Dixieland that he hoped would have even more popular appeal. By 1956, the proprietor of the Winchester Lido Ballroom was able to report that, with the new rock and roll craze still gathering momentum and of uncertain longevity, "traditional jazz is the established 'order of the day.' "[10]

Chris Barber also mentored the trad revival's single most successful artist: the clarinetist Acker Bilk, a man who almost single-handedly inspired a resurgence of interest in goatees, bowler hats, and waistcoats as fashion accessories for British men. In many ways Bilk personified trad's awkward synthesis of southern antiquarian chic and British music hall kitsch. As George Melly, himself a flamboyant jazz vocalist as well as a shrewd observer of British pop culture, noted, there was something faintly ridiculous about Bilk and the whole British impulse to revive—as opposed to revere—the music of turn-of-the-century New Orleans. As Melly put it, "In effect then the public was asked to accept a cider-drinking, belching, West Country contemporary dressed as an Edwardian music hall *lion comique*, and playing the music of an oppressed racial minority as it had evolved in an American city some fifty years before. More surprisingly, they did accept it. Acker was soon a national idol."[11]

Melly was amused and intrigued, rather than appalled and offended, by the dislocated southern nostalgia at the heart of the trad revival. Some critics, however, had always been uncomfortable with trad's tendency to romanticize a bygone South. A report of Sidney Bechet's 1949 breakthrough concert with Humphrey Lyttleton's band, for example, had praised Bechet's performance but expressed deep misgivings about the way that the show traded on old southern stereotypes. The presence of a rustically attired banjo player in Lyttleton's band was an especially unwelcome throwback. "If it is necessary to employ that anachronism, the banjo, is it necessary to expose the wretched exponent [Buddy Vallis] dressed as a hill-billy, right in front of the stage?" asked the reviewer.[12]

Other British jazz buffs, including many of those associated with *Melody Maker*, where the vogue was for bebop or cool jazz, also objected to Dixieland on aesthetic grounds that were often explicitly linked to the regional source of the music. While trad's devotees warmed to the sense of roots and tradition they found in Dixieland, its detractors often deemed this a reactionary development, founded upon a dangerously romantic attachment to a crude and unsophisticated form of music emanating from a crude and unsophisticated part of the world. "Dixieland jazz was born in the streets and riverboats of the Southern States of America; it was played by people who didn't want to be burdened by music stands, even if they'd known what they were for," carped one *Melody Maker* columnist. "The Dixielanders," he maintained, "were primitives, and they played the Dixieland style because they didn't know of any other." Moreover, he insisted that the trad craze was fundamentally inauthentic, a commercially driven fabrication—this despite trad's deep sense of its own musical and commercial integrity. It had "nothing to do with streets, riverboats or the South, it is played by musicians in dinner jackets who are trying to convince us that they are recreating the spirit of jazz as it was played before some of them were born."[13]

The internecine strife that trad provoked within the British jazz fraternity was a serious business. In his 1959 novel *Absolute Beginners*, Colin MacInnes brilliantly evoked the bitter musical rivalries between London's young jazz modernists and those who were drawn to both trad and the skiffle movement that eventually evolved from it. MacInnes's anonymous narrator describes the differences between two young habitués of the Chez Nobody coffee bar, Dean Swift and the Misery Kid. "These two don't mix in public, on account of the Dean being a sharp modern jazz creation, and the Kid just a skiffle survival, with horrible leanings to the trad thing. That is to say, the Kid admires the groups that play what is supposed to be the authentic music of old New Orleans, i.e., combos of booking-office clerks and quantity-surveyors' assistants who've handed in their cards, and dedicated themselves to blowing what they believe to be the same notes as the wonderful Creoles who invented the whole thing, when it all long ago began."[14]

MacInnes appreciated the essentially—but barely—white-collar audience for trad in Britain ("booking-office clerks and quantity-surveyors' assistants"). In an age of drab austerity, leisure time identification with the musical stylings of a flamboyant and marginalized section of the turn-of-the-century South represented a low-risk, neatly compartmentalized gesture of nonconformity from the work-a-day world of trad's largely middle- and lower-middle-class adherents. Moreover, in the early to mid-1950s, when trad first really became a mass commercial phenomenon, British admiration for southern musical traditions still tended to revolve around nostalgic invocations of the region frozen in time and conveniently stripped of its more unsavory and retrogressive aspects. It was still possible to revel in images of an exotic hybrid South ("the wonderful Creoles") without seriously contemplating the real nature of southern race relations. As the decade wore on, however, fans of Dixieland and other southern-based music were forced to reconsider the connections between their love for the music and their frequently romanticized and anachronistic conceptions of the region.

Sometime during the early 1950s, Chris Barber became rather bored with the Dixieland-by-numbers style he had done much to popularize. While retaining his love of early jazz, Barber, with the support of his singing spouse, Ottilie Patterson, steadily moved his band (and elements of his audience) more in the direction of blues, gospel, and folk influences. This broadening of repertoire to embrace other overwhelmingly southern roots music laid the foundations for the skiffle boom of the mid-1950s. Surfacing just months before the civil rights conflagrations threw disturbing light onto the darker side of southern life, skiffle was generally spared the anti-southern slurs later leveled against rock and roll by some of its British opponents. Indeed, skiffle represented something of a last yee-ha for romantic notions of southern pastoral bliss.

The most important figure in the success of skiffle was Glaswegian Lonnie Donegan. A fan of Dixieland, the southern country blues of Josh White, Blind Lemon Jefferson, and Leadbelly, as well as of Oklahoma-born folk singer Woodie Guthrie and old-time country artists like the Carter Family, Donegan had formerly fronted his own band and worked as a banjoist and guitarist with Dixieland pioneers Ken Colyer and Chris Barber. During the intermission between sets by these trad bands, Donegan would perform a few southern folk and blues staples like "Frankie and Johnny" and "House of the Rising Sun," backed by a rudimentary rhythm section of stand-up bass and drums. These interludes became increasingly popular, and in 1955 Donegan was allowed to include a few such songs on the Chris Barber Jazz Band's *New Orleans Joys* album. This Decca release sold a remarkable sixty thousand copies at a time when the Barber band had probably not played before sixty thousand people in their entire career. One of the Donegan songs, a full-throttle reworking of Leadbelly's "Rock Island Line," proved especially popular and was released as a single in February 1956. It eventually sold some 3 million copies, making the British top ten and, more astonishingly, the American top twenty—a very rare achievement by any British artist at that time.

Powered by the classic skiffle line-up of propulsive rhythm guitar, a manically scraped washboard, and a fiercely slapped upright bass—replaced in more impecunious bands by a tea-chest bass where the bass line was picked out on a single piece of string attached to the top of a broomstick which in turn was mounted on an upturned tea-chest—"Rock Island Line" inspired a massive outbreak of primitive youthful music making in Britain. Initially, much of the skiffle repertoire comprised traditional southern blues and country songs, or new songs cast in a similar style. Donegan himself recorded much more southern folk material, like "John Henry," "Pick a Bale of Cotton," "Cumberland Gap," and A. P. Carter's "Wabash Cannonball." These recordings, together with his regular live shows and appearances on British television and radio, did much to popularize both skiffle and its American antecedents among a new generation of fans.

Like both their trad predecessors and their rock and roll heirs, skiffle fans registered their impatience with some of the dominant social conventions of the day by very consciously adopting alien musical and cultural styles rooted in the South. Skiffle's substitution of southern musical standards for those associated with classical music and the more mainstream popular music fare of the day was an obvious enough declaration of this independence. Yet these southern affectations went beyond simply mimicking the region's favorite musical devices. Barely months before the rise of Massive Resistance seriously tarnished the

South's image, it was still possible to revel fairly uncritically in southern style and use it to show a rather cool detachment from middle Britain and its values. As Britain's foremost folk singer, Ewan MacColl, said of the skiffle groups that suddenly swarmed the country, emptying the kitchens of the land in their feverish search for washboards, thimbles, rope, and broomsticks, "With the guitar went the frayed and faded blue-jeans with the washed-out horizontal stripes which proclaimed you a fugitive from a chain-gang. The more extreme cultivators of the American image sent to the U.S. for those little sacks of Bull Durham tobacco and learned to roll their own with one hand. . . . And everywhere, in every dialect of English, Scots and Welsh you heard the 'Rock Island Line,' 'The Midnight Special,' and 'The House of the Rising Sun.'" Few of these disciples of Dixie paused long to consider the real implications of southern chain gangs, or to dwell upon the mixture of poverty and racism that had spawned much of the region's most impressive music.[15]

Clearly there was a common understanding in Britain that skiffle, with its rudimentary instrumentation and direct lyrics, was derived from the rural South. Sometimes this carried connotations that were more hick than hip, but most still found charm and sincerity, rather than ignorance and barbarism, in the music's apparent simplicity and lack of guile. Fans embraced the idea that skiffle was rooted in earthy, unadulterated, and largely spontaneous forms of southern music that had somehow evaded the cynical and contaminating touch of the mass popular music industry. In the village of Brewood, near Wolverhampton, for example, bassist Mo Foster's first group proudly called themselves the Peasants, jettisoning the name only when their playing matured and they traded the raw energy of skiffle for a more sophisticated pop sound.[16] The tabloid *Daily Mirror* also recognized the craze's southern lineage. "It dates back to the days of slavery in the Southern States of America when every Friday—rent day—groups of musicians would go round with homemade instruments, singing the old prison and slavery jazz songs to raise enough money to pay the rent. They were called Skiffleboys."[17] Years later, George Harrison would reiterate this line, claiming simply that skiffle was rooted in "black slave culture."[18]

If such accounts left something to be desired in terms of historical accuracy—not too many slaves paid rent on Friday, or any other day for that matter, and none of them played anything that might reasonably be called jazz—it nonetheless helped to cement in place the notion that skiffle had a real southern heritage. Moreover, the *Mirror* clearly saw nothing problematic or unsavory in acknowledging the style's indebtedness to black culture. This attitude would later sharply distinguish British critics of rock and roll from many of their American counterparts.

The heyday of skiffle lasted barely eighteen months, although its influence was felt for much longer, registered in the birth of a thousand eager British bands. Ultimately, skiffle appealed to the same youngsters who were inspired by Elvis Presley, Fats Domino, Little Richard, Buddy Holly, and the other American rock and rollers who stormed the British charts after 1956. Indeed, once rock and roll had burst upon the scene, the main British musical response was to apply skiffle's Do-It-Yourself musical techniques to that idiom. What little there was that was distinctive or potent about British rock and roll music of the late 1950s and early 1960s was the result of blending these two southern-derived musical forms.

As in America, rock and roll music was initially greeted in Britain with a combination of rapture and revulsion. On both sides of the Atlantic much of the hostility congealed around objections to its raw sexuality, fears that the frenzied responses it produced among its delirious young fans might herald a wider outbreak of teenage rebellion and anti-social behavior, and abhorrence of what was viewed as its crude musicianship and cheap commercialism. "Do we want this shockin rockin?" asked the *Daily Mirror*, speculating on whether a music that "has been blamed for starting riots, rape and alcoholism among the youngsters" could have a similar impact in Britain.[19] Meanwhile, Steve Race, the *Melody Maker*'s influential jazz critic, performer, and broadcaster, snootily dismissed rock and roll for its "cheap, nasty lyrics." Loathing the way that the style seemed to eschew traditional hallmarks of good musicianship, and the fact that it was dramatically eroding the audience and radio airtime for jazz, Race declared that "Viewed as a social phenomenon, the current craze for rock 'n' roll material is one of the most terrifying things ever to happen to popular music."[20]

None of this early criticism had a specifically southern focus. Indeed, whereas Dixieland and skiffle had immediately been identified with southern musical influences and cultural affectations, there were initially few signs of any British awareness of the southern roots of rock and roll among either supporters or opponents of the style. Given that the kiss-curled Yankee imposter Bill Haley and his "Rock Around the Clock" was the music's first great emissary in Britain, this was perhaps not surprising. It would take the emergence of Elvis Presley to cement the connection between rock and roll and the American South in British minds. After Presley's debut on the U.K. record charts in May 1956 with "Heartbreak Hotel," rock and roll's southern credentials gradually became more conspicuous, although the reputation of neither the music nor the region necessarily benefited from the association.

The rise of rock and roll and Presley coincided with a series of racially charged events in the American South that significantly altered British attitudes toward the region. In late 1955 and especially in early 1956, highly publicized civil rights confrontations in Montgomery, Tuscaloosa, and elsewhere highlighted southern prejudice and racial repression, the depths of which most trad and skiffle fans had been unaware, or at least able to ignore. One incident that had a particularly profound effect on British perceptions of the modern South occurred in Birmingham, Alabama, and involved one of the Britain's foremost dance bands, the Ted Heath Orchestra.

Ted Heath visited America in the spring of 1956 as part of an integrated "Show of Stars" package headlined by the elegant jazz pianist-cum-balladeer Nat King Cole. From the outset the tour had attracted an unusual level of interest in Britain. Heath's orchestra was the first British act to play live in the United States in some twenty years, during which time the dispute between the two countries' musicians' unions had effectively barred transatlantic exchanges of talent. *Melody Maker* featured weekly reports from Heath on the road, while many other newspapers kept close tabs on his progress. In the wake of press coverage of the *Brown* decisions, the ongoing bus boycott in Montgomery, and the efforts of Autherine Lucy to integrate the University of Alabama, there was a good deal of interest in how Heath and the tour would fare in the South, where most of the concerts were scheduled. There was even optimism that this integrated tour might actually help to ease racial divisions and tensions in the region. When the show reached San Antonio, for example, it was hailed by the *Melody Maker* as "a smash hit" which "smashed the colour bar." At the first desegregated concert ever to be held at the city's Municipal Auditorium, "Negroes and whites together gave the British musician an enthusiastic welcome."[21]

If the San Antonio concert conjured up comforting images of racial progress and interracial bonhomie founded upon shared musical tastes, events in Birmingham offered much less edifying images. At a segregated, whites-only concert at the Municipal Auditorium on April 10, Nat King Cole was roughed up on-stage by members of Asa Carter's Alabama White Citizens Council before being rescued by local policemen. Most American press reports interpreted the assault as part of a Council campaign that was really directed against rock and roll music, with Cole serving as an unfortunate surrogate in the wrong place at the wrong time. To Carter and his followers, rock and roll with its black and white stylistic influences, black and white artists, and black and white fans, represented a lewd metaphor for the sort of mongrelized and debased South they feared would emerge if integration was allowed to proceed.[22]

While few contemporary American reports dwelt long on the connection between the Council's physical attack on Cole, its extended publicity campaign against rock and roll, and its dedicated resistance to the desegregation of the South, the British press focused heavily on those links. The Cole incident seemed to confirm just how retrograde southern racial practices were at a time when the civil rights movement was just beginning to garner increased British attention and sympathy. Indeed, whereas Nat King Cole himself repeatedly tried to downplay the political aspects of the assault to American journalists, failing to associate it with the intensification of Massive Resistance and expressing incredulity that he should be attacked when he was "not a crusader" for civil rights, he was much more forthcoming about the real motivations of the attackers when speaking to Christopher Dobson of the *Daily Express*. "The attack was not a personal affront," Cole agreed, but it did symbolize desperate white efforts to preserve Jim Crow. "It was part of the fuss over Autherine Lucy at the University of Alabama and the bus boycott in Montgomery," he explained. Similarly, Cole and the American press were keen to portray the incident as an act of aberrant hooliganism; they uniformly stressed the sympathetic ovation the singer had received from the mortified white audience in Birmingham when he returned to the stage to announce that he could no longer continue. The *Daily Express* complicated this image of southern contrition by noting that "through the cheering could be heard some booing and shouts of 'Nigger go home!' "[23]

Most British accounts emphasized that the attack on Cole had happened in a South that was clinging to an anachronistic system of racial oppression with no parallel at home. The most elaborate discussion of the incident and its transatlantic implications came from jazz expert Steve Race in his *Melody Maker* column. Race noted the irony of the fact that the Cole attack took place barely three weeks after American bandleader Stan Kenton had assured him that integrating his orchestra had aroused no opposition. "Fortunately, we do not have any more problems like that in the States," Kenton explained, "It seems like the battle has been won—at least in music." Race picked up on Kenton's rider that prejudice was dead "at least in music," as if to stress that the attack on Cole had come from beyond the allegedly more equalitarian world of music fans. More significantly, Race argued that such an incident was virtually inconceivable in Britain. And even if something similar had occurred in Britain, he insisted that there would have been a very different audience response. "We, who live in a country where society not only considers all men equal but tries to treat them as such, have reason to be proud that no coloured musician here need fear for his safety. Anyone who tried to attack a Negro on a British stage would have to contend with the entire audience as well as 15 policemen." While Race accepted that most Americans were appalled by the Cole attack, the implication was that far too many of those southerners attending the Birmingham concert accepted—or at least failed to oppose—the racism of which the assault was but an extreme and dramatic manifestation.[24]

Much of this served to reinforce a rather smug British confidence that they were somehow immune to American-style racial prejudices. This view persisted more or less unchallenged until 1958, when race riots in Nottingham and Notting Hill and the exposure of blatant color-bars operating in many British nightclubs punctured some of that complacency. Nonetheless, Race at least sounded several less self-congratulatory notes, foreshadowing some of the British debates on race relations and immigration policies that characterized the 1960s—debates which would frequently take place with one eye firmly on the unfolding racial situation in America. First he reminded British jazz fans that they carried a special responsibility to take a firm stand against racial discrimination wherever they found it. There was, he wrote "no excuse for the person who deliberately hides his head in the sand when such evils are around; least of all the Jazz enthusiast, who owes much more than he can repay to the Negro and his music. That is why racial intolerance, whenever and wherever it occurs, is the business of this paper and of this columnist. And of you."[25]

Second, Race reiterated comments made earlier in the *Observer* newspaper concerning Autherine Lucy's attempt to desegregate the University of Alabama in February 1956. The paper had pointed out that at least Lucy's right to attend the previously segregated university was now protected in law, even if the enforcement of that law in the face of white mob violence in Tuscaloosa had left much to be desired. Race and the *Observer* both reminded their readers that there was no counterpart to this legal protection against segregation in those British African territories where apartheid still reigned: "It will be a long time before we see a Miss Lucy able to claim similar rights in South Africa, or indeed, in Rhodesia and Kenya." Anxious to puncture misplaced British condescension toward the United States regarding its racial record, the *Observer* noted that "If an African girl who defied segregation were sure of the backing, not only of the law but of the British press and public opinion—as Miss Lucy has the support of the federal law and most of the press and public opinion in the Northern States—the British Commonwealth would be as advanced in matters of racial liberalism as the United States of America." What was needed to hasten the legal protection of civil rights for peoples of color in Commonwealth Africa was for British people of goodwill to "play the role the American northerners have played from the Civil War onwards" and support African rights. Moreover, Race assigned to music fans and artists a special role in challenging racism wherever they encountered it, at home or abroad. Referring to British Commonwealth policy, he urged music fans to "keep a keen eye on developments, and bring to bear on our representatives the pressure which is the birthright of free citizens in a still free country. We owe it to our fellow men—the ones with darker skins than ours happen to be. And at the very least, we owe it to Jazz."[26]

Race's heartfelt plea may have been hopelessly over-optimistic about the level of concern among jazz fans, let alone other Britains, for the plight of Africans in the Commonwealth, certainly in the days before the Sharpeville massacre in South Africa. And it painted a rather simplistic and rosy picture of racial toleration in the northern states of America. More significantly, it also had the rhetorical effect of placing all right-thinking Britains, especially music fans, in potential opposition to an intransigent, wrong-headed South—a region whose whites were increasingly equated with the embarrassing and unpalatable guardians of apartheid in Commonwealth Africa. Coinciding with the reports of racial unrest from elsewhere in the region, the Cole incident helped to push the more odious discriminatory aspects of southern history to the forefront of British consciousness, where it began to eclipse the comfortable nostalgia and Old South romanticism that had long dominated attitudes toward the region. In turn, images of southern racism revitalized all sorts of stereotypes of southern uncouthness, violence, moral laxity, and general backwardness.

This trend was even evident in Ted Heath's own reports, which, perhaps not surprisingly, became increasingly jaundiced toward the region following the Cole attack. Heath even managed to criticize the poor quality of southern highways. "The roads in the South are no better than those in England," he commented archly. Given the generally woeful state of British roads and the fact that the new Eisenhower interstates, conveyor belts for all those enviably sleek chromed and finned cars, were a potent symbol of American technological prowess and high living standards, this was about as stinging an indictment as one could imagine.[27] In his postmortem on the tour, Heath continued to suggest that the South lagged behind the rest of the nation not just in amenities but also in basic refinement and taste. The South, Heath complained, did not really have the sophistication necessary to appreciate quality entertainment. "Remember, we've just played in the hillbilly areas of Kentucky, the Dixieland area of New Orleans, the Cow-Boy song area of Texas, and missed the keen awareness of good jazz that you get in such cities as St. Louis and New York."[28]

There was nothing new in the British recognition that the South was not like the rest of the United States. The difference was that after the spring of 1956 there was much greater sensitivity to the fact that some aspects of southern distinctiveness were more a curse than a blessing. While this added some healthy realism to excessively romantic images of the South, the new focus on southern flaws could sometimes spill over into an excessive demonization of the region. Once associated primarily with magnolia and moonlight, the region was in danger of becoming almost exclusively associated with mayhem and malevolence. While never absolute, this shift of emphasis within a discourse of the South where violence and honor, crudeness and grace had always coexisted, had particular significance when rock and roll first burst upon the British scene. Seeking ammunition with which to attack the new style for its alleged sexual impropriety, encouragement of antisocial behavior, and musical primitivism, many British critics saw its southern origins as potent part of their armory. In this changing climate of opinion about the region, simply drawing attention to rock and roll's southern roots was sometimes enough to raise serious doubts about the music's basic morality. Conversely, many of the more lurid tales emerging from the rock and roll scene seemed merely to confirm the accuracy of stereotypes about the depraved nature of the South.

In September 1956, the *Times* noted that Elvis Presley had ousted Bill Haley as leader of the rock and roll craze. Indeed, the newspaper admitted that all previous teen sensations "paled before the delirious triumphs of a raw young southerner, Elvis Presley, now only 21, whose combination of a hill-billy style of wailing with bodily contortions which are supposed to suggest the 'fundamental human drive,' took him even beyond the peaks of popularity enjoyed most recently by the tearful Mr. Johnny Ray and Mr. Frank Sinatra." The article continued by describing Presley in his "real element"—the "personal performances which have filled halls all over the country, mostly in the south and south-west, with excited teenagers—the great majority seem to be girls—many of whom he reduces to shrieks and outbursts of weeping by his moaning and sinuous swayings."[29]

The language used here, especially the adjectives, revealed much about attitudes toward rock and roll in polite British society, but also toward the South from whence it and Elvis came. "Raw," "delirious," "bodily contortions," and "sinuous swayings" all evoked the sensual and visceral side of the South, hinting at the source of much of its appeal to British teenagers. In the wake of Montgomery, Tuscaloosa, and the Cole incident, however, such language could also conjure up images of lost self-control; and lost control was now accepted as a typically southern vice that manifested itself in both rock and roll's unrestrained sexuality—and the frenetic dancing which acted as both expression and surrogate for that "fundamental human drive"—and in the unrestrained mob violence associated with Massive Resistance.

The *Times*'s language also implied that Presley's music was from a region so full of blood and passion that everyone before him—Ray, Sinatra, Haley—paled by comparison. Maybe this pallor-sanguine contrast was a subtle acknowledgment of rock and roll's huge debts to African American musical style, but those links were not explored, or even hinted at elsewhere in the *Times*'s article. Unlike in so many American critiques, there was no effort to trace Presley's potent and deeply disturbing sexual charge to the lascivious influence of black music. Indeed, what was missing—or much muted—in British opposition to rock and roll was the deep sense of racial transgression that dominated attacks on rock and roll in America, especially in the South. The Reverend Albert Carter of Nottingham may have sounded much like Asa Carter of the Alabama White Citizens Council when he ranted that "the effect of this music on young people is to turn them into devil worshippers; to stimulate self-expression through sex, to provoke lawlessness, to impair nervous stability and to destroy the sanctity of marriage." Reverend Carter, however, did not try to explain the grave threat rock and roll clearly posed to western civilization in terms of its racial provenance.[30]

As with skiffle, most British commentators, irrespective of whether or not they were favorably inclined toward rock and roll, tended to acknowledge the style's black influences rather matter-of-factly, with no overt or implied criticism. The *Daily Mirror*, for example, simply noted, "this new boogie-style rhythm has been described as a mixture of western music and Negro jazz."[31] The *Times* similarly observed that rock and roll "derives from Negro church music."[32] It is also important to remember that in many British minds during the mid- to late 1950s, simply acknowledging the black roots of rock and roll had the effect of intensifying any association with the South. This was a time when, as one young fan recalled, many—if by no means all, Britains—"understood that 'negroes' were entirely from the South." Outside a coterie of British aficionados it was often assumed that even popular northern-based black rock and rollers like Chuck Berry and Bo Diddley lived and recorded in the South.[33]

Generally unalarmed by rock and roll's black influences, critics seemed much more concerned that British kids should be besotted by music from a place where the despicable treatment of African Americans was seen as symptomatic of a much deeper moral malaise and ignorance. If anything, the relative absence of anxiety about rock and roll's mixed racial heritage had the effect of making its regional and class credentials much more significant as lightning rods for British criticism. Certainly the *Times*'s dismissive description of Presley's uninhibited singing as a "hill-billy style of wailing" explicitly invoked his white lower-class credentials. It also had the effect of linking rock and roll, like skiffle before it, to a specifically rural southern heritage. Yet it was apparent that in the year or so separating the emergence of the two styles the implications of that rural link had changed in tandem with changing attitudes toward the region. Whereas skiffle's folk roots had inspired a pastoral nostalgia with positive images of rural simplicity and homespun honesty, rock and roll's country dimension was usually invoked to characterize the style as crude and unsophisticated, an emblem of pervasive southern backwardness.

What made this stress on rock and roll's rural primitivism particularly ironic was that, unlike much of the black and white southern folk music that inspired skiffle, it was primarily an urban phenomenon; the product of black and white migrations off the land into the cities of the South, most famously the Memphis of Sun Records. This misapprehension was even reflected in the early marketing of rock and roll in Britain. When Sun recording star Roy Orbison had his first British release on London Records in 1957, the four-song disk was titled *Hillbilly Rock*. The cover art featured a sketch of a bearded country yokel in suspenders reclining on a flour sack while he picked an acoustic guitar and sucked on a corncob pipe. This was light years away from the ultra cool self-image of Orbison and the other habitués of Sun Records, with their penchant for blue suede shoes and the most feline of cat clothes. Moreover, British rock and roll fans were generally uninterested in revisiting the bucolic southern yokeldom of yore; they were thrilled by the buzz of the music's urban electricity and captivated by the sharp urbanity and bold sexual swagger of its artists.[34]

At least the *Times* appreciated that Presley had come a long way from the farm—or more accurately, from small-town Tupelo, Mississippi. Yet, it still depicted him as an unsophisticated rube who exhibited the tasteless, if highly conspicuous, consumption of the newly monied. Presley, the paper noted, is "now the proud owner of three Cadillacs and hundreds of the violent sports shirts he affects." The condescending coverage continued with a verbatim reproduction of Presley's comments on his future career plans. Given that few British fans would have actually heard Presley speak prior to the release later in the year of his first film, *Love Me Tender*—itself a hackneyed Civil War drama set on the southern domestic front—this was an important step in casting him and rock and roll as quintessentially southern. "I wouldn't want no regular spots on no T.V. programme," Elvis explained. "Movies are the things. I love to act. I don't care nothing whatsoever about singing in no movie...." In case its readers—well-used to reading immaculately parsed Queen's English in every paragraph—did not immediately appreciate that the *Times* was poking fun at the King's English, the piece ended with the snide observation that "Mr. Presley adds . . . that English was what he liked best at school."[35]

Presley's humble beginnings and meager formal education provided countless opportunities for the British press to belittle the singer, his musical idiom, and his region of birth. In 1958, the *Times*, for example, gratuitously reprinted the comments of Millyon Bowers, head of the Memphis draft board, which inducted Elvis into the army: "after all, when you take him out of the entertainment business what have you got left? A truck driver."[36] The *Times*'s disdain for Presley's lower-class southern roots and the diction and grammar that in British minds appeared to betray it was neither an isolated incident, nor a habit restricted to the "quality" press. British stereotypes of southern backwardness, ignorance, and even moral lassitude were always closely associated with the sound of the southern drawl, in which it seemed that southern minds and tongues were forever at odds, stumbling uncertainly toward something that might be identified as an intelligent thought. This linkage became even clearer in the coverage of Jerry Lee Lewis's aborted British tour in the spring of 1958.

Lewis arrived in England in late May, eager to capitalize on the success of his recordings "Whole Lot of Shaking Going On," "Great Balls of Fire," and "Breathless" by joining a nationwide package tour. Intrigued by advance publicity about the wild piano-pumping rock and roller raised in Ferriday, Louisiana, representatives from most of the British press were on hand as Lewis and his entourage flew into Heathrow on May 22. One member of that entourage was his young wife, Myra. When reporters asked how old she was, Jerry Lee replied, "Fifteen." The following day, the *Daily Herald* sported the headline "Rock Star's Wife Is 15: And Its His Third Marriage." *Daily Mirror* journalist John Rolls elaborated on the story following an interview with Myra at London's

Westbury Hotel. "I didn't tell my parents for a fortnight," admitted Myra. "When they knew, they had a fit," she confessed. Still, those parental misgivings seemed a thing of the past, since it transpired that Myra's mother Lois and her father J. W. Brown, were also on the tour, with J. W. playing bass in Lewis's back-up band. When Myra was asked if she thought she was too young to marry, she was quite affronted. "Gosh, no, back home you can marry at ten. One girl got wed at nine."[37]

As if this was not enough to scandalize vast sections of the British public, worse was to follow. Further investigations revealed that young Myra was not fifteen years old at all. She was just thirteen. Then it turned out she was actually Jerry Lee's cousin. To cap it all, the marriage was bigamous: the wedding had taken place five months before Lewis's previous marriage was legally annulled. As Jerry Lee tried to explain himself to the press, he became ever more deeply mired in cliché and stereotype. At one point he admitted that he had been remiss in not asking Myra's father for prior permission to wed his daughter, and in failing to wait until his own divorce had come through. Yet he excused himself with reference to his fierce religious beliefs. Declaring that he and Myra were both members of the Pentecostal church and therefore against "make-up, drink, tobacco and divorce," the twice divorced, hard-drinking Lewis explained, "I consider that Myra is my wife morally. . . . My divorce is a matter for God."[38]

A day later, Jerry Lee had changed his story again. He explained to journalist Anne Lloyd, "It was only mah second marriage which wasn't legal." Rather like the *Times* with Presley, the *Mirror* saw fit to print a phonetic version of Lewis's explanation of his matrimonial career to an incredulous British public. "Ah was a bigamist when ah was 16. Ah was 14 when ah was first married," he announced. "That lasted a year. Dorothy was a good girl, but she was too good for me. She was 17. Then ah met Jane. One day she said she was gonna have mah child. Ah was real worried. Her father threatened me. Her brothers were hunting me with whips."[39] This last point provided an important twist. These events took place long before 1976, when Jerry Lee immortalized himself as a true gun-toting son of the South by accidentally shooting his bass player Norman "Butch" Owens, and then turning up drunk at

Elvis Presley's Graceland home brandishing a loaded pistol.[40] It was all very well marrying a barely pubescent cousin, but until this point the Lewis story was rather lacking in the violent overtones long associated with the South. Coverage of contemporary civil rights events—especially of the mob violence at Little Rock in 1957—made sure that such associations were very much to the forefront of British minds.

Anyway, the threat of violence to satisfy besmirched family honor was apparently enough to encourage Jerry Lee Lewis to marry the pregnant Jane Mitchum. Although Mitchum would later deny his version of events, Lewis claimed that his second marriage had taken place a week before his divorce from Dorothy, his first wife, had come through. Employing inscrutable logic, Lewis argued that since his second marriage had been illegal, he could not possibly have committed bigamy when he took Myra as his third bride. Somewhat dolefully he concluded by suggesting, "Mah father should have put his foot on mah neck and whipped the hide off me."[41] That was certainly what Iain Murray recommended in a letter to the *Melody Maker*: "Any adult who leads a girl of 13 into what can only be described as sin should be horsewhipped."[42]

The Lewis saga played neatly into a whole range of stereotypes about unsuppressed southern sexual appetites and unhealthy regional predilections for incest and child brides that had titillated British audiences for some time. A front-page story in the *Daily Mirror* for March 9, 1956, had featured a picture of the recently married Susie Goode from Spartanburg, South Carolina. Just twelve years old, Susie was shown clutching a baby doll in a clear allusion to the recent film *Baby Doll*, in which Carol Baker had epitomized the steamy allure of sexually precocious southern nymphets. Not that it was only young southern women who suffered from such stereotyping. When a reporter from the *Daily Herald* managed to smooth talk his way into Myra's mother's hotel room, he delighted in the cheap salaciousness of the scene, portraying Lois Brown like some kind of down-market Blanche DuBois: "*She lay in bed, nylon-nightie clad, smoothing her dark hair with one hand and holding a sheet close to her throat with the other.*" When the same reporter knocked on the door of Myra and Jerry Lee Lewis's room, the Killer shouted, "*I can't come out, I haven't got any clothes on.*"[43]

This was all a very long way from visions of chivalrous cavaliers and chaste belles, or even of honest yeoman farmers and their pious, hard-working spouses. To British audiences, it seemed as if the Lewises and Browns, like many white southerners in the midst of the civil rights maelstrom, simply did not know how to control their baser instincts and behave in a civilized manner. And rock and roll was their music. The *Daily Sketch*'s review of one Lewis concert offered a striking image of primal, almost feral, redneck activity as it described how, "Drooling at the piano, Lewis moans, grunts, wails and sneezes so close to the microphone he might be eating it."[44]

Battered by the rising tide of adverse publicity, the Lewis tour disintegrated. The *People* newspaper called for a boycott of the shows and for the home secretary to institute deportation proceedings.[45] While the police checked the legality of the Lewises' paperwork, Minister of Labour Sir Frank Medlicott rose in the House of Lords to denounce the rock and roller's visit and formally raise the subject of deportation. Protests began to mount at the theatres where Lewis was appearing. Cries of "baby snatcher" could be heard from the audience at a May 26 concert in Tooting. While headlines in the *Daily Sketch* screamed, "Get Out Lewis!" the paper explained, "We have a lot of time for Americans. We also have time—but not nearly so much—for rock'n'roll." The paper made it clear that it was the South, increasingly cast as a debauched and sordid netherworld, somehow adrift from the rest of America and civilization, which was the source and site of this affront to common decency. "Where did this story begin?" it asked rhetorically. "In the Southern United States, where early marriage is common," the paper reminded its readers. That was "where Jerry Lee Lewis began his rocket-like career to stardom."[46]

After a couple of days of this incessant criticism, the Rank Organization cancelled Lewis's appearances for the remainder of the tour. Young Myra was relieved. "Ah don't wanna see no more of Britain," she said. "Ah just wanna get back to mah lovely home in Memphis, Tennessee."[47] The following day, the couple was back in New York and Jerry Lee was answering questions on the tour and his marriage. No, he had not been deported. Yes, his wife was thirteen. "She'll be fourteen in July, but she's ALL woman," he assured anyone who wanted to know, including those in Britain who had followed this little southern soap opera so closely.[48]

As the press treatment of Elvis Presley and Jerry Lee Lewis revealed, British critics of rock and roll often referred to its "typically" southern traits as a means to question the style's moral rectitude. For British fans of the music, however, those same "southern" traits often accounted for much of rock and roll's appeal. This at least suggested the continued existence of a broadly shared set of British ideas about the region: opponents and enthusiasts simply had different responses to many of what both factions saw as typically southern characteristics. For example, while critics ridiculed southern performers for their speech and for the undesirable regional and class characteristics that this speech supposedly revealed, their fans adored them for having exotic diction and a vocabulary whose very strangeness announced that they, their music, and their social values came from somewhere far beyond the mainstream of British—and, indeed, American—society. Thus rock and roll's initial appeal depended largely on its outsider credentials. British fans found in rock and roll a variant on what their trad and skiffle predecessors had also found in southern musical culture: a marker of social difference and a vehicle for some measure of cultural and generational rebellion. The way in which this worked was clearly evident among the Teddy Boys, who represented Britain's most conspicuous early rock and roll fans. Indeed, as Christopher Booker wrote from the perspective of the late 1960s, "Only three things did the revivalist jazz fans have in common with the Teddy Boys of South London—their youth . . . their sense of apartness from conventional society and their reverence for a particular romantic image of America."[49]

The working-class Teddy Boys scene, with its stylistic and very occasionally violent rebellion against conventional values and established authority, predated the rock and roll explosion by several years. Highly visible because of their curious sartorial blend of Edwardian formal wear and the American city slicker duds associated with frontier villains and riverboat gamblers, the Teds had struggled to find a suitable musical accompaniment to their counter-cultural posturing. Modern jazz was too rarified and too associated with a despised intellectual elite. Trad was too closely linked with an equally reviled radical politics—the Teds were generally a-political and hostile to most formal ideologies and social crusades, preferring to register their boredom and vague resentment of the status quo by means of their loud style politics and occasional acts of hooliganism. Skiffle sounded closer to the mark, as did some of the uptown southern country sounds associated with the likes of Hank Williams, but both styles retained their rustic overtones and lacked the requisite slick urbanity. Consequently, there was an especially intense response, an outpouring of relief almost, when after years of searching, rock and roll appeared as the long overdue soundtrack to a working-class youth movement which had always had a special reverence for Hollywood-style southern chic. As sociologist Simon Frith observed, "chronologically, the teds' look predated ted music and rock 'n' roll, but these teenagers were already committed to a fantasy of hillbilly cool—the move from Tennessee Ernie Ford to Elvis Presley was no more peculiar in London's Elephant and Castle than it had been in Tennessee itself."[50]

The Teds were enraptured by a music and a set of performers who embodied their own sense of rebelliousness, of being outsiders who were busy creating a parallel universe in which they were the insiders, the cognoscenti, the definers of a brash style and founts of cool wisdom. Most of their heroes—Elvis Presley, Jerry Lee Lewis, Carl Perkins, Little Richard—were hard-rocking southern artists who, much like their initial audiences, felt themselves to be excluded from the levers of power and prestige in American life as a consequence of their race, region, youth, or class—or of some combination of these factors.

Significantly, unlike trad and skiffle fans, the Teds and other British fans of early rock and roll appeared to have no qualms about the unabashed commercialism of their favorite music. They welcomed its novelty and saw the rapid turnover of new artists, dance crazes, and one-hit wonders less as a sign of superficiality than of vibrancy. Above all, they enjoyed the pleasures of conspicuous consumption—consumption of the records, distinctive clothing, and other paraphernalia that loudly announced both their devotion to the music and their distance from their parents and less hip peers. After all, rock and roll came from the South—America *in extremis*, a region that was simultaneously admired and despaired of for its brashness, its gaudiness, the size of its sensual appetites, and the enormity of its passions. In this world, it made perfect sense that Presley would sport "violent shirts" and flamboyant gold lame suits ("snazzy, jazzy outfits," as his first British advertisement put it), and own more Cadillacs than most of his British fans owned neckties.[51] And of course Little Richard, the extravagant "Georgia Peach," would pile his pompadour sky-high and ladle mascara, lipstick, and rouge onto his face. They were after all southerners, glamorous mavericks, steeped in the redemptive joys of excess, keen to party and eager to dazzle. Little wonder, then, that the hero of MacInnes's *Absolute Beginners* should adopt Elvis as the patron saint of his search for kicks, swearing, "By Elvis and all the saints that this last teenage year of mine was going to be a real rave."[52]

Although not all British fans of rock and roll in the late 1950s were comb-carrying Teddy Boys, to a greater or lesser extent most shared the Teds' sense that the music initially represented a musical sign of individuality and nonconformity, and that the South was the prime source of that rebellious élan, that attractive sense of outsiderhood. John Gustafson, bassist with Merseybeat pioneers The Big Three, explained the mix of bewilderment and exhilaration that accompanied his first exposure to this alien, exotic southern sound on the radio. "On came a record by Little Richard called 'Rip It Up,' and that changed my whole life.... I thought: 'What is this? Music from outer space or what? What is it?' I was so excited that I couldn't sleep at all that night."[53]

Gustafson's fellow Liverpudlian John Lennon similarly recalled "having my hair stand on end" the first time he heard Presley's "Heartbreak Hotel" in 1956. "We'd never heard American voices singing like that. They'd always be like Sinatra or enunciated very well. Suddenly there's this hillbilly hiccupping on tape echo and all this bluesy background going on. And we didn't know what the hell Presley was singing about." For Lennon as for many of his contemporaries, the sheer emotional power of the recording, its visceral power, obviated any need for a literal understanding of the lyrics. The strange, barely decipherable cadences of the voice simply added to the mystique. "It took a long time to work out what was going on. To us, it just sounded like a noise that was great."[54]

Such responses were hardly unique. Indeed, one could do worse than consider each of the Beatles' most important early musical inspirations to demonstrate the sheer pervasiveness of southern influences on their generation of British musicians.[55] However, that generation's deep admiration for southern music and its rebel rockers was often tempered by a much greater appreciation of the region's racial shortcomings. While youngsters like John, Paul, George, and Ringo could easily accept the music's lower-class southern credentials, embracing them along with its perceived sexual abandon and disregard for other middle-class niceties as part of their own gestures of nonconformity, they often found it less easy to ignore the continuing disregard for black rights in the region. In effect, what had happened was that press coverage of the early civil rights movement and the rise of Massive Resistance, coupled with a growing awareness of racial problems at home and in the Commonwealth, had changed the context and raised the stakes for British fans of southern-derived music forms. It became much more difficult to cling uncritically to romantic visions of southern charm, honor, grace, rural idyllicism, or even urban outlaw cool as stories from Montgomery, Tuscaloosa, Birmingham, Little Rock, and Clinton rolled off the presses and flickered across the television screens. Certainly, while black southern artists like Little Richard, Fats Domino, and Larry Williams were celebrated in Britain alongside their white counterparts, Elvis, Jerry Lee, Carl Perkins, and Buddy Holly, it became virtually impossible to hear the marvelously hybrid sounds of the South as the unproblematic products of joyous interracial cultural exchanges.

The author gratefully acknowledges the assistance of Steve Klinge, Helen McQuinn, Andreu Walker, Colin Ward, and Jenny Ward while researching aspects of this essay.

Afterword

On the Irrelevance of Knights

MICHAEL O'BRIEN

If the originating symposium for this book had been held about a hundred years ago in Oxford, Mississippi, it would have looked very different. Almost certainly, it would have been a celebration of Anglo-Saxon unity. There would have been much talk of civilization and German forests, the white man's burden, England's green and pleasant land, southern manners and hospitality, and the inestimable gift of the English language. Perhaps there might have been a concert, where they would have played Edward Elgar's *Land of Hope and Glory*, which had recently been written. Perhaps LeRoy Percy might have come over from Greenville, reminisced about Harry Hotspur, and quoted Shakespeare about summoning spirits from the vasty deep. Perhaps there might have been talk of a shared democracy, though (considering the recent disfranchisement movement in Mississippi) perhaps not. The talismanic meaning of there being an Oxford, both here and there, would almost inevitably have been invoked.

Whatever one might think of that vision—and it is hard to think well of it—it would have had an intellectual coherence, a unity of myth, a rationale. All that has gone now. For now there are no Anglo-Saxons, there or here, save in the imagination of a few French intellectuals and politicians. This being so, what gives coherence to the topic of Britain and the American South in 2003, instead of 1903?

First a caveat, to do with the matter of "Britain." Almost everyone is familiar with the difficulty of the term *the South*. Many a Porter Fortune Symposium has gotten itself into a knot over what, if anything, that phrase means. But the instability of the term *Britain* is also pertinent. For, at best, *Britain* is a geographical expression, the name of an island. There is also something wider called *Great Britain*, which is an archipelago or collection of islands. At different times, on those islands, there have been various polities—Wessex, Mercia, Fife, England, Wales, Scotland, Ireland, the Isle of Man, Sark, Northern Ireland, the Irish Free State, Eire—which have fluctuated in their relationships, have come and gone, and interacted asymmetrically.[1] At best, of late, there has been something that (excluding Eire) can be regarded as a federal structure, a unity of kingdoms as the United States is a unity of republics, though the United Kingdom is a federation of dazzling illogicality, of almost Austro-Hungarian confusion. This illogicality has deepened in recent years, with the advent of the European Union above the nation state (if that is what the United Kingdom is), the coming of Scottish and Welsh devolution below or beside it, and the regular appearing and disappearing of Northern Ireland as a polity. The result is that the British have little idea of who they are and are getting more confused by the year.

An anecdote illustrates the point. Some years ago, in the early 1990s, I acquired American citizenship. I was then living in Ohio. The U.S. Congress had begun to be unpleasant towards resident aliens, so my immigration lawyer advised that having dual citizenship would offer more safety. So off I trotted to the federal courthouse in Cincinnati, there to be sworn in by a judge, who explained the meaning of the American republic with much inaccuracy. That was not unexpected. But a strange scene was enacted. The clerk of the court required of the immigrants, seated in rows on hard benches, that when she called out our names, we should each stand up, repeat our names, state our country of origin, and then sit down. I happened to be about the second or third person to be called. I had to decide quickly what was my country of origin. This was not self-evident. I decided that, legally, I was from the United Kingdom. I had a fleeting memory that, on the Security Council in the United Nations, that was the name on the little plaque in front of the British ambassador. So I stood up, said my name, announced "the United Kingdom," and resumed my seat. I suppose I should have said "the United Kingdom of Great Britain and Northern Ireland," which has been the country's official name since 1927, but that would have been pedantic, even for a historian. Others followed, but very rapidly (because it seemed redundant) they stopped repeating their names, so they only stood up and said their countries. Nigeria, India, Cambodia, Nicaragua, and so forth were shouted out in a roll call of allegiances foresworn. But I noticed that those from the British Isles were indecisive. A few said "England." Someone agreed with me on the "United Kingdom." Somebody said "Britain." A defiant old lady said "Great Britain," with an emphasis that betokened a want of enthusiasm for her new passport. No one, I noticed, said Scotland or Wales, but that may have been a fluke, that no one came from there, or it is possible that "Britain" is what you say at such an event, if you are not English. Someone from Ulster would have been much vexed to know what to say and, I suppose, their response might have depended on their religion—"Britain" for the Protestant, "Ireland" for the Catholic. My own decision was, after all, arbitrary. Where you think you come from need not be a legal matter. Legally, there is nowhere called the South, though many imagine it to be a place they come from.

I mention this story because these scholarly essays are, because of this historical complexity, necessarily wavering in what they understand to be contrapuntal to the South. The colonialists speak almost exclusively of England. Anglicization is Max Edelson's topic, the Church of England that of Franklin Lambert, the transmission of English concepts of property and power that of Holly Brewer. Almost nowhere does one find discussion of the Scots, the Welsh, and the Irish. Perhaps the omission of the Welsh is not an immense loss, for they came in very small numbers, but one of those Welsh families was called Jefferson, so their influence was not insignificant. (One might read the *Summary View of the Rights of British America* as a very Welsh document.) But the Irish and the Scots are another matter. One could, quite easily, have put together parallel books on the southern connection to Scotland and to Ireland, with papers on Presbyterianism, Scottish philosophy, Irish laborers, Adam Smith and classical economics, the North-South divide in British culture, and the ideology of Unionism.

The later essays in this volume, logically, tend to be more acquainted with the construct of Britain and draw their evidence from more than England. Even so, Marcus Wood gives us an essay on English print satire, not Scottish. Richard Blackett talks at length about Liverpool, but seems here to have little interest in Glasgow, Cork, or Cardiff, though they, too, had opinions about the Confederacy and were all, in 1863, British places.[2] (It is worth conceding, however, that Liverpool was more than a place where only the English lived.) Hugh Wilford does, perhaps, best in escaping the English hegemony, because he is peculiarly interested in the Labour Party, which had great strength in the "Celtic fringe," so Welsh and Scottish names occur in his discussion: Aneurin Bevan, a miners' gala in Cardiff, and so on pop up. And Brian Ward knows what Scottish schoolchildren thought of Elvis Presley and knows that Lonnie Donegan came from Glasgow.

I mention this matter, not much to observe a lacuna, but mostly to indicate that both the South and Britain have been moving targets, not fixed points, each a mix of cultures much in flux. As a result, the southern/British connections one might identify have come and gone, and changed in their nature. For example, since there was no "South" before the nineteenth century, in any meaningful sense, Edelson, Lambert, and Brewer rightly and inescapably deal with South Carolina and Virginia, not with the wider South. That they relate these colonies, at least after the Act of Union in 1707, to England and not Britain may be less inescapable. But the case made by Linda Colley that the eighteenth century made a British nation needs to be regarded with much skepticism.[3] Yet even the matter of England is not straightforward. Jamestown, 1607, and all that do not stand now, as they did in 1903. The old narrative of American history saw English culture as foundational, as making the presumptions which survived and civilized the infusion of other immigrant cultures, which is why many years ago American history departments always had an English medieval historian and a Tudor-Stuart historian, people who had read Frederic Maitland and knew about the Rough Wooing. Arthur M. Schlesinger Jr. seems still to believe this story, but he is now in a hopeless minority among historians, if less so among the general public.[4] As a number of the essays, especially that of Kathryn Braund, indicate, colonial culture is not now understood as an inception, but as a convergence. The South, to use the anachronistic term, was in 1650 or 1750 a space into which (from different directions) many differing cultures—Indian, Spanish, French,

English, Dutch, African—had moved and a space wherein they struggled for power, interacted, and changed one another. To be sure, those of English origin and descent gained the greatest social power, but it was shared with other Europeans (Germans, Sephardic Jews, Huguenots, Scots, Scotch-Irish).

Further, it is not always clear what one might usefully understand as English, considering how disparate in the seventeenth century was custom, law, language, and economic behavior in places so different as East Anglia, London, Yorkshire, or Cornwall.[5] What is more clear, especially from the Edelson and Lambert essays, is that the invention of Englishness was, in part and often unsuccessfully, a venture of the colonial mind.[6] This accords with recent developments in British historiography, which has grown very interested in how the imperial experience dialectically formed metropolitan understandings.[7] It will be pertinent to add that the invention of Englishness was in the nineteenth century also to be a venture of the southern postcolonial mind, one of the ways by which southerners came to configure what they imagined they had been, as a predicate to understanding what they had become and might yet be.

Let me try to suggest a chronology, though scarcely a framework, for the cultural understandings implicated in the southern/British equation. I discern four phases: the colonial period from 1607 to 1776; that from 1776 to the early 1840s; that from the early 1840s to the end of the Second World War; then, lastly, the late twentieth century. But, before sketching these, it will be important to reiterate—the theme appears in many of these essays—that often Britain and the South have had little to do with one another and, when they have, have usually demonstrated remarkable ignorance and obtuseness about the other. Both are large and complicated cultures, with many preoccupations and interests, with many other exogenous cultures to address at those moments when the outward gaze was required. So much has been oblique.

One might think, with some justice, that this obtuseness was less evident in the earliest period, when the colonies were crowded with migrants from the British Isles, but even then the metropolis seems to have been vague about what they did in Virginia, where it was, and whether it mattered. Holly Brewer's essay, though it plausibly argues for a continuity with late medieval and early modern English legal culture and reasoning, suggests that Virginia had much independence and discretion, that continuity should be understood as an invention, as well as a fate. Still, it is very clear that up to the 1770s the southern/British connection was powerful and significant, though more so for the settlers, less for the metropolitan British. For the next seventy years or so, that connection palpably weakened. The South is more remarkable for Anglophobia than Anglophilia in the late eighteenth and early nineteenth centuries. Aside from the political struggle, the little matter of British troops burning the White House, and the Battle of New Orleans, the growing British patronage of the antislavery movement drove a great wedge between the two cultures, as Richard Blackett shows. Marcus Wood, too, gives compelling evidence for this mutual dislike and, indeed, his essay makes much intelligible in the British response to the South even in the twentieth century, when the idea of the lazy, ignorant, violent, and cruel southerner persists, even unto the days of Jerry Lee Lewis.

But, even if earlier the British had not placed themselves in the forefront of the antislavery movement and there had been harmony between Britain and the South over slavery, I suspect that Anglophobia would have been powerful, anyway. The independent South was in a postcolonial phase and very anxious to fashion its cultural meaning out of local materials, but also to look beyond Britain to other cultural influences—the North, France, Germany, Italy, and elsewhere. John Randolph, who was a fierce Anglophile, was very much an oddity in the 1820s and 1830s. Very few southern intellectuals and political leaders spent much time in Britain in the early decades of the nineteenth century. A partial exception to this, however, needs to be noted. Scottish culture, in both its Enlightenment and Romantic incarnations—Adam Smith, Thomas Reid, Walter Scott—remained attractive for southerners, but this was only a confirmation of Anglophobia, for the Scots offered the precedent of a provincial society which, by commerce and intellect, had made a powerful society that compelled respect, and (as a not-incidental bonus) one that was antipathetic to the English.

This Anglophobia began to change in about the 1840s, though partially. Slavery remained a deep irritant, of course. But the Webster-Ashburton Treaty of 1842 removed Britain as a political and military competitor in the southern part of North America. And the South, perhaps the most aggressively imperialist part of the United States, took advantage of the opportunities thus licensed.

Though even after 1783 British writers had never ceased to be popular, because they offered nostalgia for a vanished order (reading Laurence Sterne) or provided guides to new ideas (reading the *Edinburgh Review*), the newer crop after the 1820s were read with closer sympathy. This change was subtle, but palpable. Thackeray, Dickens, Tennyson, Carlyle, all the mid-Victorians, evoked a sympathetic response in southerners like John Pendleton Kennedy, John R. Thompson, and William Henry Trescot. Thackeray came and admired the South (then caroused with Trescot at the Café de Paris), Kennedy went to London and corresponded with Macaulay, Thompson visited Carlyle in Cheyne Row, Josiah Nott became an Honorary Fellow of the Anthropological Society of London.[8] These people liked each other, took one another to gentleman's clubs, were capital fellows together. The world was being made that eventually produced Woodrow Wilson, the southerner who was a Gladstonian, and Walter Hines Page, the North Carolinian who became ambassador to the Court of Saint James and insisted that the United States and Britain should stand together as English-speaking bulwarks against the ravages of Teutonic evil.[9]

Imperialism and race were at the center of the transformation. Both Britain and the South had by 1850 accepted a sense of themselves as imperial and racialist cultures. This was a contested matter in both places, but the British who eventually proclaimed their queen as Empress of India and the southerners who planted the American flag on the ramparts of Mexico City knew with clarity that they had an expansionist mission, which involved remaking the world in their image. They also knew that this process involved subjugating and exploiting assorted alien peoples. Slavery was, before the Civil War, a difficulty in retarding a sense of comity, but one that many in the British and southern intelligentsias were doing their best, even before 1860, to diminish. The proslavery argument had arrived at the point, by the mid-1850s, of seeing slavery as only an incidental variant on systems of labor and racial control, and writers like Carlyle were speaking freely of the "nigger question." With emancipation, there was little to inhibit a rampant sense of comity.

Here one must note the pertinence of a development within the South. By far the most important inhibitor of the Anglo-Saxon myth before 1865 was the very heterogeneity of the southern population. Huguenots, Jews, Scots, Acadians, Scotch-Irish, Germans—let alone African-Americans and Native Americans—had no particular reason to embrace the idea that the South was an Anglo-Saxon culture; they were more remarkable in 1830 for cultivating their own ethnic and racial identities. But, by the end of the nineteenth century, the secular trends of cultural assimilation, especially high levels of intermarriage, when combined with the wrenching experiences of the Civil War and Reconstruction, and then the racial bonding impelled by the formalization of segregation, made southern identity itself more central to those who lived in the southeastern United States. Being southern had been far less important before 1860, but after 1865 it became imperative to find a historical grounding for the idea of a unitary southern culture. Of the various possible myths, the English one was most available. A significant nuance here is that the Civil War was to give Virginia an especial cultural authority in the postwar era, and even before 1860, for obvious reasons, the Virginians had been more susceptible to the English myth. Hence, after 1880 or so, the narrative from Jamestown was freshly pertinent. So eventually we get that dreadful pageant about the lost colony of Roanoke, so eventually Mr. Rockefeller thought it important that Williamsburg be remade, so Virginian heiresses started showing up in London to marry lords, who were very glad to be so married and began to think well of the College of William and Mary, as they made their way to the bank. If one wished to write a history of this phase, one would go from Thomas Carlyle to Winston Churchill, from John Pendleton Kennedy to John Crowe Ransom. In this story, T. S. Eliot and Allen Tate would need to feature largely, and figures like Lady Astor.

The era since 1945 has been very different, largely because Britain began to enter a post-imperial phase. The South, of course, did not and has still not entered such a phase. The United States has waxed as a great imperial power—indeed, the greatest of such powers—and southerners, as politicians and cultural agents, as Lyndon Johnson and Elvis Presley, have been immensely significant in that process. Hence an asymmetry has developed, which is worth exploring briefly, for southern interest in Britain has lessened, while British interest in the South has grown.

It is my impression that, even now, some southerners have retained a sanitized version of the Anglo-Saxon myth. Certainly, in the last thirty-odd years of traveling in the South, I have frequently encountered a puzzlingly warm Anglophilia, though it seems to be a upper-middle-class phenomenon, issuing from people who collect antiques and remember Mrs Miniver. I have not encountered it much in diners and gas stations, though often in Charlestonian drawing rooms. But I think this Anglophilia, as elsewhere in American culture, has been steadily receding. Certainly, I have never found it wise, when around southerners, to presume any particular knowledge of British literature or politics, which (if I had lived in 1850 or 1940) I might once safely have assumed. This is not to say I have not encountered such knowledge, but the modern dynamics of southern society no longer naturally produce it. There is no particular reason, any more, why it should, other than the accessibility offered by a shared language. But English, of course, is no longer just a possession of what Churchill called the English-speaking peoples.

On the other hand, as Brian Ward and Hugh Wilford help us to see, British interest in the South is greater than it was, certainly in academic circles, but in popular culture, too. Though this phenomenon has nuances peculiar to Britain, I would see this as a local variant on the widespread influence of American culture in the modern world. We could look at German or Hindi or Australian culture and see similar patterns, see country-and-western singers and jazz musicians and rock musicians in Hamburg, New Delhi, and Sydney, see bemused academics in Tokyo and Cairo trying to grapple with Faulkner's prose. It is possible that the British are a touch more aware of the distinction between southerners and other Americans than are some other cultures—the French may be more aware, though—but I have had enough experiences in Britain to make me doubtful even of that. So it is symptomatic that, in this book, the earlier essays tend to be concerned with what the South thought of Britain, but the later essays deal with what Britain thinks of the South; cultural authority first moved from east to west, but now often runs from west to east.

In this recent phase, race has remained central, though differently. Race used to be an idea propounded in Britain, but mostly an experience elsewhere. Gravely complacent men in London institutions once drew up charts of human evolution, in which it was explained how Leamington Spa and Tunbridge Wells were superior to Kandahar and Lagos, yet those men had little occasion at home to encounter an Afghan or a Nigerian. But the eventual harvest of Empire brought many "non-white" peoples to Britain—Jamaicans and Kenyans, Pakistanis and Chinese—and Britain is now, though less so than the United States, a multicultural society. Notting Hill riots and Notting Hill festivals have changed understandings. To comprehend these fresh realities, some Britons have grown interested in the southern experience, in slavery, segregation, and civil rights, in William Faulkner and Louis Armstrong. But it will be important to stress that this is part of a wider interest, in African history, in the Indian experience, and in diasporas. There has been a widespread sense that the indigenous intellectual and aesthetic traditions of British culture do not help much in the endeavor of understanding race. Jane Austen is no longer enough. Even *Othello* is not enough.

But now a different sort of Briton is involved in this dialogue. This is no longer just a conversation among white people. In truth, it never was, though the whites seldom noticed. Olaudah Equiano, Frederick Douglass, William Wells Brown, and Alexander Crummell all once had significant British experiences. Equiano passed from southern Nigeria to the West Indies and Virginia, but ended up as a Methodist married to an Englishwoman and living in London. Douglass went from a Maryland plantation to refuge in the North, but his visits to Britain famously provided him with a comparative perspective on American racism. Brown went from slavery in Kentucky and Missouri to Canada and, eventually, to writing travel accounts of Britain. Crummell, a northern free black, studied at the University of Cambridge before becoming an Episcopalian missionary in Liberia and a minister back in the United States, where he wrote extensively on southern society.[10]

It is an incident in the life of Crummell that catches the ambivalence of Victorian Britain about race, the confused impulses that led many to oppose the Confederacy and many to support it. A story of Crummell's graduation at Cambridge in 1853 is told in A. C. Benson's life of his father. It begins, "On a certain Degree day in 1850 or thereabouts, a West African undergraduate named Crummell, of Queens', a man of colour, appeared in the Senate House to take his degree." No doubt, it is symptomatic that an English clergyman—Benson himself was relaying an anecdote furnished by the Reverend J. Bowman of New Southgate—would presume that a black attendant at Cambridge would come from Africa, not from the United States. It continues, "A boisterous individual in the gallery called out 'Three groans for the Queens' nigger.'" Here Victorian racism is palpable. But, "A pale slim undergraduate, very youthful-looking, in the front of the gallery . . . became scarlet with indignation, and shouted in a voice which re-echoed through the building, 'Shame, shame! Three groans for you, Sir!' and immediately afterwards, 'Three cheers for Crummell!' This was taken up in all directions . . . and the original offender had to stoop down to hide himself from the storm of groans and hisses that broke out all around him." The defender was E. W. Benson of Trinity College, who went on to become Archbishop of Canterbury.[11] The message of the story is complacent, but it is doubtful that these cheers for Alexander Crummell signaled a transcendence of racism, merely that an English gentleman should not stoop to cheap insults of even inferiors. The young men of Cambridge, who went forth from the Senate House in 1853 to quash the Indian mutiny and to govern their empire were not remarkable for advancing racial equality.

The triangulation of Africa, the Americas, and western Europe goes to the heart of the southern/British equation. It was the British attitude towards and experience of Africa (and Asia beyond) which predicated much in their understanding of the South. The British saw in the South a caricature of what they feared they themselves might be in South Africa and elsewhere, or an affirmation of what they felt they needed to be to sustain their mastery, or a complacent reassurance that a British empire was a more moral thing than a southern one. Concomitantly, the white southern experience of African-Americans structured much in how the former envisioned a pertinence for the British experience. For white southerners, Britain became a sort of historical touchstone. To claim the title of Anglo-Saxon in 1890 was to assert that slavery had made no difference, that there was nothing in being southern that needed an explanation drawn from the longstanding presence of adjacent Africans. In that sense, the British idea for southerners served the great purpose of self-denial.

Many people have worked to efface that self-denial. Not insignificant, of late, has been the distinguished body of writing by those from the Caribbean and Africa, who are resident in Britain as migrants or the children of migrants, for whom the South has sometimes provided a point of reference, if one enfolded in the wider pattern of the black, brown, and beige Atlantic. I am thinking of Paul Gilroy, of course, but also figures like V. S. Naipaul, Caryl Phillips, and, in an earlier generation, the great C. L. R. James. One of the youngest of these is Gary Younge, a journalist for the *Guardian* in London, who in 1999 published a book called *No Place Like Home: A Black Briton's Journey Through the American South*.[12] Richard Blackett himself—born in Trinidad, educated in Manchester, living in Nashville—can partly be seen as contributing to this tradition.

Here the asymmetry between British perceptions of the South and southern perceptions of Britain is most marked. On the whole, in recent times, elite southerners have drawn from Britain an image of conservative hierarchy, but have not often been nourished by the radical side of British society. As Ransom put it in 1930, "England was . . . the model employed by the South, in so far as Southern culture was not quite indigenous. And there is in the South even today an Anglophile sentiment quite anomalous in the American scene. . . . The customs and institutions of England seem to the American observer very fixed and ancient."¹³ This sympathy, of course, marked a change from those expressed by many southerners in the eighteenth and early nineteenth centuries, when the Commonwealth republican tradition of James Harrington and Algernon Sidney had been resonant in places like Virginia and South Carolina. To be sure, there have been a few modern instances of southerners turning a little to the left by having learned something from Britain. Rupert Vance was influenced by Patrick Geddes, who was among the founders of British sociology and urban planning; the Highlander Folk School and Black Mountain College were nourished by the British workers' education movement (and the Scandinavian); and the musicological researches of John Lomax were much impelled by the antecedent work of British students of "folk music."¹⁴ Still, the mainstream has been more conservative. Today at golf tournaments on Hilton Head Island they play the bagpipes, but not many people are interested in Scottish socialism. The British, on the other hand, after their imperial phase, have mostly turned to the dissident elements in southern culture, to jazz, the blues, rock music, and radical political activism. The University of Newcastle takes a singular pride in having awarded an honorary degree to Martin Luther King Jr. in 1967. Oddly, then, the South may have done much to make Britain a more eclectic, even humane place, but I doubt that British influence on the South has been so salutary.

Since this is 2003 and not 1903, LeRoy Percy cannot speak his piece and rebuke the observations above. Instead he lies in his grave in Greenville, and over him broods the bronze statue of an English knight, leaning on his broadsword and encased in chain mail and armor. Upon the tomb are written words from Matthew Arnold's poem "The Last Word," which speak of battle, loss, and honorable death. To LeRoy's son, William Alexander Percy, who commissioned the statue and the tomb in the early 1930s, the chivalric and English iconography seemed apposite, even moving.¹⁵ It would be pleasant to reflect that, today, the imagery has become irrelevant. It would be still more agreeable to imagine a time when a southern tomb might be guarded by the statue of a Tolpuddle Martyr. But that seems an improbability.

Notes

Notes to VIRGINIA'S RELIGIOUS REVOLUTION
by Franklin T. Lambert

1. "New Lights" was a derogatory term for evangelicals who supported the religious revival known as the Great Awakening, which swept much of New England and the middle colonies in the late 1730s and early 1740s. The so-called Log College at Neshaminy, Pennsylvania, was the principal seminary for training New Light itinerants, such as Davies.

2. William Perry, ed., *Historical Collections Relating to the American Colonial Church*, 5 vols. (1870; reprint, New York: AMS Press, 1969), 1:372.

3. Thomas Jefferson, *Notes on the State of Virginia*, ed. William Peden (Chapel Hill: Univ. of North Carolina Press, 1982).

4. Sociologists Roger Finke and Rodney Stark have given this approach much of its theoretical form. They write, "Religious economies are like commercial economies in that they consist of a market made up of a set of current and potential customers and a set of firms seeking to serve that market. The fate of these firms will depend upon (1) aspects of their organizational structures, (2) their sales representatives, (3) their product, and (4) their marketing techniques." Roger Finke and Rodney Stark, *The Churching of America, 1776–1990: Winners and Losers in Our Religious Economy* (New Brunswick, N.J.: Rutgers Univ. Press, 1992), 17.

5. Adam Smith, *An Inquiry into the Nature and Causes of the Wealth of Nations*, eds. R. H. Campbell and A. S. Skinner, 2 vols. (Indianapolis: Liberty Classics, 1981), 2:797.

6. Paul Ford, ed., *The Writings of Thomas Jefferson*, 12 vols. (New York: G. P. Putnam's Sons, 1904), 1:61–62.

7. Smith, *The Wealth of Nations*, 2:792–93.

8. Ibid.

9. For the best study of Virginia's political culture on the eve of the Revolution, see Rhys Isaac, *The Transformation of Virginia, 1740–1790* (New York: W. W. Norton, 1982).

10. Cited in Henry Bettenson, ed., *Documents of the Christian Church*, 2d ed. (New York: Oxford Univ. Press, 1970), 235.

11. Samuel Hopkins, *The Puritans: The Church, Court, and Parliament of England, During the Reigns of Edward VI and Queen Elizabeth*, 3 vols. (Boston: Gould and Lincoln, 1860), 2:486–89.

12. William W. Hening, ed., *The Statutes at Large Being a Collection of all the Laws of Virginia, From the First Session of the Legislature in the Year 1619*, 13 vols. (Richmond: Samuel Pleasants, Printer to the Commonwealth, 1810), 1:23.

13. *A Collection of All the Acts of Assembly, Now in Force, in the Colony of Virginia* (Williamsburg: William Parks, 1733), 2–3.

14. J. Franklin Jameson, ed., *Johnson's Wonder-Working Providence, 1628–1651* (New York: C. Scribner's Sons, 1910), 265.

15. Louis Wright, ed., *The History and Present State of Virginia, By Robert Beverley* (Chapel Hill: Univ. of North Carolina Press, 1947), 65–68, 261.

16. Hening, ed., *[Virginia] Statutes at Large*, 1:312–15.

17. C. G. Chamberlayne, ed., *The Vestry Book of St. Paul's Parish, Hanover County, Virginia, 1706–1786* (Richmond: The Library Board, 1940), 376.

18. Gabriel Thomas, *An Historical and Geographical Account of the Province and Country of Pennsylvania* (London: Society of Friends, 1698), 23–45.

19. Richard Hooker, ed., *The Carolina Backcountry on the Eve of the Revolution: The Journal and Other Writings of Charles Woodmason, Anglican Itinerant* (Chapel Hill: Univ. of North Carolina Press, 1953), xix, 13.

20. Ibid.

21. Ibid.

22. See Robert Leland Bidwell, "The Morris Reading-Houses: A Study in Dissent," MSS 7:3, Virginia Historical Society, 7–9, 23–24, 29.

23. Ibid., 34.

24. Ibid., 29–30.

25. John Gillies, *Historical Collections Relating to Remarkable Periods of the Success of the Gospel*, 2 vols. (Glasgow: Robert Andrews Foulis, 1754), 2:332–33.

26. Hooker, *Carolina Backcountry*, 42–43, 111–13.

27. Ibid., 90.

28. Ford, *Works of Thomas Jefferson*, 1:62.

29. Cited in Karen Kupperman, ed., *Major Problems in American Colonial History* (Lexington, Mass.: D. C. Heath, 1993), 374–75.

30. Ibid., 373.

31. John Leland, *The Virginia Chronicle* (Norfolk: Prentis and Baxter, 1789), 3–4.

32. John Leland, *The Rights of Conscience Inalienable* (Richmond: T. Nicolson, 1793), 4.

33. Christine Heyrman, *Southern Cross: The Beginnings of the Bible Belt* (New York: A. A. Knopf, 1997), 14.

34. *Virginia Gazette*, November 14 to November 21, 1745.

35. Ibid.

36. Ibid., March 5, 1752.

37. Ibid., March 5, 1752.

38. Ibid., April 3, 1752.

39. Jefferson, *Notes on the State of Virginia*, 157.

40. Charles James, ed., *Documentary History of the Struggle for Religious Liberty in Virginia* (New York: Da Cappo Press, 1971), 76–77.

41. Ibid., 68–69.
42. William Henry Foote, *Sketches of Virginia, Historical and Biographical* (Philadelphia: William S. Martien, 1850), 323–24.
43. James, ed., *Documentary History*, 80–81.
44. Ibid., 92–94, 100.
45. Ibid., 129.
46. Cited in L. F. Greene, ed., *The Writings of John Leland* (New York: Arno Press, 1969), 184.
47. Cited in Michael Kammen, ed., *The Origins of the American Constitution: A Documentary History* (New York: Penguin, 1986), 369.
48. James Madison to Robert Walsh, March 2, 1819, *Letters and Other Writings of James Madison*, 4 vols. (New York: B. Lippincott and Co., 1884), 3:121–26.

Notes to POWER AND AUTHORITY IN THE COLONIAL SOUTH
by Holly Brewer

1. See John Marshall Mitnick, "From Neighbor-Witness to Judge of Proofs: The Transformation of the English Civil Juror," *American Journal of Legal History* 32 (1988): 201–35; Barbara J. Shapiro, *Beyond Reasonable Doubt and Probable Cause* (Berkeley, Calif.: Univ. of California Press, 1991); Thomas Andrew Green, *Verdict According to Conscience: Perspectives on the English Trial Jury, 1200–1800* (Chicago, Ill.: Univ. of Chicago Press, 1985).

2. Robert Filmer, *The Freeholder's Grand Inquest* (London, 1648), in *Patriarcha and Other Writings*, ed. Johann P. Sommerville (Cambridge, U.K.: Cambridge Univ. Press, 1991) 69–130, esp. 69–80; this is the main point of the pamphlet.

3. Reprinted in David Wooten, ed., *Divine Right and Democracy* (London: Penguin Books, 1986), 104.

4. Thomas Paine, *Common Sense* (1776) in *Thomas Paine Reader*, ed. Michael Foot and Isaac Kramnick (London: Penguin Books, 1987), 101. "Virtue is not hereditary" was one of his tamer statements. He effectively makes "hereditary right" seem ridiculous.

5. *5 Eliz. c. 4., 1563 [Statute of Artificers] c. 3, 5, 17, 28*. On service in husbandry during this period, see especially Ann Kussmaul, *Servants in Husbandry in Early Modern England* (Cambridge, U.K.: Cambridge Univ. Press, 1981); Paul Griffiths, *Youth and Authority: Formative Experiences in England, 1560–1640* (Oxford, U.K.: Oxford Univ. Press, 1996); Ilana Krausman Ben-Amos, *Adolescence and Youth in Early Modern England* (New Haven, Conn.: Yale Univ. Press, 1994). Most of the children entering service seem to have been older than ten, although the research on this question is still far from complete. See e.g. Ben-Amos, *Adolescence and Youth*, 260 n 125.

None of these books emphasize the point I do here, about what it means to indenture children in this manner, in terms of hereditary status. Susan Reynolds's *Fiefs and Vassals: The Medieval Evidence Reinterpreted* (Oxford, U.K.: Oxford Univ. Press, 1994), esp. chapters 1 and 8, challenges the conception that pure feudalism ever existed in England. Still, it is clear that villeins by the legal norms did pass on their status to their children, just as the lord of the manor did to his eldest son, in particular.

6. [Thomas Cramner], *Boke of Common Prayer, and Administracion of the Sacramentes and other Rites and Ceremonies in the Churche of Englande* (London, 1549), reprinted in F. E. Brightman, ed., *The English Rite* (London: Rivingtons, 1921), 2:784–85. The 1552 and later official versions were similar.

7. Stephen Marshall, *A Sermon of the Baptizing of Infants: Preached in the Abbey Church at Westminster at the Morning Lecture, Appointed by the Honourable House of Commons* (London: Richard Cotes, 1644), 7, 8, 14–15. Marshall was a key compromise player in the religious disputes of the 1640s. He was appointed by the House of Lords in 1641, for example, to a committee to reconcile Presbyterians to the Anglican Church. While he distanced himself, as the 1640s progressed, from the Anglican church's episcopal hierarchy, he adhered to the Anglican position in many other ways. s.v. "Stephen Marshall," in Leslie Stephen et al., eds., *Dictionary of National Biography* (Oxford, U.K.: Oxford Univ. Press, 1917), 12:1128–1132.

8. Holly Brewer, "Entailing Aristocracy in Colonial Virginia: 'Ancient Feudal Restraints' and Revolutionary Reforms," *William and Mary Quarterly*, 3d ser., 54 (1997): 307–46.

9. J. G. A. Pocock, *The Ancient Constitution and the Feudal Law: A Study of English Historical Thought in the Seventeenth Century: A Reissue with Retrospect* (Cambridge, U.K.: Cambridge Univ. Press, 1987), esp. 64–66, 68, 74, 82, 119–23, 243.

10. Reynolds, *Fiefs and Vassals*, chapters 1 and 8.

11. John Milton, *The Tenure of Kings and Magistrates: Proving That it is Lawfull, and hath been so through all Ages, for Any, Who Have the Power, to Call to Account a Tyrant. . . .* (London: Matthew Simmons, 1649); for the Putney debates, see Wooten, ed., *Divine Right and Democracy,* 286. Also see Christopher Hill, *Intellectual Origins of the English Revolution Revisited* (Oxford, U.K.: Clarendon Press, 1997), especially chapter 8.

12. [John Tombes], *An Examen of the Sermon . . .* (London: George Whitington, 1645), 54; Tombes, *An Apologie for the Two Treatises,* published as part of *Two Treatises and an Appendix to them Concerning Infant Baptism* (London: George Whitington, 1646), 87.

13. Locke was cited more than any other author in American newspapers in the 1770s, to give only one example. See Donald S. Lutz, "The Relative Influence of European Writers on Late Eighteenth-Century American Political Thought," *American Political Science Review* 78 (1984): 189–97. Locke's writings on government and on human understanding were widely read in the eighteenth century and influenced a whole range of other authors, from philosophical to religious and legal

(e.g., Thomas Reid and Hutcheson, the Third Earl of Shaftesbury [grandson to Locke's mentor], were Locke's students). See, in part, David Lundberg and Henry F. May, "The Enlightened Reader in America," *American Quarterly* 28 (1976): 262-93. William Blackstone cites Locke repeatedly in his *Commentaries on the Law of England* (London, 1765-1769). On religious dissenters and political dissent in the 1680s, see among others, Richard Ashcraft, *Revolutionary Politics and John Locke's Two Treatises of Government* (Princeton, N.J.: Princeton Univ. Press, 1986), especially chapter 2. Also see Holly Brewer, *By Birth or Consent: Children, Law, and Revolution in England and America, 1550-1820* (Chapel Hill, N.C.: Univ. of North Carolina Press for the Institute of Early American History and Culture, 2003), chapter 3.

14. [John Trenchard and Thomas Gordon], *Cato's Letters or Essays on Liberty, Civil and Religious . . .* , 3d ed., 4 vols. (London: W. Wilkins, 1733), 2:89.

15. John Locke, *A Letter Concerning Toleration* (1685), in *John Locke: Political Writings*, ed. David Wooten (New York: Penguin, 1993), 396.

16. John Locke, *Two Treatises of Government*, book 2, chapter 16, "Of Conquest," para. 188 and 189, ed. Peter Laslett (Cambridge, U.K.: Cambridge Univ. Press, 1988), 393.

17. Ibid., para. 189.

18. Other scholars (notably Edmund Morgan in *American Slavery, American Freedom: The Ordeal of Colonial Virginia* [New York: Norton, 1975], esp. chapters 15 and 16) have pointed to several pieces of evidence to argue that Locke supported slavery and hereditary right: he wrote the *Fundamental Constitutions of Carolina* in 1669 that set up a hierarchical, semi-feudal system of hereditary status; he briefly owned shares in the Royal African Company (which had monopoly power from the British government to import slaves into their colonies in the New World) in 1674 and 1675; and he drafted a revision of the poor law in 1697 that forced poor children, as young as three, to labor. For the first, he wrote the *Fundamental Constitutions* while secretary to Shaftesbury, one of the original proprietors, and clearly under the direction of all eight proprietors (one of whom was William Berkeley, governor of Virginia, a staunch Royalist and supporter of hierarchy). We can hardly call this a pure expression of his own ideals. For the second, his buying shares in the Royal African Company certainly seems damning. But he did not own them long. While it is important to acknowledge that he bought those shares, he sold them quickly.

Locke seems to have developed his opposition to hereditary right only gradually. He became more radical over time. His two essays on toleration, for example, written almost twenty years apart, in 1667 and 1685, were very different. The first advocated only limited toleration and supported hierarchy. The latter argued for significant toleration and advocated free consent in religious matters. His drafting of the *Fundamental Constitutions* and buying and selling of RAC stock preceded the writing of his two treatises of government by a decade. Perhaps they even helped to shape his opinions there against slavery and hereditary right. See Ashcraft,

Revolutionary Politics and Locke's Two Treatises of Government, esp. 409n and 413n (on Royal African Company) and chapter 3 (on Locke's increasing radicalism). On the extent of Locke's authorship of the *Fundamental Constitutions of Carolina,* see K. H. D. Haley, *The First Earl of Shaftesbury* (Oxford, U.K.: Oxford Univ. Press, 1968), 242–48.

19. Richard S. Dunn, ed., *The Laws and Liberties of Massachusetts,* photostat of edition published in Cambridge in 1648 (San Marino, Calif.: Huntington Library, 1998), 4. On the capture and sale of Indians into slavery, see especially Jill Lepore, *In the Name of War* (New York: Knopf, 1998), 159–63.

20. See William Waller Hening, ed., *[Virginia] Statutes and Laws* (New York: Bartow, 1819–1823), 3:304–6 [1705].

21. Rowland Berthoff and John Murrin, "Feudalism, Communism, and the Yeoman Freeholder: The American Revolution Considered as a Social Accident," in *Essays on the American Revolution,* ed. Stephen G. Kurtz and James H. Hutson (Chapel Hill, N.C.: Univ. of North Carolina Press, 1973), esp. 266–68.

22. On the development of slavery in Virginia before 1660 and the gradual move toward making service life-long, see especially Winthrop Jordan, *White over Black: American Attitudes toward the Negro, 1550–1812* (Chapel Hill, N.C.: Institute of Early American History and Culture, 1968), and also T. H. Breen and Stephen Innes, *"Myne owne Ground": Race and Freedom on Virginia's Eastern Shore, 1640–1676* (New York: Oxford Univ. Press, 1980). On Barbados, see Richard S. Dunn, *Sugar and Slaves: The Rise of the Planter Class in the English West Indies, 1624–1713* (Chapel Hill, N.C.: Univ. of North Carolina Press, 1972), esp. 238–41, and Gary A. Puckrein, *Little England: Plantation Society and Anglo-Barbadian Politics, 1627–1700* (New York: New York Univ. Press, 1984), especially chapters 2 and 5. While Puckrein gives some wonderful detailed analysis of the politics on the island, he tends to naturalize slavery and to see the laws as irrelevant. Slavery itself does not need to be explained (see, for example, page 75, where he claims that the "planter patriarch" had virtually unlimited control over his slaves with little "interference" from "the state." Yet the government, of course, provided the means to control the slaves and to repress rebellions.).

23. Hening, ed., *[Virginia] Statutes and Laws,* 1:359–61 [1649]. In 1651 Berkeley was still speaking defiantly of the need to fight the soldiers that Parliament was sending to subdue the colony: "Gentlemen" he said to the Burgesses, "by the Grace of God we will not so tamely part with our King [Charles II]." The Assembly then passed another series of resolutions pledging their loyalty to Charles II and threatening to punish any who disagreed.

24. Public Record Office, CO1-26-77, as cited by Thomas J. Wertenbaker, *Virginia under the Stuarts* (Princeton, N.J.: Princeton Univ. Press, 1914), 144.

25. One might quibble that it is important that the status of children born to slavery was determined by their mother, a point explored extensively by Katherine Brown, who argues in *Good Wives, Nasty Wenches, and Anxious Patriarchs: Gender, Race, and Power in Colonial Virginia* (Chapel Hill, N.C.: Institute of Early American

History and Culture, 1996) that worries over paternal responsibility and even access to costless sex were part of why the law was so written. While undoubtedly there is some connection here, *this* practice had roots in English law, where illegitimate children had the status of the mother, and could not inherit from their father (unless some special provision was made). Regardless, I do not believe that the few cases of paternity support explain the timing of the legal change. One might as easily argue that the cases of paternity support were an outgrowth of the Puritan influence on Virginia in the 1650s. Even in the 1750s, paternity support for white illegitimate children was sharply limited in Virginia, as I have shown elsewhere.

26. Richard Ligon, *A True and Exact History of the Island of Barbados* (1647–1650), abridged, ed. Philip Sherlock (Mona, Jamaica: Univ. College of the West Indies, 1949), 16–17; Charles de Rochefort [before 1658], *The History of the Carriby-Islands*, trans. by John Davies (London, 1666), book 2, chapter 4, pp. 200–201. Ligon began as a slave trader, then owned a plantation in Barbados between 1647 and 1650, and then took up slave trading again; Dunn, *Sugar and Slaves*, 231. Ligon wrote his manuscript while imprisoned for debt in London in 1653. He differentiated clearly between servants and slaves in his account of Barbados, claiming that slavery was already perpetual and hereditary there: "The Iland is divided into three sorts of men, viz., Masters, Servants, and slaves. The slaves and their posterity, being subject to their masters for ever, are kept and preserv'd with greater care then the servants, who are theirs but for five years, according to the custom of the Iland"; Ligon, "A True and Exact History," 10. The difference in treatment was undoubtedly based to some degree on the Spanish and Portuguese practices, from whom Ligon and others purchased most of their slaves.

27. Puckrein, *Little England,* tries to dispute earlier historians' understanding of this issue, arguing that the politics of Barbados was only local. But his own evidence actually supports these earlier accounts (he does not actually seem very aware of the political or ideological debates in England and for him plantation society emerges full blown, with no need for justification). For the earlier accounts, see Vincent Harlowe, *History of Barbados* (1926; reprint, New York: Negro Universities Press, 1969), and N. Darnell Davis, *The Cavaliers and Roundheads of Barbados* (Georgetown, British Guiana: Argosy Press, 1887).

28. Holly Brewer, "Age of Reason? Children, Testimony, and Consent in Early America," in *The Many Legalities of Early America*, ed. Christopher L. Tomlins and Bruce Mann (Chapel Hill, N.C.: Univ. of North Carolina Press, 2001), 293–336, esp. 316–23.

29. There is a substantial literature on kidnaping. See Peter Coldham Wilson, "The 'Spiriting' of London Children to Virginia, 1648–1685," *Virginia Magazine of History and Biography* 83 (1975), 280–87; Coldham, *Emigrants in Chains: A Social History of Forced Emigration to the Americas of Felons, Destitute Children, Political and Religious Non-Conformists, Vagabonds, Beggars, and other Undesirables, 1607–1776* (Baltimore: Johns Hopkins Univ. Press, 1992), esp. chapter 7; Richard B. Morris,

Government and Labor in Early America (New York: Columbia Univ. Press, 1946), 340, 342; Holly Brewer, "Age of Reason?" esp. 316–22.

30. Bernard Bailyn, "Politics and Social Structure in Virginia," in *Seventeenth-Century America: Essays in Colonial History*, ed. James Morton Smith (Williamsburg, Va.: Institute of Early American History and Culture, 1959).

31. Hening, ed., *[Virginia] Statutes at Large*, 2:169–70, acts 11, 12.

32. For these laws, see Brewer, "Entailing Aristocracy." For one examination of the treatment of entailed slaves, see Lorena Walsh, *From Calabar to Carter's Grove: The History of a Virginia Slave Community* (Charlottesville, Va.: Univ. of Virginia Press, 1997), 44–45, 148, 211–13, 223, 310 n 11. Clearly the restrictions on the sale of entailed slaves could be avoided in some cases.

33. Thomas D. Morris, *Southern Slavery and the Law, 1619–1860* (Chapel Hill, N.C.: Univ of North Carolina Press, 1996), 39; St. George Tucker, *Blackstone's Commentaries* . . . (Philadelphia, Pa.: 1803); Brewer, "Entailing Aristocracy," 307–8, 338.

34. Richard Beale Davis, *William Fitzhugh and His Chesapeake World: The Fitzhugh Letters and Other Documents* (Chapel Hill, N.C.: Univ. of North Carolina Press, 1963), 33.

35. Louis B. Wright, ed., *Letters of Robert Carter, 1720–1727: The Commercial Interests of a Virginia Gentleman* (Westport, Conn.: Greenwood Press, 1940), vii, 8, 118; Brewer, "Entailing Aristocracy," 328–31.

36. Brewer, "Entailing Aristocracy," 307–46.

37. On the power of the Anglican Church in Virginia, see John Nelson, *"A Blessed Company: Parishes, Parsons, Parishioners, in Anglican Virginia, 1690–1776.* (Chapel Hill, N.C.: Univ. of North Carolina Press, 2002). On the question of divine right in English catechisms, see, among others, Ian Green, *The Christian's ABC: Catechisms and Catechizing in England, c. 1530–1740* (Oxford, 1996). [Richard Allestree], *The Whole Duty of Man* (London: William Norton, 1703), e.g. 104; Thomas Bacon, "Sermon to Slaves," in *Religion in American History: A Reader*, ed. Jon Butler and Harry S. Stout (New York: Oxford Univ. Press, 1998), 74–87.

38. As should be clear, I disagree with Morgan's interpretation of republican ideology in *American Slavery, American Freedom*, where he portrays it as justifying slavery. Morgan does not recognize any alternative ideology to republican; he does not see what Locke and others were arguing against. Therefore he missed the larger debate. Betty Wood's *The Origins of American Slavery: Freedom and Bondage in the English Colonies* (New York: Hill and Wang, 1997) provides a good summary of traditional interpretations, one which neatly blurs any ideological issues. Her reading of Massachusetts's statute on slavery in its *Body of Liberties* of 1641, for example, ignores the first, critical statement condemning slavery and villenage (p. 104). Karen Kupperman's *Providence Island, 1630–1641: The Other Puritan Colony* (Cambridge, U.K.: Cambridge Univ. Press, 1993) contends that Puritans owned slaves in their unsuccessful settlement in the Carribean, and thus contends that ideology cannot be the explanation for slavery. However the Providence Island settlement, while financed and

owned by proprietors who were Puritans, was not, by and large, settled by them. The settlement was intended as a base to attack Spaniards—slaves were obtained largely through raids on Spanish bases. Most of the settlers were soldiers who could participate in such attacks. The colony ended when it was finally overcome by the Spanish in 1641. For the Puritan lords who were involved in the Providence Island enterprise, attacking the Spanish Catholic empire was the most important goal. The slaves were imported against their instructions (see, e.g., Kupperman, *Providence Island*, 172).

Notes to "LIKE A STONE WALL NEVER TO BE BROKE"
by Kathryn E. Holland Braund

1. J. Brian Harley, "Rereading the Maps of the Columbian Encounter," *Annals of the Association of American Geographers* 82 (1992): 522, 529, 532.

2. These were held at Augusta (1763), Pensacola (1765), Fort Picolata (1765), Augusta (1768), Pensacola (1771), and Augusta (1773). Dorothy V. Jones, *License for Empire: Colonialism by Treaty in Early America* (Chicago: Univ. of Chicago Press, 1982), examines the post-1763 congresses from the imperial perspective.

3. "A Talk from the Headmen and Warriors of the Upper Creek Nation to John Stuart," July 15, 1771, Great Britain, Public Record Office, Colonial Office, America and West Indies, Series 5, vol. 72, fol. 348, hereafter cited as CO5.

4. Allen D. Candler, Kenneth Coleman, and Milton Ready, eds., *The Colonial Records of the State of Georgia*, 28 vols. (Atlanta: C. Byrd, 1904–16; Athens: Univ. of Georgia Press, 1974–76), 10:568, hereafter cited as *CRG*. "At a Meeting of the Abekas, Tallippooses, and Alibamas at the Little Tallassies the 4th February 1774," CO5/75, fol. 69.

5. Gregory A. Waselkov and Kathryn E. Holland Braund, eds., *William Bartram on the Southeastern Indians* (Lincoln: Univ. of Nebraska Press, 1995), 173. Peter Nabokov and Robert Easton, *Native American Architecture* (New York: Oxford Univ. Press, 1989), 104–14, provide the best overview of the Creek town.

6. *CRG*, 8:432. A later talk from the Lower Creeks reaffirmed that the "three Rivers [Tallapoosa, Coosa and Chattahoochee] are all one People." William L. Saunders, ed., *The Colonial Records of North Carolina*, 16 vols. (Raleigh: Josephus Daniels, 1886–1890), 11:167, hereafter cited as *CRNC*.

7. For example, at a meeting of Upper Creek towns held at Okchai on April 5, 1763, the Handsome Fellow of the Okfuskees related "there are two head men from every Town in the Upper Creeks at this Meeting and that he is going to say the Sentiments of them all." *CRG*, 9:72.

8. Kathryn E. Holland Braund, *Deerskins and Duffels: Creek Indian Trade with Anglo-America, 1685–1815* (Lincoln: Univ. of Nebraska Press, 1993), 139–40.

9. Dunbar Rowland, ed., *Mississippi Provincial Archives, 1763–1766, English Dominion*, vol. 1 (Nashville, Tenn.: Mississippi Department of Archives and History, 1911), 94–97, hereafter cited as *MPAED*.

10. Kenneth G. Davies, ed., Speech of Emisteseguo, "Proceedings of a Congress with the Upper Creeks," *Documents of the American Revolution, 1770–1783*, 20 vols. (Dublin: Irish Univ. Press, 1972–79), 3:217, hereafter cited as *DAR*.

11. *DAR*, 3:217. It was a theme he would repeat: "The lands are not the property of the head warriors but of the whole nation in common; every boy has a right in the disposal of them" (*DAR*, 3:218).

12. Waselkov and Braund, eds., *William Bartram on the Southeastern Indians*, 155–56.

13. *DAR*, 3:217.

14. Other public structures included a winter council house—or "hot house"—and a chunky field, the site of games, dances, and other public events.

15. Gregory A. Waselkov, "Changing Strategies of Indian Field Location in the Early Historic Southeast," in *People, Plants, and Landscapes: Studies in Paleobotany*, ed. Kristen J. Gremillion (Tuscaloosa: Univ. of Alabama Press, 1997), 179–94.

16. The Creeks were not only matrilineal, but matrilocal as well.

17. Waselkov and Braund, eds., *William Bartram on the Southeastern Indians*, 158. David Taitt reported that the Creeks built their houses among the fields and constructed a fence around the entire town to protect the crops from horses and cattle. Remarks by Bernard Romans and David Taitt, "A Map of West Florida part of Et. Florida, Georgia part of So. Carolina," 1773 (Stuart-Gage Map), William L. Clements Library. I wish to thank Professor Louis De Vorsey Jr., who kindly allowed me to photocopy his copy of this map for study purposes.

18. Waselkov and Braund, eds., *William Bartram on the Southeastern Indians*, 159.

19. Waselkov and Braund, eds., *William Bartram on the Southeastern Indians*, 46; *DAR*, 6:191; C. L. Grant, ed., *Letters, Journals, and Writings of Benjamin Hawkins*, 2 vols. (Savannah: Beehive Press, 1980), 1:42, 51, 294, 303; Philip Georg Friedrich von Reck, *Von Reck's Voyage: Drawings and Journal of Philip Georg Friedrich von Reck*, ed. Kristian Hvidt (Savannah: Beehive Press, 1980), 50, 116–17.

20. Waselkov and Braund, eds., *William Bartram on the Southeastern Indians*, 156.

21. Alan Gallay, ed., *Colonial Wars of North America, 1512–1763: An Encyclopedia* (New York: Garland, 1996), s.v. "Creek-Cherokee Wars" (c. 1716–1754).

22. Report of John Stuart to the Lords Commissioners of Trade and Plantations on the Southern Indian Department, March 9, 1764. CO323/17, hereafter cited at Stuart's 1764 Report.

23. Bernard Romans, *A Concise Natural History of East and West Florida* (New York, 1775), 277, 280.

24. Braund, *Duffels and Deerskins*, 6; LeClerc Milfort, *Memoirs or a Quick Glance at my various Travels and my Sojourn in the Creek Nation*, trans. by Ben C. McCary (Kennesaw, Ga.: Continental Book Company, 1959), 62–63. See also pp. 163–67.

Notes 239

25. *CRG*, vol. 28, pt. 1, 429.
26. *CRG*, 9:71–72.
27. *CRG*, 9:76.
28. *CRG*, 9:71, 72, 74.
29. *CRG*, 9:73.
30. *CRG*, 9:72. The first Creek treaty with Georgia confined the colony to the tidewater, with the exception of a fort on the Savannah River along the trade path. David H. Corkran, *The Creek Frontier: 1540–1783* (Norman: Univ. of Oklahoma Press, 1967), 84.
31. *CRG*, 9:74–76, quotation from p. 76.
32. *CRG*, 9:73.
33. *MPAED*, 137. At Pensacola, the Creek emissaries presented Lieutenant Colonel Augustine Prevost with "some white feathers." These were the tail feathers of the bald eagle, given only by authorized representatives of the Creek people, a fact Prevost failed to appreciate.
34. *MPAED*, 137; James W. Covington, "The British Meet the Seminoles," *Contributions of the Florida State Museum*, Number 7 (Gainesville: Univ. of Florida Press, 1961), 5–14; Robin Fabel, "St. Mark's, Apalache and the Creeks," *Gulf Coast Historical Review* 1 (spring 1986): 4–22.
35. Related by Peter Chester in a letter to the Earl of Hillsborough, March 9, 1771, *DAR*, 3:65.
36. Charles J. Kappler, ed., *Indian Affairs: Laws and Treaties*, 7 vols., reprint ed. (Washington, D.C.: Government Printing Office, 1975–1979), 4:1172–3.
37. *CRG*, 9:74 and 77.
38. Louis De Vorsey Jr., *The Indian Boundary in the Southern Colonies, 1763–1775* (Chapel Hill: Univ. of North Carolina Press, 1961), is the definitive study of the topic. See quotation on page 3.
39. *CRG*, 10:566–71.
40. *MPAED*, 194.
41. *MPAED*, 12; "At a Meeting of Head Men at Little Talsey, April 10, 1764," Gage Papers. The British did occupy Fort Tombeckbe, in Choctaw territory.
42. *MPAED*, 196.
43. See *CRNC*, 11:184; *MPAED*, 199; *CRG*, 10:568; Samuel Thomas to David Taitt, December 10, 1774, CO5/76, fol. 33
44. *CRNC*, 11:184.
45. The grant in question was made by the Wolf of Muccolossus, a Tallapoosa elder, to Captain Robert Mackinnen. For details on the treaty, see Corkran, *Creek Frontier*, 246; John R. Alden, *John Stuart and the Southern Colonial Frontier: A Study of Indian Relations, War, Trade, and Land Problems in the Southern Wilderness, 1754–1775* (Ann Arbor: University of Michigan, 1944), 194. See *MPAED*, 207, for a reference to the felling of trees. See also Milo B. Howard Jr. and Robert R. Rea, eds. and trans., *The*

Mémoire Justificatif of the Chevalier Montault de Monberaut: Indian Diplomacy in British West Florida, 1763–1765 (Tuscaloosa: Univ. of Alabama Press, 1965), 11.

46. *DAR*, 3:118. In deploying the term elder brother, the Cussita King was reminding the Upper Creeks of the relative order among Creek towns. For an examination of kinship and gender language in southeastern Indian diplomacy, see Nancy Shoemaker, "An Alliance between Men: Gender Metaphors in Eighteenth-Century American Indian Diplomacy East of the Mississippi," *Ethnohistory* 46 (spring 1999): 239–63. Cussita origin stories explained their status by their war prowess. See Grant, ed., *Letters, Journals, and Writings of Benjamin Hawkins*, 1:326–27. See Claudio Saunt, *A New Order of Things: Property, Power, and the Transformation of the Creek Indians, 1733–1816* (Cambridge: Cambridge Univ. Press, 1999), 12–17, for a discussion of Creek origin stories.

47. John Stuart to Earl of Egremont, December 5, 1763, CO5/65, pt. 2, fol. 69.

48. *CRG*, 9:148. Emisteseguo reported the "Cussaty King . . . being their elder brother. We therefore consented to everything he proposed" (*DAR*, 3:118). For a discussion of the use of fictive kinship in southeastern Indian diplomatic ritual, see Patricia Galloway, "The Chief Who Is Your Father: Choctaw and French Views of the Diplomatic Relation," in *Powhatan's Mantle: Indians in the Colonial Southeast*, ed. Peter Wood, Gregory Waselkov, and Thomas Hatley (Lincoln: Univ. of Nebraska Press, 1889), 254–78.

49. *MPAED*, 187, 201. Captain Alick, the Young Lieutenant, and White Cabin led the Lower Creek delegation. *CRG*, 28, pt. 2, 113.

50. For details on the congress, see Kathryn E. Holland Braund, "Ye Congress Held in A Pavilion: John Bartram and the Indian Congress at Fort Picolata, East Florida," in John Bartram, *Proceedings of the American Philosophical Society* (forthcoming). For a list of signatories and their towns, see Covington, ed., "The British Meet the Seminoles," 38. *DAR*, 14:148.

51. Some of the Apalachee settled on Mobile Bay. Their land was included in the Upper Creek cession at Pensacola. For information on the Apalachee, see John H. Hann, *Apalachee: The Land between the Rivers* (Gainesville: Univ. of Florida Press, 1988). See also Gregory A. Waselkov and Bonnie L. Gums, *Plantation Archaeology at Rivière Aux Chiens, ca. 1725–1848* (Mobile: University of South Alabama Center for Archaeological Studies, 2000), 26–29.

52. De Vorsey, *Indian Boundary Line*, 188–89. Stuart's conference with the Lower Creek towns was September 25–28, 1764. Fabel, "St. Mark's, Apalache, and the Creeks," *Gulf Coast Historical Review* (1986), 1:10.

53. Most likely with Coweta and Cussita knowledge. At the Congress of Augusta, Tallechea restricted the British to the same land the Spanish had occupied. *CRNC*, 11:185.

54. "At a Meeting of Head Men at Little Talsey, April 10, 1764," Gage Papers.

55. The colonies of Georgia and South Carolina had awarded special "commissions" to leading men prior to this date. Steven C. Hann, "The Invention of the

Creek Nation: A Political History of the South's Imperial Era, 1540–1763" (Ph.D. diss., Emory Univ., 2000), 306–8.

56. Some scholars have generally interpreted the medal chiefs as "client chiefs" of the British, whose authority rested solely upon their ability to procure goods and favors from the British and have generally taken the view that the British system was an attempt to bypass or thwart traditional leadership, particularly among the Choctaw. This is clearly not the case among the Creek Indians.

57. "At a Congress of the Principal Chiefs & Warriors of the Creek Nation held at Fort Augusta in Georgia, the 12th November 1768," CO5/70, fol. 86.

58. *DAR*, 3:213.

59. Presumably, the designation of the royal family as Tygers came to pass as a result of the royal symbol, the lion. Philemon Kemp to the Governor of Georgia with Talks from Emistesiguo and Gun Merchant, June 6, 1771, *DAR*, 3:119. Interestingly, Emisteseguo told the Georgians that "all of the Tyger Family are of royal Descent." See *CRG*, 10:582.

60. *MPAED*, 186.

61. The cession was carefully described by both the Creeks and the British at the congress, and all the headmen present were specifically asked in public if they understood the boundary (*CRNC*, 11:194–95). The boundary is described in detail in Article 4 of the treaty. The Creeks also renounced possession of any of the sea islands, a thorn in Creek-Georgia relations for a number of years (*CRNC*, 11:201–2). The manner in which Creeks were queried on their understanding of the proposed boundary suggests that it was not of their own devising. Lobbying efforts by Georgians prior to the congress seem to have been undertaken without the knowledge of Stuart (see Corkran, *Creek Frontier*, 239; and Edward Cashin, *Lachlan McGillivray, Indian Trader: The Shaping of the Southern Colonial Frontier* [Athens: Univ. of Georgia Press, 1992], 221–22; *DAR*, 3:119; John Stuart to Sir Thomas Gage, October 4, 1763, Gage Papers). Among the Upper Creeks pardoned was the Mortar, who was responsible for the death of a number of British subjects. His execution as satisfaction for the deaths would have been impossible.

62. Corkran, *Creek Frontier*, 239; Alden, *John Stuart*, 185.

63. *CRNC*, 11:976; Alden, *John Stuart*, 186. See also John Stuart to Lord Egremont, December 5, 1763, CO5/65, pt. 2, fol. 69.

64. "At a Meeting at Little Tallassee 15th July 1764," Gage Papers (first quotation); John Stuart to Earl of Egremont, December 5, 1763, CO5/65, pt. 2, fol. 69 (second quotation).

65. Some of the lands ceded by the Choctaw were claimed by the Mobilian, Naniaba, and Tomé Indians. These tribes, with the withdrawal of the French, had settled among the Chickasawhay (Six Towns) division of the Choctaw. The Chickasawhay claimed the right to cede the land, and they explicitly excluded some land claimed by the Naniaba and Mobilians. Although the speakers acknowledged the

authority of those who made the cession, it was not popular. See *MPAED*, 238–42; Richard White, *The Roots of Dependency: Subsistence, Environment, and Social Change among the Choctaws, Pawnees, and Navajos* (Lincoln: Univ. of Nebraska Press, 1983), 74.

66. The printed transcript of the congress can be found in *MPAED*, 188–214. For discussions of the congress, see Corkran, *Creek Frontier*, 247–50; Alden, *John Stuart*, 205–7; De Vorsey, *Indian Boundary Line*, 212–15; *Mémoire Justificatif*, 28–43; Braund, *Deerskins and Duffels*, 128, 144–5.

67. *MPAED*, 187; De Vorsey, *Indian Boundary Line*, 215. See John Stuart to John Pownall, August 24, 1765, CO5/66, fol. 356.

68. "In a Council Held in the Council Chamber at Pensacola the Third August 1771," CO5/72, fol. 681.

69. Bartram, "Diary," 51. For a complete explanation of the complex boundary in East Florida, see De Vorsey, *Indian Boundary*, 190–203.

70. "At a Meeting of Head Men at Little Talsey, April 10, 1764," Gage Papers.

71. Howard and Rea, ed. and trans., *Mémoire Justificatif*, 172. The time period was specified at four years at the congress (*MPAED*, 202). In 1771, Emisteseguo of the Little Tallassee was reported to have invoked a seven-year period (see *DAR*, 3:217).

72. "At a Congress of the Principal Chiefs & Warriors of the Creek Nation, held at Fort Augusta in Georgia, the 12th November 1768," CO5/70, fol. 86.

73. *DAR*, 3:214.

74. See Waselkov and Gums, *Plantation Archaeology*, 6–62, for the best account of the historic tribes of Mobile Bay.

75. The Naniaba and Tomé settled with the Chickasawhay component of the Choctaw confederacy. Waselkov and Gums, *Plantation Archaeology*, 37–38; De Vorsey, *Indian Boundary Line*, 209.

76. *DAR*, 5:33.

77. They also claimed the deserted fields and villages of the Towasa Indians, who settled among the Tallapoosa and Alabama towns. Waselkov and Gums, *Plantation Archaeology*, 31–32.

78. See ibid., 32–33, for an overview of Taensa history and land claims.

79. De Vorsey, *Indian Boundary Line*, 205–6; Alden, *John Stuart*, 194.

80. *DAR*, 3:214.

81. *DAR*, 3:217–18.

82. *DAR*, 3:218–19.

83. *DAR*, 3:219.

84. *DAR*, 3:220.

85. *DAR*, 3:221.

86. *DAR*, 3:222.

87. The land north of the stream respectively called Byuck Connonga by the Choctaw and Hitesia by the Creeks (the course of which formed the triangle of

Notes

land known as Naniaba Island) was not ceded by the Creeks, and remained contested territory.

88. *DAR*, 3:223 and 229.

89. Peter Chester to Earl of Hillsborough, December 28, 1771, *DAR*, 3:280.

90. "At a meeting held in Oak Choys 19th April 1772," CO5/73, fol. 268. See also David Taitt to John Stuart, March 16, 1772, CO5/73, fol. 259, and David Taitt to John Stuart, May 4, 1772, CO5/73, fol. 263.

91. Gallay, ed., *Colonial Wars of North America*, s.v. "Creek-Cherokee Wars (c. 1716–1754)." While the precise extent of the Creek domain toward the north and northwest is unclear, extant records do reveal that the Creeks worked out border agreements with both the Chickasaw and Cherokee. In time, they would establish the Tennessee River as their northern limit. Grant, ed., *Letters, Journals, and Writings of Benjamin Hawkins*, 2:541.

92. For a discussion of the New Purchase cession, see Braund, *Deerskins and Duffels*, 150–53.

93. Harper, ed., *Travels of William Bartram*, 308.

94. There were, in fact, two parcels. The northern tract lay along the Broad River. The more southerly portion lay between the Ogeechee and Altamaha Rivers—clearly Creek land. De Vorsey, *Indian Boundary Line*, 175.

95. Braund, *Deerskins and Duffels*, 159–63.

96. "At a meeting held in Oak Choys 19th April 1772," CO5/73, fol. 268; Creeks to Governor Johnstone, 1767, CO5/68, fol. 90; *CRG*, 10:569.

97. *DAR*, 5:74.

98. "At a meeting held in Oak Choys 19th April 1772," CO5/73, fol. 268. Women were the ones who usually dispatched cattle that wandered into the corn fields and vegetable patches. See Saunt, *A New Order of Things*, 46–50, for a discussion of Creek views on cattle.

99. Harper, ed., *Travels of William Bartram*, 312; Braund, *Deerskins and Duffels*, 191–92.

100. *DAR*, 3:120.

101. John Stuart to Hillsborough, September 23, 1772, CO5/73, fol. 403.

102. John Stuart to Hillsborough, January 3, 1769, CO5/70, fol. 105.

103. Governor Chester specifically stated that he believed it would be difficult to convince the Creeks to extend the boundary once it was marked. *DAR*, 5:165; John Stuart to Hillsborough, September 23, 1772, CO5/73, fol. 403.

104. Harper, ed., *Travels of William Bartram*, 26; *CRG*, 10:303.

105. *DAR*, 3:118 and 120.

106. Talk to John Stuart from Emisteseguo, July 12, 1769, CO5/70, fol. 262. More natural to the Creek people was Emisteseguo's characterization of the boundary as "a tree which you are not to climb over" (*DAR*, 5:74). The stone wall analogy was

suggested by John Stuart (*DAR,* 3:217). "A Talk from the Headmen & Warriors of the Creek Nation to John Stuart, Esq. dated the 15th July 1771," CO5/72, fol. 348.

107. "Answer from the Headmen of the Lower Creek Nation to a Talk sent to them by John Stuart, Esq.," September 19, 1767, CO5/69, fol. 135.

108. Alan Gallay, *The Formation of a Planter Elite: Jonathan Bryan and the Southern Colonial Frontier* (Athens: Univ. of Georgia Press, 1989), chapter 6.

109. Robbie Ethridge, "Creek Country: The Creek Indians and Their World, 1796–1816," (Chapel Hill: Univ. of North Carolina Press, in press), explores the boundaries of the Creek country in the period after the American Revolution.

110. "Some Account of the Creeks," *The American Museum, or, Universal Magazine* 7 (April 1790): 185.

111. For the Mortar's remarks, see *CRG,* 9:72–73. For the Cussita King's remarks, see *DAR,* 3:118.

112. "At a Meeting of the Abekas, Tallapoosas, and Alibamas at the Little Tallassies the 4 Day of February 1774," CO5/75, fol. 69.

Notes to CAROLINIANS ABROAD
by S. Max Edelson

1. Peter Manigault to [Anne] Manigault, [c. 1750?], Manigault Family Papers, folder 10, South Carolina Historical Society, Charleston.

2. On colonial cultural dependence on metropolitan forms and the psychological insecurities this relationship produced, see Jack P. Greene, "The Search for Identity: An Interpretation of the Meaning of Selected Patterns of Social Response in Eighteenth-Century America," in *Imperatives, Behaviors, and Identities: Essays in Early American Cultural History* (Charlottesville: Univ. Press of Virginia, 1992), 143–73.

3. On the connection between food, eating, and early modern medical theory, see Trudy Eden, "'Makes Like, Makes Unlike': Food, Health and Identity in the Early Chesapeake" (Ph.D. diss., Johns Hopkins University, 1999); Henry Laurens to Lachlan McIntosh, September 27, 1774, *The Papers of Henry Laurens,* Philip Hamer, George C. Rogers, David Chestnut et al., eds., 16 vols. (Columbia: Univ. of South Carolina Press, 1968–2003), 9:578. A similar instance is related by Sidney W. Mintz, who noted that at one British almshouse in the late eighteenth century, impoverished consumers demanded the right to purchase tea and sugar, foods with positive class associations (*Sweetness and Power: The Place of Sugar in Modern History* [New York, Penguin, 1985], 172).

4. Eliza Lucas Pinckney to Mr. Gerrard, [c. August 1758?], *The Letterbook of Eliza Lucas Pinckney,* ed. Elise Pinckney (Chapel Hill, Univ. of North Carolina Press, 1972), 97; Elias Ball to Elias Ball Jr., September 6, 1785, Ball Family Papers, folder 2, South

Caroliniana Library, University of South Carolina, Columbia; Elias Ball to Elias Ball Jr., April 29, 1785, ibid.

5. See, for example, A. G. Roeber, "Authority, Law, and Custom: The Rituals of Court Day in Tidewater, Virginia, 1720 to 1750," *William and Mary Quarterly*, 3d ser., 27 (1980): 29–52; Jack P. Greene, "Political Mimesis: A Consideration of the Historical and Cultural Roots of Legislative Behavior in the British Colonies," in *Negotiated Authorities: Essays in Colonial Political and Constitutional History* (Charlottesville: Univ. Press of Virginia, 1994), 185–214.

6. On wealth, see Peter A. Coclanis, *The Shadow of a Dream: Economic Life and Death in the South Carolina Low Country* (New York: Oxford Univ. Press, 1989), 82–91.

7. C[hristopher] G[asden] to [William?] Drayton, June 1, 1788, Copies of Correspondence, Robert Scott Small Library, Special Collections, College of Charleston; on the diminished value of owning land without slaves, see "Report of William Bull to the Lords Commissioners for Trade and Plantation," James Glen Papers, South Caroliniana Library; Robert Raper to John Colleton, May 13, 1761, Robert Raper Letterbook (photoduplicate of original in West Sussex Record Office, U.K.), South Carolina Historical Society.

8. Peter Manigault to Ralph Izard, September 6, 1769, Peter Manigault Letterbook, South Carolina Historical Society; [Alexander] Hewit, "An Historical Account of the Rise and Progress of the Colonies of South Carolina and Georgia," in *Historical Collections of South Carolina*, ed. B. R. Carroll, 2 vols. (London, 1836 [1779]), 1:420–21.

9. On the "wishful and occasionally even extravagant boasting" and "arcadian conceits" with which colonists attempted to envision provincial societies as superior to English society, see Greene, "Search for Identity," 162–64.

10. [Robert Horne], "A Brief Description of the Province of Carolina" (1666), in Carroll, ed., *Historical Collections*, 2:16; John Archdale, "A New Description of that Fertile and Pleasant Province of Carolina" (1707), in Alexander S. Salley Jr., ed., *Narratives of Early Carolina* (New York: Charles Scribner's Sons, 1911), 290; John Stewart to William Dunlop, June 23, 1690, "Letters from John Stewart to William Dunlop," *South Carolina Historical Magazine* 32 (1931): 110, 93.

11. John Martin [Sr.] to John Martin [Jr.], February 17, 1788, July 1, 1788, John Martin Estate Papers, folder 1, South Carolina Historical Society; Isaac Danford to John Martin [Jr.], December 6, 1790, ibid., folder 2.

12. J[ohn] Channing to [Edward Telfair], August 10, 1786, Edward Telfair Papers, William R. Perkins Library, Special Collections, Duke University, Durham, N.C.; Henry Laurens to Ralph Izard, November 6, 1777, quoted in David D. Wallace, *The Life of Henry Laurens With a Sketch of the Life of Lieutenant-Colonel John Laurens* (New York: G. P. Putnam's Sons, 1915), 45.

13. James Grant to Earl of Egmont, February 9, 1769, quoted in Daniel C. Littlefield, *Rice and Slaves: Ethnicity and the Slave Trade in Colonial South Carolina*

(Baton Rouge: Louisiana State Univ. Press, 1981), 70; Margaret Colleton to Robert Raper, July 13, 1777, Colleton Manuscripts, folder 4, South Caroliniana Library; Petition of Joseph Townsend et al. "for knowing and setting a Yearly Value of the Lands and plantations . . . which did belong to Charles Burnham," April 1730, Miscellaneous Manuscripts Collection, South Carolina Historical Society. Note the discrepancies as to the expected and actual value of annual rice crops in "Account of John Drayton with James Glen," Glen Papers, folder: MS, 1764–1767; Josiah Smith Jr. to George Austin, January 31, 1774, Josiah Smith, Jr., Letterbook, Southern Historical Collection, University of North Carolina, Chapel Hill. Before moving his family to England in 1753, Charles Pinckney assigned landed and slave property a rent value "For raising Funds . . . for the support of myself and my Family in England," "Account Book 1753 of Charles Pinckney," Benjamin Rutledge Huger Family Papers, folder 21, South Carolina Historical Society. Disappointing returns prompted Pinckney to return to South Carolina to sell his property. See Eliza Lucas Pinckney to [Lady Carew], February 7, 1757, Eliza Lucas Pinckney to [Mr. Morly], March 14, 1760, *Pinckney Letterbook*, 87–88, 143–44; see also contrasting views of expectations for an indebted Carolina estate, Richard H[ill] to John Guerard, September 16, 1743, Richard Hill Letterbook, William R. Perkins Library, Special Collections, Duke University.

14. Henry Laurens to Cowles and Harford, July 17, 1764, *Papers of Henry Laurens*, 4:343–44.

15. For remarks on English servants, see Peter Manigault to [Anne] Manigault, February 20, [1750 or 1751], Manigault Family Papers, folder 6, South Carolina Historical Society; A. Kinloch to Cleland Kinloch, October 3, 1787, Kinloch Correspondence, folder 3, South Carolina Historical Society; Elias Ball to Elias Ball Jr., April 29, 1785, Ball Family Papers, folder 2.

16. Louisa Susannah Wells, *The Journal of a Voyage from Charlestown, S.C., to London* . . . (New York: New York Historical Society, 1906), 11; Peter Manigault to [Anne] Manigault, November 1, 1750, Manigault Family Papers, folder 6, South Carolina Historical Society; Peter Manigault to [Anne] Manigault, February 20, [1750 or 1751], ibid.

17. Peter Manigault to [Anne] Manigault, August 30, 1754, "Peter Manigault's Letters," ed. Mabel Webber, *South Carolina Historical Magazine* 32 (1931): 248; Peter Manigault to [Anne] Manigault, June 26, 1750, "Six Letters of Peter Manigault," *South Carolina Historical Magazine* 15 (1914): 114.

18. Peter Manigault to Gabriel Manigault, March 29, 1754, "Peter Manigault's Letters," *South Carolina Historical Magazine* 33 (1932), 55–56; Peter Manigault to [Anne] Manigault, February 20, 1750 [1751?], Manigault Family Papers, folder 6, South Carolina Historical Society.

19. Robert Olwell, *Masters, Slaves, and Subjects: The Culture of Power in the South Carolina Low Country, 1740–1790* (Ithaca: Cornell Univ. Press, 1998), 37; Robert M.

Weir, " 'The Harmony We Were Famous For': An Interpretation of Pre-Revolutionary South Carolina Politics," *William and Mary Quarterly*, 3d ser., 26 (1969): 481–82; Elias Ball to Elias Ball, May 15, 1784, Elias Ball XIV Family Papers, South Carolina Historical Society.

20. Hewit, "Historical Account," 378; *South-Carolina Gazette*, June 27, 1744.

21. Henry Laurens to Levi Durand, July 18, 1763, *Papers of Henry Laurens*, 3:501; Harriott Pinckney to ___, April 1766, Pinckney Letterbook, Ravenel and Pinckney-Lowndes Papers, folder 8, South Carolina Historical Society; J[oseph] Manigault to Gabriel Manigault, January 5, 1787, Manigault Family Papers, box II, folder 14, South Caroliniana Library.

22. Josiah Quincy Jr., "Journal of Josiah Quincy, Junior, 1773," Massachusetts Historical Society *Proceedings*, 49 (1915–1916): 450, 456; on prevailing standards for polite discourse that tended to exclude discussions of economic matters, see David S. Shields, *Civil Tongues and Polite Letters in British America* (Chapel Hill: Univ. of North Carolina Press, 1997).

23. Thomas Pinckney to Har[r]iot Horry, January 3, 1777, Pinckney Family Papers, series 1, box 6, Manuscripts Division, Library of Congress, Washington, D.C.

24. Wells, *Journal of a Voyage from Charlestown*, 29, 48.

25. Edward Fenwicke to John Fenwicke, August 14, 1726, July 8, 1727, Edward Fenwicke Letterbook, South Carolina Historical Society.

26. Will of Charles Cotesworth Pinckney (1778), Huger Family Papers, folder 27, South Carolina Historical Society.

27. Will of John Vanderhorst (1786), John Vanderhorst Papers, folder 3, South Carolina Historical Society.

28. Indenture, January 10, 1756, Manigault Family Papers, Box I (letter), folder 3, South Caroliniana Library.

29. Richard Waterhouse, "The Development of Elite Culture in the Colonial American South: A Study of Charles Town, 1670–1770," *Australian Journal of Politics and History* 28 (1982): 392; Edward Fenwicke to John Fenwicke, July 8, 1727, Fenwicke Letterbook; Quincy, "Journal," 447, 449.

30. Waterhouse, "Development of Elite Culture," 392.

31. Quoted in Michael Zuckerman, "Penmanship Exercises for Saucy Sons: Some Thoughts on the Colonial Southern Family," *South Carolina Historical Magazine* 84 (1983): 154; see ibid., passim., on fears of ungovernable male children.

32. Babut and Laboucher to Robert Cochran, January 15, 1779, Cochran Family Papers, South Carolina Historical Society; Mary Cochran to [Charles Cochran], August 16, 1779, July 16, 1781, ibid.

33. [Sarah Gibbes] to John Gibbes, August 13, 1783, Sarah R. Gibbes Letters, folder 4, South Carolina Historical Society; Ralph Izard to [Alice Izard?], December 28, 1782, Ralph Izard Papers, box: Originals and Photostats 1765–1803 and n.d.,

folder 1, South Caroliniana Library; Henry Laurens to Monkhouse Davison, October 15, 1762, *Papers of Henry Laurens*, 3:139.

34. John Drayton to James Glen, October 11, 1761, December 24, 1769, March 14, 1770, February 6, 1773, Glen Papers.

35. Henry Laurens to Thomas Savage, December 5, 1771, *Papers of Henry Laurens*, 8:75; Henry Laurens to John Rose, December 28, 1771, ibid., 8:140–41; Henry Laurens to James Laurens, January 1, 1772, ibid., 8:147–49. In part because of his critique of English boarding schools, Laurens sent one of his sons to Geneva for his education. See also A. Leath and Maurie D. McInnes, "'To Blend Pleausre with Knowledge': The Cultural Odyssey of Charlestonians Abroad," in *In Pursuit of Refinement: Charlestonians Abroad, 1740–1860*, ed. Maurie D. McInnes (Columbia: Univ. of South Carolina Press, 1999), 11–13.

36. Henry Laurens to Devonsheir, Reeve, and Lloyd, June 24, 1755, *Papers of Henry Laurens*, 1:271–72.

37. Wells, *Journal of a Voyage from Charlestown*, 4, 34, 61, 38.

38. *South-Carolina Gazette*, February 8, 1735.

39. A. Capers to Mrs. Russell, March 25, 1791, Edith Mitchell Dabbs Papers, Southern Historical Collection.

40. Brian Simon, *The Two Nations and the Educational Structure, 1780–1870*, vol. 1, Studies in the History of Education Series (London: Lawrence and Wishart, 1960), 28, 32–34.

41. See the example of Paul Mazyck, a resident of Kings County, Ireland: Stephen Mazyck to [Paul Mazyck], February 7, 1776, September 5, 1766, Daniel Elliott Huger Smith Papers, folders 20, 21, South Carolina Historical Society.

42. For a general discussion of the effects of the war on South Carolina, see Jerome J. Nadelhaft, *The Disorders of War: The Revolution in South Carolina* (Orono: Univ. of Maine Press, 1981); on the disruption that accompanied the British invasion of South Carolina, see John S. Pancake, *This Destructive War: The British Campaign in the Carolinas, 1780–1782* (Tuscaloosa: Univ. of Alabama Press, 1985); on slave resistance during the war, see Sylvia R. Frey, *Water from the Rock: Black Resistance in a Revolutionary Age* (Princeton: Princeton Univ. Press, 1991), 118–20, 163–64; see also Stephen Mazyck to [Paul Mazyck], February 7, 1776, Smith Papers; William Piercy to Lady Huntingdon, January 15, 1781, Letters 1767–83, Piercy Letters, Papers of Henry Laurens, South Carolina Historical Society.

43. Kathryn Roe Coker, "Absentees as Loyalists in Revolutionary War South Carolina," *South Carolina Historical Magazine* 96 (1995): 119; Josiah Smith Jr. to James Poyas, November 30, 1778, Smith Letterbook; Gabriel Manigault to Gabriel Manigault, June 2, 1778, Manigault Family Papers, box 1 (letter), folder 9, South Caroliniana Library.

44. Louisa Ojier to Harriet Hyrne, November 21, 1781, Baker Family Correspondence, folder 12, South Carolina Historical Society.

45. Elias Ball to Elias Ball Jr., September 6, 1785, Ball Family Papers, folder 2. The father of "John Bull" was most likely William Bull, the last royal lieutenant governor of South Carolina and the leader of the South Carolina loyalist community in London. See Mary Beth Norton, *The British-Americans: The Loyalist Exiles in England, 1774–1789* (Boston: Little, Brown, 1972), 72.

46. In 1782, the Assembly confiscated more than two hundred loyalist estates but provided that some absentees might regain theirs on payment of a 12 percent amercement, a concession secured for absentees after aggressive lobbying on the part of resident relatives and friends. In partial compliance with Treaty of Paris stipulations, the commission that was formed to manage and sell confiscated estates considered petitions from absentees seeking the reinstatement of their property after 1783. Thus, at the close of the war, a second contingent of lowcountry planters left England for South Carolina. Coker, "Absentees as Loyalists," 119; Jerome J. Nadlehaft, *Disorders of War: The Revolution in South Carolina* (Orono, Maine: Univ. of Maine Press, 1981), 73–85; Robert M. Weir, *Colonial South Carolina: A History* (Millwood, N.Y.: KTO Press, 1983), 336–37; Josiah Smith Jr. to James Poyas, January 31, 1784, Smith Letterbook.

47. J[oseph] Manigault to G[abriel] Manigault, April 8, 1784, Manigault Family Papers, box 1 (letter), folder 12, South Caroliniana Library; Elias Ball to Elias Ball Jr., September 6, 1785, Ball Family Papers, folder 2; see also Peter Manigault's reflections on disease environments in South Carolina and Britain: Peter Manigault to [Anne] Manigault, April 15, 1751, Manigault Family Papers, folder 7, South Carolina Historical Society; Peter Manigault to [Anne Manigault], February 26, 1754, Manigault-Burnet Papers, South Carolina Historical Society; Peter Manigault to Anne Manigault, September 11, 1773, Manigault Family Papers, folder 10, South Carolina Historical Society.

48. Wells, *Journal of a Voyage from Charlestown*, 64–65, 68. On the cultural implications of physical "seasoning" in the lowcountry disease environment, see Joyce E. Chaplin, *An Anxious Pursuit: Agricultural Innovation and Modernity in the Lower South, 1730–1815* (Chapel Hill: Univ. of North Carolina Press, 1993), 93–108.

49. Louisa Ojier to Harriet Hyrne, November 21, 1781, Baker Family Correspondence, folder 12; Elias Ball to Elias Ball Jr., April 29, 1785, Ball Family Papers, folder 2. Wambaw plantation was owned jointly during the 1760s by Henry Laurens and John Coming Ball. After John Coming Ball's death, Elias Ball Jr., Ball's eldest son, purchased Laurens's share as well as the shares owned by his sisters to reintegrate the plantation under his sole ownership. *Papers of Henry Laurens*, 4:493n.

50. On European observers' critiques of lowcountry agriculture, see Chaplin, *Anxious Pursuit*, 77–84. For a widely read example of this literature of critique, see Henry J. Carman, ed., *American Husbandry: Containing an Account of the Soil, Climate, Production and Agriculture, of the British Colonies in North America* (New York: Columbia Univ. Press, 1939 [1775]).

51. Elias Ball to Elias Ball Jr., April 29, 1785, Ball Family Papers, folder 2; on production capacity at Comingtee plantation, see Elias Ball to [Elias Ball], June 6, 1790, Elias Ball XIV Family Papers, folder 7.

52. A. Kinloch to Cleland Kinloch, October 3, 1787, and n.d., Cleland Kinloch Correspondence, folder 3; Wells, *Journal of a Voyage from Charlestown*, 69, 68.

53. On planters' changing perceptions of the lowcountry landscape, see S. Max Edelson, "Planting the Lowcountry: Agricultural Enterprise and Economic Experience in the Lower South, 1695–1785" (Ph.D. diss., Johns Hopkins University, 1998), 36–70.

54. Elias Ball to [Elias Ball?], November 22, 1784, Ball Family Papers, folder 1; Elias Ball to Elias Ball, March 10, 1785, Elias Ball XIV Family Papers, folder 7.

55. On loyalists' social isolation and the separation of loyalist social circles oriented around a colonial point of origin, see Norton, *The British-Americans*, 66–72.

56. Elias Ball to [Elias Ball?], Ball Family Papers, November 22, 1784, folder 1; [Elias Ball] to Elias Ball Jr., September 19, 1785, Ball Family Papers, folder 2; for another example of genealogical interest in English family roots, see Barnard Elliott to Richard Bohoun Baker, May 10, 1764, Baker Family Correspondence, folder 5.

57. Elias Ball to [Elias Ball?], November 22, 1784, Ball Family Papers, folder 1.

58. Elias Ball to Elias Ball Jr., September 6, 1785, Ball Family Papers, folder 2. Just as Elias Ball reckoned time in terms of the South Carolina rice harvest in this instance, Joseph Manigault remembered that April was the time when his family traveled to Goose Creek "to hunt and amuse yourself with your Country Neighbours" (J[oseph] Manigault to G[abriel] Manigault, April 8, 1784, Manigault Family Papers, box 1 [letter], folder 12, South Caroliniana Library); Elias Ball of Limerick, Elias Ball Jr.'s first cousin, provided a harrowing account of returning to Charlestown as a loyalist (Elias Ball to Elias Ball, May 15, 1784, Elias Ball XIV Family Papers, folder 7). On property and other disputes that strained relations between Elias Ball and his relatives in South Carolina, see Elias Ball to John Ball, August 27, 1786, and John Ball to Elias Ball, December 27, 1786, Elias Ball XIV Family Papers, folder 8.

59. *South-Carolina Gazette*, April 29, 1732.

60. Records in the British Public Record Office Relating to South Carolina, South Carolina Department of Archives and History, Columbia, 5:207; on Francophobic invective, note the case of Henry Laurens, himself of French (Huguenot) descent, who hoped that British forces would "reduce the pride of that haughty tyrannical People," Henry Laurens to John Knight, July 24, 1755, *Papers of Henry Laurens*, 1:300; see also Henry Laurens to Sarah Nickleson, August 1, 1755, *Papers of Henry Laurens*, 1:309.

61. Hewit, "Historical Account," 518.

62. Ralph Izard to John Strange, June 13, 1775 (photoduplicate), Ralph Izard Papers, box: Originals and Photostats 1765–1803 and n.d., folder 1; Ralph Izard to William Duer, October 8, 1777 (photoduplicate), ibid.

63. See Waterhouse, "Development of Elite Culture," 391–404.

64. Wells, *Journal of a Voyage from Charleston*, 61–62, 28.

65. Peter Manigault to [Anne] Manigault, November 1, 1750, Manigault Family Papers, folder 6, South Carolina Historical Society; Peter Manigault to Anne Manigault, August 26, 1773, ibid., folder 10.

66. See James Raven, *London Booksellers and American Customers: Transatlantic Literary Community and the Charleston Library Society, 1748–1811* (Columbia: Univ. of South Carolina Press, 2001); quoted in Jack P. Greene, "Mastery and the Definition of Cultural Space in Early America: A Perspective," in *Imperatives, Behaviors and Identities*, 9; quoted in Greene, "Social and Cultural Capital in Colonial British America: A Case Study," *Journal of Interdisciplinary History* 29 (1999): 496.

67. Roger Williams Jr. to Peter Manigault, December 2, 1750, Manigault Family Papers, Box (legal): 2 December 1750–11 November 1884 and n.d., folder 1, South Caroliniana Library.

68. Peter Manigault to [Anne] Manigault, August 30, 1754, "Peter Manigault's Letters," 248.

Notes to THE AMERICAN SOUTH AND ENGLISH PRINT SATIRE, 1760–1865
by Marcus Wood

1. The primary archive for English Print satire during the war of independence is Mary Dorothy George, *Catalogue of the Political and Personal Satires: Preserved in the Department of Prints and Drawings in the British Museum* (London: British Museum, 1935–1954), hereafter cited as George, *BMC*. For the later period see the bibliography of primary materials in Patricia Anderson, *The Printed Image and the Formation of Popular Culture* (Oxford: Oxford Univ. Press, 1991), 199–203.

2. The standard historical account remains Herbert Atherton, *Political Prints in the Age of Hogarth* (Oxford: Oxford Univ. Press, 1974). See also Mary Dorothy George, *English Political Caricature: A Study of Opinion and Propaganda to 1792* (Oxford: Clarendon Press, 1959); Mary Dorothy George, *Hogarth to Cruikshank: Social Change in Graphic Satire* (London: Allen Lane, 1967); for an invaluable cultural survey of the background, see Ronald Paulson, *Hogarth, His Life and Art*, 2 vols. (New Haven: Yale Univ. Press, published for the Paul Mellon Centre for Studies in British Art, 1971). For a survey of the American Civil War prints, see Gwyn Williams, *The Cartoon History of the American Revolution* (London: London Editions, 1977); Peter D. G. Thomas, *The English Satirical Print 1600–1832: The American Revolution* (Cambridge: Chadwyk Healey, 1986), 11–31. For the small numbers of American prints surviving from this period, see Jane R. Pomeroy, "Alexander Anderson's Life and Engravings

before 1800, with a Checklist of Publications Drawn from His Diary," *Proceedings of the American Antiquarian Society* 100, no. 1 (1990): 137–230.

3. For Gillray's impact, see Draper Hill, *Fashionable Contrasts* (London: Phaidon, 1960); Draper Hill, *Mr. Gillray the Caricaturist*. (London: Phaidon, 1965); Diana Donald, *The Age of Caricature: Satirical Prints in the Reign of George III* (New Haven and London: Yale Univ. Press, 1996), 36–37, 41–43, 155–60, 170–75. The best general survey of print manufacture and publishing is George, *English Political Caricature*, 150–70; see also Vincent Caretta, *George III and the Satirists from Hogarth to Byron* (Athens and London: Univ. of Georgia Press, 1990), 1–41.

4. For Victorian periodical printing and satire, see Anderson, *Printed Image* (Oxford: Oxford Univ. Press, 1990); Brian Maidmant, *Reading Popular Prints 1790–1870* (Manchester: Manchester Univ. Press, 1996); Robert L. Patten, *George Cruikshank: A Revaluation* (Princeton: Princeton Univ. Press, 1974); Robert L. Patten, *George Cruikshank's Life, Times, and Art*, 2 vols. (Cambridge: Lutterworth, 1992 and 1996), 2:196–205, 422–511.

5. For the social history of *Punch*, see M. J. H. Spielmann, *The History of "Punch"* (New York, 1895); R. G. G. Price, *The History of Punch* (London: Collins, 1957); Patten, *George Cruikshank's Life, Times, and Art*, 2:199–200, 504–5. For the Victorian periodical press, see Mason Jackson, *The Pictorial Press: Its Origin and Progress* (London, 1885); Louis James, *English Popular Literature, 1819–1851* (New York: Columbia Univ. Press, 1976); Louis James, *Fiction for the Working Man* (London: Penguin, [1963] 1974); Laurel Brake and Aled Jones, eds., *Investigating Victorian Journalism* (New York: St. Martin's Press, 1990); Laurel Brake, *Subjugated Knowledges: Journalism, Gender, and Literature in the Nineteenth Century* (London: Macmillan, 1994); *Victorian Periodicals Review* (1968–   ).

6. For the decline of the single-sheet satire, see Marcus Wood, *Radical Satire and Print Culture, 1790–1822* (Oxford: Clarendon Press, 1994), 269–71; George, *English Political Caricature: A Study of Opinion and Propaganda to 1792*, 208–40; George, BMC, vol. 10, intro., xl–xlviii.

7. For moral attitudes in the nineteenth-century press, see Aled Jones, *Powers of the Press, Newspapers, and the Public in Nineteenth-Century England* (London: Scolar Press, 1996), 73–140; Maidment, *Popular Prints* (Manchester: Manchester Univ. Press), 101–75.

8. Atherton, *Political Prints*, 89.

9. See Atherton, *Political Prints*, 89; Thomas, *American Revolution*, 70–71, 82–83, 106–7, 116–17; George, BMC, 5526, 5534; Williams, *Cartoon History*, 24–27, 46–49.

10. For the political background to this print, see George, BMC, 4128.

11. For commentary on this print, see George, BMC, 5226; George, *English Political Caricature: A Study of Opinion and Propaganda to 1792*, 150–51; Williams, *Cartoon History*, 46–48, gives the English print and American variants.

12. This print is discussed in Atherton, *Political Prints*, 92, 96, 104, 188; George, BMC, 3069.

Notes

13. George, *English Political Caricature: A Study of Opinion and Propaganda to 1792*, 150–70.

14. For the intricate shifts in political loyalties in the papers of the period, see the meticulous Hannah Barker, *Newspaper, Politics, and Public Opinion in Late Eighteenth-Century England* (Oxford: Clarendon Press, 1998).

15. For personified and animalised representations of the colonies, see George, *English Political Caricature: A Study of Opinion and Propaganda to 1792*, 133–39, 142, 150–59; George, *BMC*, 4124, 4128, 4183, 5226, 5334, 5472, 5487, 5631, 5644.

16. See George, *BMC*, 5487, and George, *English Political Caricature: A Study of Opinion and Propaganda to 1792*, 156.

17. George Henry Preble, *Our Flag* (New York, 1872), 204–17.

18. Ibid., 214–15.

19. Williams, *Cartoon History*, 156–57.

20. For Darley's activities, see David Alexander, *Richard Newton and English Caricature in the 1790s*, exhibition cat. (Manchester: Manchester Univ. Press, 1998), 11; George, *English Political Caricature: A Study of Opinion and Propaganda to 1792*, pp. 101–4, 115–17, 147–48, 154–56, 175–77.

21. For other Darley prints showing America in similar guise, see Thomas, *American Revolution*, 132–33, 138–39; Williams, *Cartoon History*, 72–73, 80–83.

22. *London Chronicle,* January 26, 1774.

23. For Wilkes's shifting political profile, see George Rudé, *Wilkes and Liberty* (Oxford: Clarendon Press, 1962); Wood, *Radical Satire*, 55–56, 272–90. For Wilkes in print satire, see George, *English Political Caricature: A Study of Opinion and Propaganda to 1792*, 141–49.

24. For the shift in popular publishing around 1815–1855, see Hannah Barker, *Newspapers, Politics and English Society, 1695–1855* (London: Longman, 2000), 196–223.

25. For Leech and Tenniel, see John Ruskin, "The Fireside: John Leech and John Tenniel," *The Art of England Lectures Given in Oxford*, in *The Library Edition of the Works of John Ruskin*, ed. E. T. Cook and A. Wedderburn, 39 vols. (London: George Allen, n.d.), 33; Simon Houfe, *A Dictionary of British Book Illustrators and Caricaturists 1800–1914* (Woodbridge: Antique Collector's Club, 1978), 207–8, 324–25; Price, *History of Punch*, 70–74; Patten, *George Cruikshank's Life, Times, and Art*, vol. 1:26, 35, 97, 150, 422–28, 460–64; Paul Goldman, *Victorian Illustration* (London: Scolar Press, 1996), 329, 42.

26. For the Ojjobeway and *Punch*, see vol. 6, pp. 29, 179. The best account of their British tour is Tom F. Cunningham, *The Diamond's Ace: Scotland and the Native Americans* (Edinburgh: Mainstream Publishing, 2001).

27. For the text and fine contextualising discussion, see the Yale Avalon Project, electronic text, http://www.yale.edu/lawweb/avalon/diplomacy/britian/brtreaty.htm.

28. For a discussion of the role of infantilization in print satire, see Wood, *Radical Satire*, 215–63.

29. For whole-sheet prints based on the infantilization of America, see *Punch: RIDICULOUS EXHIBITION; OR, YANKEE NOODLE PUTTING HIS HEAD INTO THE BRITISH LION'S MOUTH*, vol. 10, p. 201; *"WHAT? YOU YOUNG YANKEE NOODLE, STRIKE YOUR OWN FATHER?,"* vol. 10, p. 119; *YOUNG YANKEE-NOODLE TEACHING GRANDMOTHER BRITANNIA TO SUCK EGGS*, vol. 10, p. 131, *THE SPOILT CHILD, NAUGHTY JONATHAN*, vol. 42, p. 25; *JOHN BULL'S NEUTRALITY, COLUMBIA'S SEWING MACHINE*, vol. 47, p. 136.

30. *JOHN BULL'S NEUTRALITY, Punch* 45 (1864), 136.

31. *Liberty Equality and Fraternity Dedicated to the Smartest Nation in all Creation, Punch* 15 (1854), 204–5.

32. *THE SENSATION STRUGGLE IN AMERICA, Punch* 42 (1862), 227.

33. *THE RE-UNITED STATES, Punch* 49 (1865), 136.

34. For the operation of the Promethean myth in earlier English abolition texts, see my discussion of Shelley in *Slavery Empathy and Pornography* (Oxford: Oxford Univ. Press, 2002), 246–50.

35. *KING COTTON BOUND; Or, The Modern Prometheus, Punch* 41 (1861), 175–76.

36. See David Dabydeen, *Hogarth's Blacks* (Manchester: Manchester Univ. Press, 1987); Wood, *Blind Memory*, 151–79.

37. For the treatment of emancipated slaves in English literature and art, see Douglas Lorimer, *Colour, Class, and the Victorians: English Attitudes to the Negro in the Mid-Nineteenth Century* (Leicester: Leicester Univ. Press, 1978), 11–12, 24–29; R. J. M. Blackett, *Building an Antislavery Wall: Black Americans in the Atlantic Abolitionist Movement, 1830–1860* (Ithaca and London: Cornell Univ. Press, 1983), 21–24, 41–43, 135–39, 145–48; Wood, *Blind Memory*, 191–92.

38. For the evolution of a new form of crude Victorian, see Robert J. C. Young, *Colonial Desire Hybridity in Theory, Culture and Race* (London: Routledge, 1995), 90–142; Lorimer, *Colour, Class, and the Victorians* 108–31; H. F. Augstein, *Race: The Origins of an Idea, 1760–1850* (Bristol: Thoemmes Press, 1996).

39. For Carlyle and the nigger question, see John Stewart Mill, "The Negro Question," *Fraser's Magazine* (1850) 469. For the South's use of Carlyle in Civil War propaganda, see Simon Heffer, *Moral Desperado*, 328–29. For the American reception of "On the Nigger Question," see Jules Paul Seigel, ed., *Carlyle the Critical Heritage* (London and New York: Routledge, 1995), 310–18, 367–69; the best theoretical discussion is David Theo Goldberg, "Liberalism's Limits: Carlyle and Mill on 'The Negro Question,'" *Nineteenth Century Contexts* 22 (2000) 208–16.

40. "Punch's Police: A Very Melancholy Case," *Punch* 18 (1858), 107.

41. For an excellent discussion of Powers's work, see Jean Fagan Yellin, *Women and Sisters* (New Haven: Yale Univ. Press, 1989), 99–124.

42. *DIVORCE À VINCULO Mrs. Carolina Asserts her Right to "Larrup" her Nigger, Punch* 40 (1861), 27; *OBERON AND TITANIA, Punch* 42 (1862), 138.

43. For infantilization of the black in English print culture, see Wood, *Blind Memory*, 273-79.

44. *THE BLACK CONSCRIPTION, Punch* 45 (1863), 128; *THE BLACK DRAFT, Punch* 47 (1864), 209.

Notes to BRITISH VIEWS OF THE CONFEDERACY
by R. J. M. Blackett

1. Dudley to Seward, Liverpool, October 22, 24, 1864, Despatches from U.S. Consuls in Liverpool, England, 1790-1906; Mason to Benjamin, Paris, September 29, 1864, Records of the Confederate States of America; Henry Hotze to Benjamin, London, October 31, 1863, Hotze Papers, Library of Congress.

2. Edward F. Spence, *Bar and Buskin Being Memories of Life, Law and the Theatre* (London: E. Matthews and Marot, 1930), 1-2, 8; Mason to Benjamin, London, May 6, 1862, Records of the Confederate States of America; Hotze to Hunter, London, February 28, 1862, Hotze to Secretary of State, London, April 25, 1862, Hotze to Benjamin, London, May 9, 1863, Hotze Papers.

3. Hotze to Benjamin, London, October 31, 1863, Hotze Papers; for Prioleau's comments, see Frank Hughes, "Liverpool and the Confederate States" (M.Phil. thesis, Keele University, 1998), 112-13; Spence to Mason, Liverpool, January 22, 1864, Mason Papers, Library of Congress.

4. Spence to Mason, Liverpool, April 4, 1864, Mason Papers; Spence to Wharncliffe, Liverpool, September 15, 1864, and October 3, 1864, Wharncliffe Muniments, Sheffield Record Office; *London Times*, August 5, 1864, September 25, 1864; *Liverpool Mercury*, October 19, 20, 22, 1864, November 11, 1864.

5. *Index*, May 15, 1862; *Blackwood's*, January 1863; see Robert Botsford, "Scotland and the American Civil War" (Ph.D. diss., Edinburgh University, 1955), 605, for the final quotation.

6. *Glasgow Daily Herald*, November 27, 1863; Percy Greg, *History of the United States from the Foundation of Virginia to the Reconstruction of the Union*, 2 vols. (London: W. H. Allen, 1887), 1:133-37. Although Greg's book was written after the war, it is clear from all the evidence that the views expressed in this work were similar to those he penned in his unsigned newspaper articles.

7. *London Times*, December 12, 1864, August 12, 1861.

8. *London Times*, November 11, 21, 1862. In an earlier column Spence saw similar developments as a result of the French Revolution. "Shoeless, shirtless, paid in assignats, they, too, went onward in eager hosts. But the movement, which began with songs of liberty, ended in erecting despotism, and in piling up, as an altar to brotherly love, a hecatomb of human bones" (March 22, 1862).

9. Miles Taylor, *The Decline of British Radicalism, 1847–1860*, (Oxford: Oxford Univ. Press, 1995), 20, 195–99; see Gregory Claeys, "Mazzini, Kossuth, and British Radicalism, 1848–1854," *Journal of British Studies* 28 (1989), for a discussion of some of these issues; and Linda Colley, *Britons: Forging the Nation, 1707–1837* (New Haven, Conn.: Yale Univ. Press, 1992), 18, 50, 103.

10. *London Times*, October 9, 1861; Charles Fairbanks, *The American Conflict as Seen from a European Point of View* (Boston: George C. Rand and Avery, 1863), 12; Louis Blanc, a French radical living in England, thought the Americans took great pleasure cocking a snoot at the British: "To humiliate England has always been, for the Yankees, a luxurious and exquisite enjoyment." As a consequence, many in England take a "malicious satisfaction" in America's troubles. Louis Blanc, *Letters on England*, 2 vols. (London: Sampson Low, 1866), 1:213–14.

11. *Manchester Guardian*, May 18, 1861; Wilbur S. Shepperson, *Emigration and Disenchantment: Portraits of Englishmen Repatriated from the United States* (Norman, Okla.: Oklahoma Univ. Press, 1965), 24–25, 29.

12. Henry Pelling, *America and the British Left from Bright to Bevan* (New York: New York Univ. Press, 1957), 2; G. D. Lillibridge, *Beacon of Freedom: The Impact of American Democracy upon Great Britain, 1830–1870* (Philadelphia: Univ. of Pennsylvania Press, 1955), 35; Ernest Jones, *The Slaveholders' War: A Lecture Delivered in the Town Hall, Ashton-under-Lyne . . . on November 16th, 1863* (Ashton-under-Lyne: Ashton-under-Lyne Union and Emancipation Society, 1863), 40; *Manchester Examiner and Times*, February 6, 1863; *Huddersfield Examiner*, November 1, 1862.

13. Walter M. Merrill, ed., *The Letters of William Lloyd Garrison*, 6 vols. (Cambridge, Mass.: Harvard Univ. Press, 1971–1981), vol. 5 (1979), 72; W. E. Adams, *The Slaveholders' War: An Argument for the North and the Negro*, (London: J. Snow, 1863), 13; *National Reformer*, December 13, 1862; see also John Stockdale's arguments in the *Bury Times*, February 21, 1863.

14. *London Times*, August 27, 1861, May 10, 1862; W. C. Corsan, *Two Months in the Confederate States: An Englishman's Travels through the South* (1863; reprint, Baton Rouge: Louisiana State Univ. Press, 1996), 94–95; Thomas Colley Grattan, *England and the Disunited States of America* (London: Ridgway, 1861), 40–41.

15. William Wyndham Malet, *An Errand to the South in the Summer of 1862* (London: Richard Bentley, 1863); Anthony Trollope, *North America*, 2 vols. (1862; reprint, London: St. Martin's Press, 1968), 2:62–70.

16. "Letters of Richard Cobden to Charles Sumner," *American Historical Review* 2, no. 2 (January 1897).

17. *Bee Hive*, March 28, 1863; *Mansfield Reporter*, March 17, 1863; *Ashton and Stalybridge Reporter*, October 1, 1864.

18. Douglas Lorimer, *Colour, Class, and the Victorians: English Attitudes to the Negro in the Mid-Nineteenth Century* (New York: Holmes and Meier, 1978); Ronald Rainger, "Race, Politics, and Science: The Anthropological Society of London in the 1860s,"

Victorian Studies 22 (autumn 1978), 51; Hotze to Benjamin, London, August 27, 1863, Hotze Papers.

19. Hotze to Benjamin, London, September 26, 1862, Hotze Papers; Alexander J. Beresford-Hope, *The American Desruption: Three Lectures Delivered by the Request of the Maidstone Literary and Mechanical Institution* (London: James Ridgway, 1862), 10, 16, 92–93; *London Times,* January 17, 1862; *Anti-Slavery Reporter,* November 2, 1863; *Maidstone Telegraph,* January 24, 1863; *Bury Times,* February 21, 1863.

20. The debate ran in the *Todmorden Times* from October 1863 to February 1864. See particularly November 21, 1863, December 19, 1863, January 2, 9, 16, 23, 1864, and February 21, 1864.

21. Spence to Mason, Liverpool, April 28, 1862, Mason Papers; *Ashton and Stalybridge Reporter,* May 3, 1862.

22. *Bee Hive,* March 28, 1863; *National Reformer,* August 30, 1862.

23. *Ashton and Stalybridge Reporter,* January 3, 1864, October 4, 1862; *Preston Guardian,* April 4, 1863; *Leicestershire Mercury,* May 9, 1863; see also the comments by a Mr. Sommerville at a meeting in Edinburgh: "We also declare our sympathy with four million of working men and women who are defrauded of the fruits of their labour, and the ownership of their bodies, because they are guilty of having 'a skin not coloured like our own' " *Caledonian Mercury,* February 20, 1863.

24. *Ashton and Stalybridge Reporter,* January 21, 1865.

25. *Glasgow Daily Herald,* November 27, 1863; *London Times,* January 16, 1863; James Spence, *The American Union: Its Effect on National Character and Policy, with an Inquiry into Secession as a Constitutional Right and the Causes of Desruption* (London: Richard Bentley, 1862), 132; *Leicester Free Press,* December 12, 1863.

26. *London Times,* October 12, 1864, December 12, 1864; *Index,* October 6, 1864; Spence to Wharncliffe, Liverpool, August 25, 1865, Wharncliffe Muniments; Joseph Parker, *A Report from Mr. Joseph Parker of Manchester, to Sir Henry De Hoghton, Bart., on His Mission as Bearer of the Peace Address from the People of Great Britain and Ireland to the People of the United States of America* (N.p.: n.p., 1865).

27. *Reports of the Select Committee of the House of Commons on Public Petitions, Session 1864* (London, 1864); *Manchester Examiner and Times,* July 19, 1864.

28. *Sheffield and Rotherham Independent,* June 11, 1863; *Richmond Daily Dispatch,* October 26, 27, 1875; James M. Morgan Jr., *The Jackson-Hope and the Society of the Cincinnati Medals of the Virginia Military Institute* (Verona, Va.: McClure Press, 1979), 2–5.

29. Hughes, "Liverpool and the Confederate States," 502–24; Dudley to Seward, Liverpool, January 13, 1865, Despatches from U.S. Consuls in Liverpool, England, 1790–1906; *Liverpool Mercury,* December 23, 1864; *Liverpool Courier,* January 12, 1865; *London Times,* December 26, 1864; *New York Times,* December 9, 1864.

30. Spence to Wharncliffe, Liverpool, January 28, July 29, September 6, 1865, August 22, 1868, Wharncliffe Muniments; George Green Shackleford, *George Wythe*

Randolph and the Confederate Elite (Athens, Ga.: Univ. of Georgia Press, 1988), 152-57; Eli N. Evans, *Judah P. Benjamin: The Jewish Confederate* (New York: The Free Press, 1988), 329; Spence, *Bar and Buskin*, 14.

31. *London Times,* May 19, 1862.

32. *Boston Commonwealth,* July 17, 1863; Moncure D. Conway, *Autobiography, Memories, and Experiences of Moncure D. Conway,* 2 vols. (London: Cassell and Co., 1904), 1:362-63.

Notes to THE SOUTH AND THE BRITISH LEFT, 1930-1960
by Hugh Wilford

1. Cleanth Brooks, "The British Reception of Faulkner's Work," in *William Faulkner: Prevailing Verities and World Literature,* ed. Wolodymyr T. Zyla and Wendell M. Aycock (Lubbock, Texas: Texas Tech University, 1973), 45-46, 41.

2. Patricia Hollis, *Jennie Lee: A Life* (Oxford: Oxford Univ. Press, 1997), 75.

3. Richard Crossman, "The Black Scar," *The New Statesman and Nation,* 30 April 1949, 424-25.

4. Woodrow Wyatt, *Confessions of an Optimist* (London: Collins, 1985), 188.

5. Quoted in Giora Goodman, "'Who is anti-American?': The British Left and the United States, 1945-1956" (Ph.D. diss., University College London, 1996), 55.

6. Quoted in Isaac Kramnick and Barry Sheerman, *Harold Laski: A Life on the Left* (London: Hamish Hamilton, 1993), 568.

7. See, for example, Harold Laski, *The American Democracy: A Commentary and an Interpretation* (London: George Allen and Unwin, 1949), 44.

8. Ibid., 428-30. For a recent appraisal of the New Criticism which emphasizes its political motivation, see Marc Jancovich, "The Southern New Critics," in *The Cambridge History of Literary Criticism,* vol. 7, *Modernism and the New Criticism,* ed. A. Walton Litz, Louis Menand, and Lawrence Rainey (Cambridge: Cambridge Univ. Press, 2000), 200-218.

9. Laski, 468, 471. There are interesting comparisons to be made between Laski's analysis of southern conditions and that of the Trinidadian-born black writer and radical C. L. R. James, who began drafting his *Notes on American Civilization* in 1949. Like Laski, James, who had traveled extensively in the South, noted such signs of positive change as "the terrific struggles of the Negroes" and the federal government's growing inclination to protect African-American civil rights. He was, however, doubtful that these developments would upset the interrelated system of vested economic interests, local political oligarchies, and white racism that held down southern blacks. C. L. R. James, *American Civilization* (Oxford: Blackwell, 1993), 204.

10. Laski, 457-62, 463, 466.

11. Tony Benn, *Years of Hope: Diaries, Letters and Papers, 1940–1962* (London: Hutchinson, 1994), 119; Bryan Magee, *Go West, Young Man* (London: Eyre and Spottiswoode, 1958), 148.

12. Kingsley Martin, "Letter to an American Liberal," *The New Statesman and Nation*, 19 January 1946, 39.

13. Herbert Hill, "A Negro in Notting Hill," *The New Statesman*, 9 May 1959, 635–36.

14. For more on this group, see Jonathan Schneer, *Labour's Conscience: The Labour Left, 1945–1951* (London: Unwin Hyman, 1988).

15. See Radhika Desai, *Intellectuals and Socialism: "Social Democrats" and the Labour Party* (London: Lawrence and Wishart, 1994).

16. For examples of this "Gaitskellite" tendency to talk up improvements in southern race relations, see Denis Healey, *The Time of My Life* (London: Michael Joseph, 1989), 204; Roy Jenkins, "The Negro in the United States," *Plebs* 46 (January 1954): 1–2; Rita Hinden, "Hope in the Negro South," *Socialist Commentary* 14 (September 1950): 210–11. *Socialist Commentary* was the principal theoretical organ of the Gaitskellites, and Hinden, an expert on colonial affairs, its editor. Whereas *The New Statesman* and the other mouthpiece of the Labour left, *Tribune*, dwelt on the problems of the South, Hinden preferred to publish pieces which emphasized positive developments in the region, even suggesting in the wake of the Supreme Court's 1954 *Brown* decision that Britain adopt the United States as a model of successful race relations. See her editorial "Colour and Equality," *Socialist Commentary* 18 (August 1954): 205–7.

17. See Stephen Brooke, "Atlantic Crossing? American Views of Capitalism and British Socialist Thought, 1932–1962," *Twentieth Century British History* 2 (1991): 120–25.

18. C. A. R. Crosland, *The Future of Socialism* (London: Jonathan Cape, 1964), 179, 186, 185, 183.

19. Anthony Crosland, "USA trip, 1954, notebook," Anthony Crosland Papers, British Library of Political and Economic Science, London.

20. During a visit to the United States in the early 1960s, Crosland noted about the South its "steady advance twds desegregation: and 'quiet cooperation' between Negroes and White Libs [sic]." Anthony Crosland, "USA, 1960–64," Crosland Papers.

21. See Walter Citrine, *My American Diary* (London: Labour Book Service, 1940), 23–39.

22. Quoted in Victor Silverman, *Imagining Internationalism in American and British Labor, 1949–1949* (Urbana: Univ. of Illinois Press, 2000), 80. See also Peter Weiler, *British Labour and the Cold War* (Stanford: Stanford Univ. Press, 1988), chapter 1.

23. See Anthony Carew, "Conflict within the ICFTU: Anti-Communism and Anti-Colonialism in the 1950s," *International Review of Social History* 41 (1996): 147–81.

24. Following a particularly egregious incident of racial injustice in Alabama (the Jimmy Wilson case, which is discussed below), the Labour Party expressed its regret that "those who wish to criticize western liberty and democracy" had been furnished with "such suitable ammunition for their propaganda." Quoted in Mary L. Dudziak, *Cold War Civil Rights: Race and the Image of American Democracy* (Princeton: Princeton Univ. Press, 2000), 5.

25. See Graham Smith, *When Jim Crow Met John Bull: Black American Soldiers in World War II* (London: Tauris, 1987), 179–81; David Reynolds, *Rich Relations: The American Occupation of Britain, 1942–1945* (London: HarperCollins, 1995), chapter 18; Christopher Thorne, "Britain and the Black GIs: Racial Issues and Anglo-American Relations in 1942," in *Race and U.S. Foreign Policy from 1900 through World War II*, ed. Michael Krenn (New York: Garland, 1998), 342–51.

26. B. A. Godwin to Walter Citrine, 15 January 1935, TUC Papers, Modern Records Centre, University of Warwick.

27. N. White (TUC Research and Economic Department) to Miss McDonald, 16 January 1935, TUC Papers; Assistant Secretary, TUC, to B. A. Godwin, 13 February 1935, TUC Papers.

28. E. Clark (Secretary of Croydon Trades Council) to Vincent Tewson (General Secretary of TUC), 23 November 1958, TUC Papers; C. J. Geddes (General Secretary of the Union of Post-Office Workers) to Vincent Tewson, 3 November 1955, TUC Papers; Vincent Tewson to S. F. Greene (General Secretary of National Union of Railwaymen), 2 July 1959, TUC Papers.

29. See, for example, Vincent Tewson to C. J. Geddes, 4 November 1955, TUC Papers, about Emmett Till. The protests about Jimmy Wilson prompted a lengthy, diplomatic correspondence with AFL-CIO officials about what action they were taking in the case. See, for example, George Woodcock to George Meany, 20 April 1959, TUC Papers.

30. D. Doxsey (Secretary, Croydon Trades Council), to the Secretary, TUC International Department, 31 January 1956, TUC Papers. See also H. Baker (Secretary, Birmingham Trades Council) to Secretary, TUC Organization Department, 6 October 1955, TUC Papers, and H. E. Newbold (Secretary, Manchester and Salford Trades Council) to Vincent Tewson, 28 May 1958, TUC Papers.

31. Secretary, TUC Organization Department, to H. Baker, 11 October 1955, TUC Papers.

32. Secretary, TUC International Department, to D. Doxsey, 31 January 1956, TUC Papers.

33. Dudziak, 34–35.

34. Quoted in Goodman, 172.

35. American Embassy, London, to Department of State, "Semi-Annual Evaluation Report, December 1–May 31, 1951," 27 July 1951, Records of the Department of State (Record Group [RG] 59), National Archives, Washington, D.C.

36. P. Bowen Evans to United States Information Agency (USIA), "USIS/United Kingdom Annual Assessment Report—October 1, 1957 through September 30, 1958," 19 January 1959, Records of the USIA (RG 306), National Archives.

37. Dudziak, 141.

38. Neil M. Ruge, American Consulate, Wales, to State, "Miners' Gala Day; Paul Robeson Theme," 13 June 1956, RG 59, National Archives.

39. Martin Bauml Duberman, *Paul Robeson* (London: Bodley Head, 1989), 227–28.

40. See Silverman, 75–80.

41. Fred Vanderschmidt, *What the English Think of Us* (London: Duality Press, 1951), 123, 125. Vanderschmidt sarcastically described the simultaneous reception by Labour MPs in the House of Commons of Joe Louis and a company of African-American actors as "Emancipation Day in Parliament" (ibid., 126).

42. There were links between racist British organizations and the Ku Klux Klan. See Mike Sewell, "British Responses to Martin Luther King, Jr., and the Civil Rights Movement," in *The Making of Martin Luther King and the Civil Rights Movement*, ed. Brian Ward and Tony Badger (Basingstoke: Macmillan, 1996), 207.

43. P. Bowen Evans to USIA, "USIS/United Kingdom Annual Assessment Report—October 1, 1957 through September 30, 1958," 19 January 1959, RG 306, National Archives.

44. R. G. Wellings, for example, a National Union of Railwaymen official and English-Speaking Union grantee, perceived the TVA as "a classical example of Socialism in a Capitalist Country." R.G. Wellings, "Study Tour of the United States of America, November-December 1954," no date, TUC Papers.

45. Derek Gladwin, "Report on Six Weeks' Tour of the United States, November 30 1955 to January 12 1956," no date, TUC Papers.

46. Dayle C. McDonough (American Consul General, Glasgow) to State, "Report on US Visit by John Lang, Scottish Labor Leader, under Smith-Mundt Program," 5 October 1951, RG 59, National Archives.

47. David Linebaugh to State, "Woodrow Wyatt's Views on the United States," 25 November 1952, RG 59, National Archives.

48. Anglo-American Council on Productivity, Productivity Team Report on "Cotton Spinning," Federation of British Industries (FBI) Papers, Modern Records Centre, University of Warwick.

49. Anglo-American Council on Productivity, Productivity Team Report on "Cotton Yarn Doubling," FBI Papers.

50. Quoted in John Bright, "Why the American Worker Earns More than the British," *Plebs* 43 (1951): 36.

51. H. G. Wells, *The Future in America: A Search After Realities* (London: Chapman and Hall, 1906), 259. While disagreeing with his strategy of voluntary racial separation, Wells was impressed by Washington as a man whose mind "can grasp the situation and destinies of a people" (ibid., 275).

52. See Peter Davison, ed., *The Complete Works of George Orwell*, vol. 16, *I Have Tried To Tell the Truth, 1934–1944* (London: Secker and Warburg, 1998), 23; quoted in ibid., 406.

53. Quoted in Barry Feinberg and Ronald Kasrils, *Bertrand Russell's America*, vol. 1, *1896–1945* (London: Allen and Unwin, 1973), 319.

54. Quoted in Barry Feinberg and Ronald Kasrils, *Bertrand Russell's America*, vol. 2, *1945–1970* (London: Allen and Unwin, 1983), 240.

55. Quoted in Mick Gidley, "Faulkner and the British: Episodes in a Literary Relationship," in *Faulkner: International Perspectives: Faulkner and Yoknapatawpha, 1982*, ed. Doreen Fowler and Ann J. Abadie (Jackson: Univ. Press of Mississippi, 1984), 75–76.

56. For an exhaustive treatment of this subject, see Gordon Price-Stephens, "The British Reception of William Faulkner, 1929–1962," *Mississippi Quarterly* 18 (1965): 119–200.

57. Quoted in Vincent Brome, *J. B. Priestley* (London: Hamish Hamilton, 1988), 209.

58. See Hugh Wilford, *The New York Intellectuals: From Vanguard to Institution* (Manchester: Manchester Univ. Press), 111.

59. Wells, 273, 270–71.

60. Quoted in Ray Monk, *Bertrand Russell, 1921–1970: The Ghost of Madness* (London: Jonathan Cape, 2000), 104.

61. See Feinberg and Kasrils, *Bertrand Russell's America*, 2:225–34.

62. Quoted in Davison, *The Complete Works of George Orwell*, 16:23.

63. Quoted in ibid., 328–29.

64. Quoted in Peter Davison, ed., *The Complete Works of George Orwell*, vol. 20, *Our Job Is To Make Life Worth Living, 1949–1950* (London: Secker and Warburg, 1998), 209.

65. See Gidley, 78–80.

66. Michael O'Brien, *The Idea of the American South, 1920–1941* (Baltimore: Johns Hopkins Univ. Press, 1979), 156–57.

67. See Stephen Spender, *Journals, 1939–1983* (London: Faber and Faber, 1985), 101–2; Stephen Spender to Allen Tate, 20 February 1953, Allen Tate Papers, Firestone Library, Princeton; Frank Kermode, *Modern Essays* (London: Fontana Press, 1990), chapter 21.

68. L.D. Lerner, "The New Criticism," in *The Craft of Letters in England: A Symposium*, ed. John Lehmann (London: Cresset Press, 1956), 142. Indeed, the title of Lerner's essay suggests that the New Criticism was considered rather more important than the New York Intellectuals, as does his list of "leading practitioners," which apart from Lionel Trilling consists entirely of New Critics, namely John Crowe Ransom, Allen Tate, Robert Penn Warren, R. P. Blackmur, and Yvor Winters.

69. See the useful discussion in Chris Baldick, *Criticism and Literary Theory, 1890 to the Present* (London: Longman, 1996), chapter 3.

70. See Alan Sinfield, *Literature, Politics and Culture in Postwar Britain* (London: Athlone Press, 1997), chapter 9.

71. Lawrence H. Schwartz, *Creating Faulkner's Reputation: The Politics of Modern Literary Criticism* (Knoxville: Univ. of Tennessee Press, 1988).

72. Frances Stonor Saunders, *Who Paid the Piper? The CIA and the Cultural Cold War* (London: Granta, 1999), chapter 15, 333–34.

73. See Sewell, 205–8.

74. Ibid., 207.

Notes to "BY ELVIS AND ALL THE SAINTS"
by Brian Ward

Epigraph: Helen Taylor, *Circling Dixie: Contemporary Southern Culture Through a Transatlantic Lens* (New Brunswick: Rutgers Univ. Press, 2001), 21.

1. *London Times*, August 20, 1977, 13.

2. Mo Foster, *Play Like Elvis: How British Musicians Bought the American Dream* (Bodmin: MPG Books, 2000), 55.

3. *London Times*, December 30, 1958, 3.

4. Ibid., November 22, 1957, 7; Grady McWhiney, *Cracker Culture: Celtic Ways in the Old South* (Tuscaloosa: Univ. of Alabama Press, 1988).

5. *The Beatles Anthology* (London: Cassell and Co, 2000), 28.

6. Jim Godbolt, *A History of Jazz in Britain, 1919–50* (London: Quartet, 1984), 17; Foster, *Play Like Elvis*, 199.

7. Foster, *Play Like Elvis*, 268.

8. *The Stage*, September 6, 1956, 7.

9. *Newcastle Evening Chronicle*, March 7, 1957, 19.

10. *The Stage*, September 13, 1956, 7.

11. George Melly, *Revolt into Style: The Pop Arts in Britain* (1970; reprint, London: Penguin, 1972), 60.

12. *Jazz Journal*, January 1950, 17.

13. *Melody Maker*, November 13, 1943, 6–7.

14. Colin MacInnes, *Absolute Beginners* (1959; reprint, London: Allison and Busby, 2001), 62.

15. Ewan MacColl, *Journeyman: An Autobiography* (London: Sidgwick and Jackson, 1990), 273.

16. Foster, *Play Like Elvis*, 191–93.

17. *Daily Mirror*, September 8, 1956, 7.

18. George Harrison, quoted in *Beatles Anthology*, 28.

19. *Daily Mirror*, August 16, 1956, 5.

20. *Melody Maker,* May 5, 1956, 8.
21. Ibid., April 7, 1956, 24.
22. For a detailed account of the Cole incident, and the links between Massive Resistance and the southern campaign against rock and roll, see Brian Ward, *Just My Soul Responding: Rhythm and Blues, Black Consciousness and Race Relations* (Berkeley: Univ. of California Press, 1998), 95–105.
23. *Daily Express,* April 12, 1956, 9.
24. *Melody Maker,* April 21, 1956, 8.
25. Ibid.
26. Ibid.
27. Ibid., April 14, 1956, 7.
28. Ibid, May 26, 1956, 3.
29. *London Times,* September 15, 1956, 4.
30. Reverend Albert Carter, quoted in Ian Whitcomb, *Whole Lotta Shakin'* (London: Arrow Books, 1985), 13. Clearly, a crucial factor here was that rock and roll's black heritage was associated specifically with African Americans, not with the Afro-Caribbeans or Asians who occupied a more conspicuous place in Britain's racial landscape and who were the subject of increasingly tense debates about race relations, immigration policies, and anti-discrimination laws.
31. *Daily Mirror,* September 5, 1956, 3.
32. *London Times,* September 15, 1956, 7.
33. Colin Ward, interview with author, June 20, 2001.
34. *Mojo,* July 2001, 138.
35. *London Times,* September 15, 1956, 4.
36. Ibid., January 6, 1958, 7.
37. *Daily Mirror,* May 23, 1958, 2; *Daily Herald,* May 23, 1958, 1. For the best coverage of Lewis's tour, see Nick Tosches, *Hellfire: The Jerry Lee Lewis Story* (New York: Dell, 1982), 151–61.
38. *Daily Mirror,* May 26, 1958, 1.
39. Jerry Lee Lewis, quoted in ibid., May 27, 1956, 10.
40. See, Tosches, *Hellfire,* 245–46.
41. Jerry Lee Lewis, quoted in *Daily Mirror,* May 27, 1956, 10.
42. *Melody Maker,* June 7, 1958, 12.
43. *Daily Herald,* May 26, 1958, 1, 3.
44. *Daily Sketch,* May 25, 1958, 5.
45. *People,* May 25, 1958, 1.
46. *Daily Sketch,* May 26, 1958, 1.
47. *Daily Mirror,* May 28 1958, 2.
48. Ibid., May 29, 1958, 2.
49. Christopher Booker, *The Neophiliacs: The Revolution in English Life in the Fifties and Sixties* (1969; 2d ed., London: Pimlico, 1992), 34–35.

50. Simon Frith, *Sound Effects: Youth, Leisure and the Politics of Rock 'n' Roll* (New York: Pantheon, 1982), 184–85.
51. *New Musical Express*, March 3, 1956, 5.
52. MacInnes, *Absolute Beginners*, 12.
53. John Gustafson, quoted in Foster, *Play Like Elvis*, 44.
54. John Lennon, quoted in *Beatles Anthology*, 192.
55. Paul McCartney, whose father led his own Dixieland combo, frequently cited Elvis and Little Richard as his greatest rock and roll idols, with Buddy Holly and the Everly Brothers not too far behind. George Harrison had similar heroes, but recalled Cajun legend Fats Domino's "I'm in Love Again" as the first rock and roll record he ever heard. Harrison credited hearing his father's copy of Jimmy Rodgers's "Waiting for a Train" with making him want to take up the guitar in the first instance; he had a similarly paternal exposure to the blues, folk, and country sounds of Josh White, Bill Broonzy, and Slim Whitman. Ringo Starr's infatuation with southern music, indeed the whole notion of the South, was if anything even more intense. "I thought about emigrating to the USA . . . I wanted to go to Texas to live with Lightin' Hopkins—the blues man, my hero. I actually went to the embassy and got the forms. This was in 1958 . . . we'd got a list of jobs to go to in Houston." *Beatles Anthology*, 27–28, 37 (Starr quote on page 37).

Notes to AFTERWORD: ON THE IRRELEVANCE OF KNIGHTS
by Michael O'Brien

1. On these matters, Alexander Grant and Keith J. Stringer, eds., *Uniting the Kingdom? The Making of British History* (London: Routledge, 1995), is helpful.
2. In his book on Britain and the Civil War, however, Blackett is very attentive to these matters. See R. J. M. Blackett, *Divided Hearts: Britain and the American Civil War* (Baton Rouge: Louisiana State Univ. Press, 2001).
3. Linda Colley, *Britons: Forging a Nation, 1707–1837* (New Haven, Conn.: Yale Univ. Press, 1992).
4. See Arthur M. Schlesinger Jr., *The Disuniting of America: Reflections on a Multicultural Society* (New York: W. W. Norton, 1992).
5. Pertinent is Keith Wrightson, *English Society, 1580–1680* (London: Unwin Hyman, 1982).
6. This would seem to support the suggestion of Anderson that nationalism was a venture of Creole culture: see Benedict Anderson, *Imagined Communities: Reflections on the Origin and Spread of Nationalism*, revised and enlarged ed. (1983; reprint, London: Verso, 1991).
7. On literary culture, see Alan Richardson and Sonia Hofkosh, eds., *Romanticism, Race, and Imperial Culture, 1780–1834* (Bloomington: Indiana Univ. Press, 1996).

More broadly, the two relevant volumes of the *Oxford History of the British Empire* are pertinent: P. J. Marshall, ed., Alaine Low, asst. ed., *The Oxford History of the British Empire*, vol. 2, *The Eighteenth Century* (Oxford: Oxford Univ. Press, 1998); and Andrew Porter, ed., Alaine Low, asst. ed., *The Oxford History of the British Empire*, vol. 3, *The Nineteenth Century* (Oxford: Oxford Univ. Press, 1999).

8. On Thackeray, see James Grant Wilson, *Thackeray in the United States, 1852–3, 1855–6: Including a Record of a Variety of Thackerayana* (1904; reprint, New York: Haskell House, 1970), 1:128, 278–96, 347–48; on Trescot, see William Henry Trescot to William Porcher Miles, 4 December 1853, William Porcher Miles Papers, Southern Historical Collection, University of North Carolina; on Thompson, entry for 4 October 1864, John R. Thompson Diary, Thompson Papers, Alderman Library, University of Virginia; on Kennedy, entries during March and April 1856, John Pendleton Kennedy Journal, and Thomas Babington Macaulay to John Pendleton Kennedy, 23 February 1856, both in Kennedy Papers, Peabody Library, Baltimore; on Nott, see the list of fellows of the Society appended to its edition of Johann Friedrich Blumenbach, *The Anthropological Treatises of Johann Friedrich Blumenbach*, edited by Thomas Bendyshe (London: Longman, Green, Longman, Roberts, and Green, 1865).

9. On Wilson's Anglophilia, see John A. Thompson, *Woodrow Wilson* (London: Longman, 2002), 15–42; on Page, see Burton J. Hendrick, *The Life and Letters of Walter H. Page* (London: William Heinemann, 1923).

10. Olaudah Equiano, *The Interesting Narrative and Other Writings*, ed. and introduced by Vincent Carretta (New York: Penguin, 1995); Alan J. Rice and Martin Crawford, eds., *Liberating Sojourn: Frederick Douglass and Transatlantic Reform* (Athens: Univ. of Georgia Press, 1999); Paul Jefferson, ed., *The Travels of William Wells Brown* (New York: Markus Wiener Publishing, 1991); Wilson Jeremiah Moses, *Alexander Crummell: A Study of Civilization and Discontent* (New York: Oxford Univ. Press, 1989); J. R. Oldfield, ed., *Civilization and Black Progress: Selected Writings of Alexander Crummell on the South,* Southern Texts Society (Charlottesville: Univ. Press of Virginia, 1995).

11. Arthur Christopher Benson, *The Life of Edward White Benson, Sometime Archbishop of Canterbury,* new edition, abridged (London: Macmillan, 1901), 43–44.

12. See Paul Gilroy, *The Black Atlantic: Modernity and Double Consciousness* (London: Verso, 1993), but especially *Small Acts: Thoughts on the Politics of Black Cultures* (London: Serpent's Tail, 1993); V. S. Naipaul, *A Turn in the South* (New York: Alfred A. Knopf, 1989); Caryl Phillips, *The Final Passage* (London: Faber, 1985), a novel of Caribbean migration to Britain, and *Cambridge* (London: Bloomsbury, 1991), another on English involvement in Caribbean slavery; C. L. R. James, *American Civilization,* ed. Anna Grimshaw and Keith Hart (Oxford: Blackwell, 1993); Gary Younge, *No Place Like Home: A Black Briton's Journey Through the American South* (London: Picador, 1999).

13. John Crowe Ransom, "Reconstructed but Unregenerate," in *I'll Take My Stand: The South and the Agrarian Tradition* (1930; reprint, Baton Rouge: Louisiana State Univ. Press, 1977), 3–4.

14. John Shelton Reed and Daniel Joseph Singal, eds., *Regionalism and the South: Selected Papers of Rupert Vance* (Chapel Hill: Univ. of North Carolina Press, 1982), 44, 46, 313, 318; Martin Duberman, *Black Mountain: An Exploration in Community* (Garden City, N.Y.: Anchor Books, 1973); Henry D. Shapiro, *Appalachia on Our Mind: The Southern Mountains and the Mountaineers in the American Consciousness, 1870–1920* (Chapel Hill: Univ. of North Carolina Press, 1978), 231–43; John Lomax, *Adventures of a Ballad Hunter* (New York: Macmillan, 1947).

15. Bertram Wyatt-Brown, *The House of Percy: Honor, Melancholy, and Imagination in a Southern Family* (New York: Oxford Univ. Press, 1994), 3–5.

Contributors

R. J. M. BLACKETT is the Andrew Jackson Professor of History at Vanderbilt University. Among his publications are *Building an Antislavery Wall: Black Americans in the Atlantic Abolitionist Movement, 1830–1860* (Louisiana State Univ. Press, 1983); *Beating against the Barriers: Biographical Essays in Nineteenth-Century Afro-American History* (Louisiana State Univ. Press, 1986); and *Divided Hearts: Britain and the American Civil War* (Louisiana State Univ. Press, 2002).

KATHRYN E. HOLLAND BRAUND is an associate professor of history at Auburn University. She is the author of *Deerskins and Duffels: The Creek Indian Trade with Anglo-America, 1685–1815* (Univ. of Nebraska Press, 1993) and the editor of Bernard Romans's, *A Concise Natural History of East and West Florida* (Univ. of Alabama Press, 1999).

HOLLY BREWER is an associate professor of history at North Carolina State University. She is the author of the prize-winning "Entailing Aristocracy in Colonial Virginia: 'Ancient Feudal Restraints' and Revolutionary Reform," *William and Mary Quarterly* 54, no. 2 (1997), and of *By Birth or Consent: Children, Law, and Revolution in England and America, 1550–1820* (Univ. of North Carolina Press, 2003).

S. MAX EDELSON is an assistant professor of history at the University of Illinois at Urbana-Champaign. He has published "Affiliation without Affinity: Skilled Slaves in Eighteenth-Century South Carolina," in Jack P. Greene, et al., eds., *Money, Trade, and Power: The Evolution of South Carolina's Plantation Society* (Univ. of South Carolina Press, 2001), and is currently revising a book manuscript that examines plantation settlement, slavery, and economic culture in colonial South Carolina.

FRANKLIN T. LAMBERT is a professor of history at Purdue University. His publications include *"Pedlar in Divinity": George Whitefield and the*

Transatlantic Revivals, 1737–1770 (Princeton Univ. Press, 1994); *Inventing the "Great Awakening"* (Princeton Univ. Press, 1999); and *The Founding Fathers and the Place of Religion in America* (Princeton Univ. Press, 2003).

MICHAEL O'BRIEN is University Lecturer in American History at the University of Cambridge and a Fellow of Jesus College. Among his publications are *The Idea of the American South, 1920–1941* (Johns Hopkins Univ. Press, 1979); *All Clever Men, Who Make Their Way: Critical Discourse in the Old South* (Univ. of Arkansas Press, 1982); and *Rethinking the South: Essays in Intellectual History* (Johns Hopkins Univ. Press, 1988).

BRIAN WARD teaches history at the University of Florida. His book, *Just My Soul Responding: Rhythm and Blues, Black Consciousness, and Race Relations* (Univ. of California Press, 1998), won an American Book Award for outstanding literary achievement and the Organization of American Historians' James A. Rawley Prize for the best book on the history of U.S. race relations.

JOSEPH P. WARD teaches British and European history at the University of Mississippi. He is the author of *Metropolitan Communities: Trade Guilds, Identity, and Change in Early Modern London* (Stanford Univ. Press, 1997), and an editor of *The Country and the City Revisited: England and the Politics of Culture, 1550–1850* (Cambridge Univ. Press, 1999) and *Protestant Identities: Religion, Society, and Self-Fashioning in Post-Reformation England* (Stanford Univ. Press, 1999).

HUGH WILFORD is a member of the Department of History at the University of Sheffield. He is the author of *The New York Intellectuals: From Vanguard to Institution* (Manchester Univ. Press, 1995) and *The CIA, the British Left and the Cold War: Calling the Tune?* (Frank Cass, 2003).

MARCUS WOOD is a painter and performance artist reader in English at the University of Sussex. He is the author of *Radical Satire and Print Culture, 1790–1822* (Oxford Univ. Press, 1994); *Blind Memory: Visual Representations of Slavery in England and America, 1780–1865* (Routledge, 1999); and *Slavery, Empathy and Pornography* (Oxford Univ. Press, 2002).

Index

Abeika Indians, 55, 74, 79
Abolition propaganda, 121, 126–27, 132, 146, 147, 150–51, 156
Absentee plantation owners, 81, 86–87, 96–97
Absolute monarchy, 28, 29, 35, 38, 39
Act of Toleration, 3, 17
Act of Uniformity, 6
Act of Union, 218
Adams, Charles Francis, 153, 158
Adams, W. E., 147, 154
Addams, Jane, 180
African slaves, 43–44, 82, 84, 98, 148, 151, 155
Agrarians, 167, 183
Aitken, William, 152–53
Alabama, 174
Alabama Indians, 55, 60, 74, 79
Alabama River, 64, 72
Alabama White Citizens Council, 198
Allestree, Richard, 48
Allick, Captain, 64
Altamaha River, 69
American Civil War, 107, 108, 121, 123, 136, 139, 141, 144, 221, 222
American Federation of Labor (AFL), 172, 173, 174
Americans for Democratic Action, 165
Anglican Church. *See* Church of England
Anglo-American Council on Productivity, 179
Anglophilia, 165, 220, 223, 226
Anglophobia, 220–21
"Angry Young Men," 184
Antebellum period, 168, 184
Anthropological Society of London, 221
Anti-Apartheid Movement, 186
Anti-Slavery Almanac, 127

Apalachee Old Fields, 59, 65, 66
Appalachicola, 67
Appleby, George, 83
Apprenticeships, 30
Aptheker, Herbert, *Negro Slave Revolts in the United States*, 168
Ardeley, Hertfordshire, England, 148
Armstrong, Louis, 224
Arnold, Matthew, "The Last Word," 227
Ashton-under-Lyne, England, 179
Association of Women Clerks and Secretaries, 174
Astor, Lady, 222
Atherton, Herbert, *Political Prints in the Age of Hogarth*, 109–10
Atlanta, Ga., 165, 166
Attlee government, 169, 170
Augusta, Ga., Congress of, 63, 65, 66, 67, 69, 70–71
Austen, Jane, 224; *Pride and Prejudice*, 32
Austin, Tex., 168
Auston, George, 94
Avon River, 99

Baby Doll, 208
Bacon's Rebellion, 40
Baker, Carol, 208
Ball, Elias, Jr., 83, 98, 99–101
Banjo, 191
Baptism, 34; infant, 31
Baptists, 15, 21
Barbados, 28, 41, 43–44, 49
Barber, Chris, 190, 191, 193, 194
Bartram, William, 55, 57, 75
Bath, Marchioness of, 143
Battle of New Orleans, 220
Bazaar in Aid of the Southern Prisoner's Relief Fund, 141, 143, 158
Beatles, 212–13
Bebop, 189, 191

271

Bechet, Sidney, 190, 191
Beesly, Edward S., 154
Belloc, Hilaire, 184
Bell, R., 151–52, 153
Benjamin, Judah, 159
Benn, Tony, 168
Bennett, Arnold, 183
Benson, A. C., 225
Benson, E. W., 225
Beresford-Hope, Alexander J., 150, 151, 155, 158, 159
Beresford-Hope, Lady Mildred, 143
Berkeley, Sir William, 8–9, 41–42, 43
Berle, A. A., 170
Bermuda, 41
Berry, Chuck, 204
Bessemer, Ala., 174
Bevan, Aneurin, 176, 218
Bevanism, 170, 172
Bevanites, 170, 171, 175, 186
Beverley, Robert, 8–9
Bevin, Ernest, 169, 175
Bible, 7, 8, 12, 38
Big Three, The, 212
Bilk, Acker, 191
Biltcliffe, Jonathan, 154
Birmingham, Ala., 166, 179, 197, 198, 199, 213
Birthright, 29, 30–31, 34, 36–37, 43, 49–50
Bishop of London, 3, 10
Black Mountain College, 227
Blackett, Richard, 226
Blackmur, R. P., 167
Blackwood's, 143
Blair, Samuel, 13
Bloomsbury literary establishment, 184–85, 186
Boggs, James, 181, 183
Bond labor, 39
Book of Common Prayer, 15, 16
Booker, Christopher, 210
Boston, Mass., 119
Boston Port Bill, 111
Bowers, Millyon, 206
Bowman, Rev. J., 226
Brazil, 134
"Breathless," 206
Brewood, England, 195

Bridgewater, Somerset, England, 187
Bright, John, 154
Britain. *See* England/Britain
British. *See* English/British
Brogan, D. W., 181
Brooks, Cleanth, 163–64, 181, 182
Brown, J. W., 207, 208
Brown, Lois, 207, 208
Brown vs. Board of Education, 172, 176, 198
Brown, William Wells, 224–25
Bryan, Jonathan, 78
Bryce, 166
Burma, 169

Calvin, John, 12
Campaign for Nuclear Disarmament, 186
Cape Breton, 113
Capers, Mrs. Richard, 95
Cardiff, Wales, 176
Carlyle, Thomas, 148, 149, 160–61, 221, 222; *On the Nigger Question*, 134
Carolinas, 41, 42, 116, 117
Carter, A., 204
Carter, A. P., 194
Carter, Asa, 198, 204
Carter Family, 193
Carter, Robert "King," 47–48
Cartography, 53, 77
Catawba, 63
Catholics, 9
Central Association for the Recognition of the Confederate States, 156
Channing, John, 87
Charles I, 29, 34, 35, 40, 41, 42, 43, 44
Charles II, 35, 40, 42, 43, 48, 49
Charleston, Va., 60, 81, 82, 83, 89, 90, 99, 103, 142, 166, 169; harbor blockade, 123
Charlotte, N.C., 179
Chartists, 146, 147
Chattahoochee River, 54, 59, 65, 66
Cherokee, 54, 58, 63, 75
Cheshire, 152
Chester, Gov. Peter, 72, 73
Chesterfield, Countess of, 143

Index

Chesterton, G. K., 184
Chickasaw Indians, 59, 63
Choctaw Indians, 58, 63, 70, 72, 74, 77
Chris Barber Jazz Band, 194
Church of England, 3–11, 13, 14, 15, 16–20, 22, 30–31, 34, 35, 37; in Virginia, 48, 236
Churchill, Winston, 187, 222, 223
CIA, 185
Cincinnati, Ohio, 216
Citrine, Walter, 172, 174
Civil rights movement, 185–86, 189, 193, 197, 198–201, 208, 209, 213, 224
Civil War. *See* American Civil War
Clarendon Code, 8, 9
Clover, S.C., 179
Cobden, Richard, 148
Cochran, Charles, 92
Cochran, Robert and Mary, 92
Coke, Sir Edward: *Institutes of the Laws of England* (*Coke Upon Littleton*), 47; *Statutes of the Realm*, 47
Cold War, 165, 170, 173, 175, 178, 184–86
Cole, Nat King, 197, 198, 199–200, 201, 203
Colyer, Ken, 190, 193
Communist movement, 164, 173, 174, 175, 177
Confederate Jazz Band, 190
Congregational churches, 8
Conica River, 73
Connolly, Cyril, 182
Conway, Moncure D., 160
Cooke, Alistair, 166
Coosa Indians. *See* Abeika Indians
Coosa River, 54, 55, 60
Copyhold, 32, 33
Cornwallis, Lord, 115
Cotton famine, 152, 153, 154, 160
Coweta, 54, 59, 66
Creek, 53–79; boundary lines, 53–54, 60, 64, 241; land ownership, 55, 56; medal chiefs, 66–67, 74; political and social structure, 54, 55, 57–60; towns, 54, 55–59, 56, 57, 238

Cresta Ballroom, 190
Cribb, Tom, 149
Cromwell, Oliver, 28, 34, 35, 36
Crosland, Anthony, 170–71; *The Future of Socialism*, 171–72
Crossman, Richard, 165, 170
Cruikshank, George, 109
Crummell, Alexander, 224–25
Crystal Palace, Great Exhibition, 134–36
"Cultural Cold War," 185
"Cumberland Gap," 194
Cussita, 54, 59, 65, 66, 79

Dabney, Virginius, 167
Daily Express, 199
Daily Herald, 206, 208
Daily Mirror, 195, 196, 206–07, 208
Daily Sketch, 209
Daily Worker, 175
Daniels, Jonathan, 167
Darley, Mathew, 117
Davies, Samuel, 3, 5, 13, 14, 19
Davis, Jefferson, 149, 154, 159
Davis, Miles, 189
Dawe, Phillip, 118, 119
De Donis Conditionalibus, 31
De Vorsey, Louis, Jr., 63
"Declaration for Liberty of Conscience and Indulgence in Religious Matters," 9
DeHoghton, Lady, 143
Delta Jazz Club, 190
Devonshire, England, 99, 100
Dickens, Charles, 221
Diddley, Bo, 204
Dissenters, 3–4, 6, 7–9, 10–15, 16–18, 19–24, 34, 35, 36, 37
Distributists, 183–84
Dixieland jazz, 188, 189–93, 197
Dixielanders, 190
Dobson, Christopher, 199
Domino, Fats, 196, 213
Donegan, Lonnie, 193–94
Douglass, Frederick, 224–25
Drayton, Charles, 93
Drayton, John, 93
Drayton, Thomas, 93
Drayton, William, 88, 93

Du Bois, W. E. B., *The Souls of Black Folk*, 180
Dudley, Thomas, 141
Dudziak, Mary L., 175
Dunning School, 168
Durbin, Evan, 171

Economy, agricultural, 82
Edinburgh Review, 221
Eisenhower, Dwight, 188
Elgar, Edward, *Land of Hope and Glory*, 215
Eliot, T. S., 184, 222
Elizabeth I, 6–7
Elizabethan Settlement, 6, 8
Emancipation Proclamation, 154
Emisteseguo of Little Tallassee, 53–54, 55, 67, 73–74, 79
Enclosure movement, 33
Encounter, 184, 185
England/Britain, 8, 9, 14, 38, 43, 104, 215, 216, 217
English Civil War, 28, 34, 35, 38, 43
English poor laws, 45
English/British: agricultural landscape, 97–100; architectural styles, 82; boarding schools, 90, 248; education, 90–96; influence on colonial America, 27–28, 39–42; law, 27–37, 47, 50–51; print satire, 107–40; revolutions, 27–28; rural landscape, 99; support of Confederacy, 141–45, 147–50, 151–55, 157–59, 160–61; textile industry, 125, 130
English-Speaking Union, 178
Entail, 31–32, 33, 38, 46, 48, 50
Episcopalians, 24
Equiano, Olaudah, 224
Escambia River, 73
Establishment, 18, 21, 22, 23
Etched print satire, 109
European Union, 216
Everglades, 59
Exchange programs, 165–66, 178–79

Fairbanks, Charles, 146
Faubus, Gov. Orval E., 176

Faulkner, William, 183, 185, 223–24; *Light in August*, 163; *Sartoris*, 163; *Soldier's Pay*, 181
Federalists, 6
Fenwicke, John, 91
Ferguson, 168
Ferriday, La., 206
Feudalism, 28, 30, 31, 32–34, 39, 41, 46–47, 50, 232
Fife, 216
Filmer, Sir Robert, 29
Finke, Roger, 229
First Continental Congress, 79
Fitzhugh, William, 47
Flint River, 66
Florida, 54, 58–59, 61, 62–63, 64, 69, 70, 74, 75, 76, 77, 172
Foley, John Henry, 158
Ford, Tennessee Ernie, 211
Fort Picolato, congress, 64, 66, 70
Fort St. Marks, 62, 64, 66
Fort Toulouse, 64
Foster, Mo, 195
Founding Fathers, 145
France, 7, 60, 108, 145
"Frankie and Johnny," 194
Franklin, Ben, 111–12, 113, 116–17
Freeholds, 39
French, 60, 61
Frith, Simon, 211

Gaitskell, Hugh, 170
Gaitskellites, 170–71, 172, 186
Galbraith, John Kenneth, 170
Garibaldi, 147
Garrison, William Lloyd, 147
Gastonia, N.C., 179
Geddes, Patrick, 227
General Assessment Bill, 23
George III, 68
Georgia, 58, 59–60, 61, 62, 65, 69, 70, 75–78, 102, 117
Georgia New Purchase, 75, 77, 78
Gibbes, Sarah, 92
Gibraltar, 112
Gidley, Mick, 183
Gillray, James, 107, 109, 115, 116, 119
Gilroy, Paul, 226
Gladwin, Derek, 178

Index

Glorious Revolution, 28, 34, 35
Gooch, William, 16–17
Goode, Susie, 208
Gordon and Trenchard, *Cato's Letters*, 36
Graceland, 208
Grant, Gov. James, 70
Gray, Henry, 87
"Great Balls of Fire," 206
Greene, Jack P., 103–04
Greensboro, N.C., 179
Greenville, Miss., 215, 227
Greg, Percy, 144
Grimshaw, Mortimer, 152
Grits, 83
Grotius, Hugo, 44
Guardian, 226
Gulf Coast, 55, 58, 62
Gustafson, John, 212
Guthrie, Woodie, 193

Haley, Bill, 197, 203
Handsome Fellow of Okfuskee, 61
Hanover County, Va., 3, 10, 12
Harley, J. Brian, 53
Harrington, James, 35, 227
Harrison, George, 188, 195
"Heartbreak Hotel," 197, 212
Heath, Ted, 197–98, 201–02
Henry VIII, 31
Henry, Patrick, 3, 4, 12, 14–15, 23
Hewit, Alexander, 102
Highlander Folk School, 227
Hill, Herbert, 169
Holly, Buddy, 196, 213
Horizon, 182
Horner, Arthur, 176
Horsfall, John B., 146
Hotspur, Harry, 215
Hotze, Henry, 142, 143, 149, 150, 152
House of Burgesses, 28, 43, 45–46, 50
House of Commons, 29, 34, 157
House of Lords, 29, 35, 50
"House of the Rising Sun," 194, 195
Howard, Ashbury, 174
Howard of Effingham, Lord, 9
Hull House, 180
Hunt, Dave, 190
Hurstfield, Betty, 187

Husbandry, 30
Hyde Park, London, 99

Imperialism, 169, 221
Indentured servitude, 37, 44–45, 232
Index, 142
India, 148, 169
Indonesia, 169
Inherited right, 34–38, 40, 42, 43
Interregnum, English, 28, 35
Ireland, 157, 216, 217
Irish, 149
Irish Free State, 216
Irish Nationalist movement, 186
"Isle of Capri," 190
Isle of Man, 216
Italwa, 54
Izard, Ralph, 102–03

Jackson, Andrew, 154
Jackson, Miss., 175
Jackson, Stonewall, 158
Jamaica, 148, 183
James, C. L. R., 226
James I, *Trew Law of Free Monarchies*, 29
James II, 9, 47
James River, 43
Jamestown, Va., 222
Jarratt, Devereux, 16
Jazz, 189, 191–92, 193, 196–97, 200, 201, 202, 211
Jefferson, Blind Lemon, 193
Jefferson, Thomas, 3–4, 5, 13, 19, 22, 23–24, 25, 33, 48
Jim Crow, 165, 167, 169, 171, 172, 173, 177, 180, 199
John Bull, 97, 124–25
"John Henry," 194
Johnson, Bunk, 189, 190
Johnson, Edward, 8
Johnson, Lyndon, 223
Johnstone, George, 64, 68
"Join or Die" image, 116–17
Jones, Ernest, 147
Jordan, Winthrop, *White Over Black*, 39
Journal of Southern History, 168
Jury, 27

Kartun, Derek, *America Go Home*, 175
Kennedy, John Pendleton, 221, 222
Kenton, Stan, 199
Kentucky, 165, 202
Kenya, 200
Kenyon Review, 185
Kermode, Frank, 184, 185
Kershaw, T. B., 157
Khrushchev, 188
Kidnaping, 44–45, 235
King, Martin Luther, Jr., 181, 185, 227
Kingsley, Charles, 160–61
Knoxville, Tenn., 178
Korean War, 175
Kossuth, 147
Ku Klux Klan, 179

Labour Party, 164, 165–72, 218
Lancashire, England, 146, 152–53
Lang, John, 179
Laski, Harold, 166–68, 170, 171, 183; *The American Democracy*, 166–68
Latchawie (Latchoway), 65
Laurens, Henry, 87, 89, 92, 93–94
Laurens, John, 93
Le Charivari, 121
Leadbelly, 193, 194
Leavis, F. R., 184
Lee, Jennie, 165, 170
Lee, Robert E., 141
Leech, John, 121
Leland, John, 15, 23, 24
Lennon, John, 212–13
Lerner, Max, 169
Lewis, C. Day, 182
Lewis, George, 190
Lewis, James, Jr., 175
Lewis, Jerry Lee, 206–10, 211, 220
Lewis, Myra, 206–10
Ligon, Richard, 43, 235
Lincoln, Abraham, 136–39, 154, 155, 157
Literary criticism, 183–86
Lithograph, 107
Little Richard, 196, 211, 212, 213
Little River, 69
Little Rock, Ark., 208, 213; Central High School, 176

Little Tallassee, 74
Littleton, 47
Liverpool, 99, 141, 154, 158, 159, 160, 190, 217, 218
Liverpool Southern Club, 142, 152, 159
Lloyd, Anne, 207
Locke, John, 35, 36–37, 38, 44, 232–34; *Essay on Toleration*, 36; *Two Treatises of Government*, 36–37
Lomax, John, 227
London, 50, 60, 63, 81, 88, 93, 96, 100, 103, 154, 163, 178, 187
London Anthropological Society, 149
London Chronicle, 117–18
London Evening News, 163
London Records, 205
London School of Economics, 166
London Times, 142, 144, 145, 146, 147, 153, 157, 203, 204, 205–06
Long, Huey, 168
Lorimer, Douglas, 149
Los Angeles Times, 181
Lothian, Marchioness of, 143
Louisiana, 144
Love Me Tender, 205
Loyalist émigrés, 96–103
Lucy, Autherine, 198, 199, 200–01
Luther, Martin, 12, 38
Lutherans, 21
Lynching, 125–26, 181
Lyttleton, Humphrey, 190, 191

MacColl, Ewan, 195
MacCormack, Martha, 179
MacInnes, Colin, *Absolute Beginners*, 192, 212
Madison, James, 4, 23, 24–25
Magee, Bryan, 168–69
Maine, 41
Maize, 83
Malet, Rev. William W., 148
Manigault, Gabriel, 91
Manigault, Joseph, 97
Manigault, Peter, 81, 88, 103
Manchester Southern Club, 150, 156
Mansfield, Lord, 111
Maps, European, 53

Index

March on Washington, 181
Marked Tree, Ark., 165
Marion, Ala., 174
Marshall Plan, 179
Marshall, Stephen, 31, 49
Martin, John, 86
Martin, J. Sella, 160
Martin, Kingsley, 169
Martinsville seven, 175
Marxism, 166–67, 168, 172
Maryland, 40, 41, 48, 144
Mason, James, 141, 159
Mason, Steve, 190
Massachusetts, 7–8, 38–39, 117, 144
Massive Resistance, 194–95, 198, 203, 213
Matthews, John, 152
Maury, Matthew, 157
Maury, Rev. James, 14, 15
McCarthyism, 171–72, 174, 175
McClelland, George, 157
McGee, Willie, 175
McGillivray, Alexander, 79
McWhiney, Grady, 187
Melly, George, 191
Melody Maker, 191, 192, 196, 197, 198, 199, 208
Memphis, Tenn., 205, 209
Medlicott, Sir Frank, 209
Mercia, 216
Mersey River, 99, 190
Merseybeat, 212
Merseyssippi Jazz Band, 190
Methodism, 16
Methodists, 14
Mickelburgh, Bobby, 190
Micos, 67
Middle East, 169
"Midnight Special, The," 195
Milton, John, 34
Mississippi, 143, 163, 165, 215
Mississippi River, 60, 76
Mitchell, Margaret, *Gone with the Wind*, xi–xii
Mitchum, Jane, 208
Mobile, Ala., 60, 62, 64, 72, 73, 190
Mobile Bay, 72
Mobile River, 64, 65
Mobilian tribe, 72

Modernism, 184–85
Molyneaux, 149
Money, Miss., 174
Montgomery, 166, 197, 198, 199, 203, 213
Moon, Jacob, 16
Morgan, Kevin, 173
Morris, Samuel, 12
Morris, Thomas D., *Southern Slavery and the Law*, 46
Mortar of Okchai, 61, 79
"Movement" poets, 184, 186
Murray, Iain, 208
Muskogean tribes, 54–55
Myrdal, Gunnar, *An American Dilemma*, 167

NAACP, 169, 174
Naipaul, V. S., 226
Naniaba, 72, 74
Naniaba Island, 73
Natchez Indians, 59
Natchez, Miss., 165, 179
National Association for the Advancement of Colored People (NAACP), 169, 174
National Union of Mineworkers, 176
Native Americans, 122–23
Nehru, 188
Neo-feudalism, 28, 30, 33, 39, 49
Neshaminy, Pa., 3
New Brunswick, N.J., 12
New Castle, Pa., 12
New Criticism, 167, 183–85
New England, 27–28, 38–39, 144
New Lights, 3, 11–13, 16, 17, 229
New Orleans, La., 166, 172, 190; French Quarter architecture, 172; jazz, 189, 191, 192, 202
New Orleans Delta, 131
New Orleans Joys, 194
New Republic, 180
"New South," 179
New Statesman and Nation, The, 169
New York, 19, 79, 90, 127, 157, 202
New York Intellectuals, 182, 184
Newsweek, 177
Newton, Richard, 109
Nicholas, Robert Carter, 22

Non-Importation Agreement, 119
Norman conquest, 33
North Lanark, England, 165
North, Lord, 111
Northern Ireland, 186, 216
Nott, Josiah, 221
Notting Hill, London, 169–70, 178, 200, 224
Nottingham, England, 200

Observer, 181, 200–01
Odger, George, 149
Ogeechee River, 69, 75
Oglethorpe, Gen. James, 60
Ojier, Louisa, 96
Ojjobeway, 122
Okefenokee, 77
Orbison, Roy, *Hillbilly Rock*, 205
Orwell, George, 181–82, 183; *The American Problem*, 181; *The Negro: His Future in America*, 180
Ory, Kid, 190
Owens, Norman "Butch," 207
Oxford, Miss., 215

Page, Walter Hines, 221
Paine, Thomas, 29
Parliament, 6, 34, 35, 36, 42, 43, 153, 157, 165
Parker, Joseph, 157
Patterson, Ottilie, 193
Peace Address, 157
Peasants, 195
Pelhams, Lord, 112
Pendleton, Edmund, 22
Penns, 41
Pennsylvania, 41; model of free religion, 4, 6, 10, 18
Pennsylvania Gazette, 116
Pensacola, Fla., 60, 62, 64, 72; Congress of, 63, 66, 70–71
People, 209
Percy, LeRoy, 215, 227
Percy, William Alexander, 227
Perkins, Carl, 211, 213
Perpetual status, 27, 28–32, 34, 39–41, 42, 43–44, 46, 48–50
Phillips, Caryl, 226
Phillips, Ulrich B., 168

"Pick a Bale of Cotton," 194
Pinckney, Charles Cotesworth, 91
Pinckney, Eliza, 83
Pinckney, Thomas, 90
Plantation agriculture, 81, 82, 85–87, 89–90, 105
Plantation economy, 95, 121
Powers, Hiram, *The Greek Slave*, 134
Presbyterian Synod of Philadelphia, 17
Presbyterians, 3, 15, 18, 21
Presley, Elvis, 187–88, 196, 197, 203, 204, 205–06, 210, 211, 212, 213, 223
Priestley, J. B., 182
Priestly, Joseph, 96
Primogeniture, 29, 31–32, 35, 36, 41, 42, 46
Prioleau, Charles, 142, 158
Prioleau, Mrs., 143
Pritchett, V. S., 183
Proclamation of 1763, 62–63
"Productivity Teams," 179–80
Protestant Episcopal Church, 23
Proud Valley, 177
Punch, 108–09, 121–39
Puritans, 7–8, 19, 34, 35, 36, 38–39, 43, 144
Putney debates, 34

Quakers, 10

Race riots, 169, 178, 200
Race, Steve, 196–97, 199–200, 201
Rainsborough, Col., 34
Randolph, George W., 159
Randolph, John, 220
Rand School, 181, 182
Ransom, John Crowe, 167, 185, 222, 226
Ray, Johnny, 203
Rebels, 188
Reconstruction, 158, 168, 222
Reformation, 38
Reid, Thomas, 220
Restoration, 8, 9, 35, 41
Revolutionary War, American, 23, 35, 48, 49, 50, 51, 78, 82, 100, 107, 109–10, 113, 114, 121, 125, 144

Index

Rhodes, Thomas, 152
Rhodesia, 200
Rice, 83
Richmond, Va., 158
"Rip It Up," 212
Roan, John, 13
Roanoke, 222
Robeson, Paul, 174, 176–77, 178
Robinson, William, 12
Rochefort, Charles de, 43–44
Rock and roll, 187, 188, 189, 191, 193, 196–97, 198, 202–06, 209, 210, 211–13
"Rock Around the Clock," 197
"Rock Island Line," 194, 195
Rockefeller, John D., 222
Rolls, John, 206–07
Roosevelt, Franklin D., 166
Rowlandson, Thomas, 109, 119
Royalists, 28, 29, 36, 37, 42, 43, 44, 47
Ruge, Neil M., 176–77
Rum, 76, 77
Russell, Bertrand, 181, 182–83
Russell, Lord John, 157

St. Augustine, 58, 62, 64
St. Johns River, 70
St. Louis, Mo., 202
St. Marys River, 69, 70
Salisbury Square, 88
San Antonio, Tex., 198
Sandwich, Lord, 111
Sark, 216
Saunders, Frances Stonor, 185
Savannah, Ga., 60
Savannah River, 54, 58, 60, 64, 69, 75
Schlesinger, Arthur M., Jr., 166
Schwartz, Lawrence H., 185
Scotland, 6, 50, 186, 216, 217
Scott, Walter, 220
Scottish culture, 220
Scrutiny, 184
Secession, 142, 146, 147, 156
Segregation, 164, 165, 171, 173, 181, 222, 224
Seminoles, 59
Semmes, Capt., 141
Sepoys, 148

Seven Years' War, 58, 60
Seward, William, 157, 158–59
Sewell, Mike, 186
Seymour, Horatio, 157
Shackleford, Roger, 12
Shakespeare, William, 215
Sharecropping, 181
Shawnee Indians, 59
Shepperson, Wilbur, 146
Sidney, Algernon, 35
Simkins, Francis B., "New Viewpoints of Southern Reconstruction," 168
Sinatra, Frank, 203, 212
Sinfield, Alan, 184–85
Single-sheet etching, 107, 252
Skiffle, 188, 189, 192, 193–96, 197, 204, 205, 210, 211
Slave code, 39, 41, 43
Slavery, 28, 37, 147, 148, 151, 164, 221; debate in England, 142, 147–54; early colonial laws, 38–39, 46–47; hereditary, 41, 43–44, 45–46; in print satire, 122–23, 124, 125–27, 131–33
Slidell, Mrs., 143
Smith, Adam, 14, 217, 220; *Wealth of Nations*, 4–6
Smith, Kinder, 152
Smith-Mundt "Leader Specialist" Award, 165–66, 179
Socialism, 170, 171
Society for Promoting the Cessation of Hostilities in America, 156
South Africa, 180, 183, 186, 200, 201
South Carolina, 10, 13, 49, 58, 59, 81, 116, 117, 143; education of children, 81, 90–96; foods, 83–84, 105; legal training, 91; planter-merchant elite, 82–85, 87–95, 102–05; rural landscape, 99, 105; slave labor, 82, 85, 86, 148; social environment, 88–90
South Carolina Provincial Congress, 96
South-Carolina Gazette, 95, 101
Southern Independence Association, 156, 157, 158
Spain, 60

Spanish, 58, 61; colonial model, 50
Spartanburg, S.C., 208
Spence, James, 141–43, 144, 145, 147, 150, 152–54, 155–56, 157, 159–60; *The American Union*, 142
Spender, Stephen, 184–85
Sphere, The, 163
Stamp tax, 110, 111, 116, 119
Stark, Rodney, 229
Statute of Artificers, 30, 33
Sterne, Laurence, 221
Stuart, John, 64, 66, 68, 69, 70, 73, 74, 75
Stuart kings, 8, 28, 40–41
Summary View of the Rights of British America, 217
Sumner, Charles, 148
Sun Records, 205
Sutherland, Duke of, 50
Swing music, 189
Sydney, Algernon, 227
Sylacauga, Ala., 179

Taensa tribe, 72
Tallachea, 71
Tallahassee. *See* Apalachee Old Fields
Tallapoosa Indians, 55, 74, 79
Tallapoosa River, 54, 55, 60
Talmadge, 168
Tampa Bay, 58
Tate, Allen, 167, 183, 184, 222
Taylor, Helen, *Circling Dixie*, 187
Taylor, Peter A., 154
Ted Heath Orchestra, 197
Teddy Boys, 210–12
Telltruthia, Tom, 18–19
Tennent, Gilbert and William, 13
Tennessee River, 55
Tennessee Valley Authority, 178
Tenniel, John, 121
Tennyson, Alfred, Lord, 221
Tensaw Old Fields, 74
Tensaw River, 72
Texas, 125–26, 202
Texas Tech University, 163
Thackeray, William, 221
Thames River, 99
Thirty-Nine Articles, 6
Thomas, Gabriel, 10

Thompson, John R., 221
Till, Emmett, 174
Tocqueville, 166
Todd, John, 14
Todmorden, England, 151, 153
Tombe, John, 34
Tombigbee River, 55, 58, 72, 73
Tomé tribe, 72, 74
Towasa, 72
Trade union movement, 164, 172–74, 186
Trades Union Congress (TUC), 172, 173, 174
Trad jazz revival, 188, 189–93, 197, 210, 211. *See also* Dixieland jazz revival
Treaty of Paris, 60, 249
Tremlett, Rev. Francis William, 157, 159
Trenholm, Fraser, 142
Trescot, William Henry, 221
Tribune, 180
Trollope, Anthony, 148, 149
Trudell, Charles, 175
Tucker, St. George, *Blackstone's Commentaries*, 46
Tudor kings, 28
Tupelo, Miss., 205
Turner, John, 154
Tuscaloosa, Ala., 197, 200, 203, 213

Ulster, 6, 217
Uncle Tom's Cabin, 134
Union and Emancipation Society, 147, 154
Unionism, 217
University College, London, 154
University of Alabama, 198, 199, 200
University of Cambridge, 90, 225
U.S. Congress, 216
Usufruct, 55

Vallis, Buddy, 191
Vance, Rupert, 227
Vanderschmidt, Fred, 177–78, 183
Verity, Rev. Edward A., 157
Vietnam, 181
Villenage, 30, 33, 46, 49
Vincent, Henry, 147

Index

Virginia, 28, 44, 90, 114, 116, 144, 158, 220, 222; Church of England, 3–11, 13, 14–15, 16–20, 22, 48; colonial law, 38, 39–41, 43, 46, 47, 48, 49; headright policy, 40; land distribution policy, 40–41, 46; political culture, 229; slavery, 46, 50, 148, 234
Virginia Assembly, 4, 8, 10, 18, 19–20
Virginia Company, 6
Virginia Gazette, 18
Virginia, Philo, 18
Virginia Statute for Religious Freedom, 4, 6
Virginia Statute of Religious Freedom, 24
Voting rights, 27, 161, 165, 179

"Wabash Cannonball," 194
Wales, 176–77, 186, 216, 217
Wallis, Bob, 190
Walsh, Robert, 24
War of Independence. *See* Revolutionary War, American
Washington, Booker T., 180
Washington, D.C., 157
Washington, George, 79, 114, 126
Washington, Henry Augustine, 46–47
"We Shall Not Be Moved," 165
Webb, George, 190
Webster-Ashburton Treaty, 122–23, 221
Wells, H. G., 180, 182
Wells, Louisa, 88, 90, 94–95, 97, 99, 103
Wells, Robert, 88

Wessex, 216
West Indian emancipation, 148, 149–50, 156, 161
Westminster, Duke of, 50
Wharncliffe, Lady, 143
Wharncliffe, Lord, 158, 159
White Citizens' Council, 179
White, Josh, 193
Whitefield, George, 12
"Who Owns America?," 184
"Whole Lot of Shaking Going on," 206
Wilkes, John, 118, 119
Williams, Hank, 211
Williams, Larry, 213
Williamsburg, Va., 117, 222
Wilson, Jimmy, 174
Wilson, Woodrow, 221
Winchester Lido Ballroom, 190
Winters, Yvor, 167
Winthrop, John, 36
Winyaw River, 86
Wolseley, Lord, 143–44
Woodcut, 107
Woodmason, Charles, 10–11, 13
Woodward, C. Vann, *Tom Watson, Agrarian Rebel*, 168
Worcell, 147
World War II, 173–74
Wortley, Lady Emmeline, 135–36
Wright, Gov. James, 60, 61, 63
Wyatt, Woodrow, 165–66, 179

Yamasee Indians, 59, 72
Younge, Gary, *No Place Like Home: A Black Briton's Journey through the American South*, 226
Yuchi Indians, 59

www.ingramcontent.com/pod-product-compliance
Lightning Source LLC
Chambersburg PA
CBHW030336240426
43661CB00052B/1655